The End of Conflict

k in your negotiations.

Really hope you like the book.

Simon

The End of Conflict
How AI Will End War and Help Us Get on Better

Simon Horton

Copyright © Simon Horton 2025

The right of Simon Horton to be identified as author of this work has been asserted by him in accordance with the Copyright, Designs and Patents Act 1988.

All rights reserved. No part of this publication may be reproduced, stored in or introduced into a retrieval system or transmitted in any form or by any means, electronic, mechanical, photocopying, recording or otherwise without prior written permission from the copyright holder.

All trademarks used herein are the property of their respective owners. The use of any trademark in this text does not vest in the author or publisher any trademark ownership rights in such trademarks, nor does the use of such trademarks imply any affiliation with or endorsement of this book by such owners.

Cover design by Jim Lawrance

ISBN: 978-1-83919-636-2

Published by The Invisible Imprint in the United Kingdom in 2025

About The Author

Simon Horton is a world-renowned expert in negotiation. For 20 years, he has taught negotiation and conflict resolution at Goldman Sachs, HM British Army and many similar world class organisations. He has taught at Oxford University and Imperial College and has regularly appeared on television and been interviewed in national press and magazines on the topic.

Previous publications include "Change Their Mind", Pearson Business (2022) and "The Leader's Guide to Negotiation", FT Publishing (2016), with testimonials:

'An entertaining, immediately useful book that goes beyond advocating for win-win - Simon Horton shows us how to get there.'

Adam Grant, Wharton Professor and New York Times bestselling author of Give and Take

'"Change Their Mind" draws on the methods of hostage negotiators, political campaigners and counsellors who work successfully with the toughest of patients. It's very practical and full of stories that show exactly how these same methods work in everyday life too.'

Daniel Finkelstein, former Executive Editor of The Times and Conservative peer of the House of Lords

Find out more at www.theendofconflict.ai and www.negotiation-mastery.com.

Excerpts From the Book*

"On one occasion, we broadcast on Facebook, then this was broadcast on television, and we had a 1.4 million audience, which was about a third of the whole country. This led directly to a ceasefire, all while polled in real-time, and to the surprise of the cynics, the Forum was created and a Government of National Unity was set up."

Colin Irwin, Research Fellow, Liverpool University

"I'm a mediator and negotiation advisor and for nearly thirty years I've been involved in processes like the Dayton Agreement, the Darfur Peace Agreement, the Colombia agreements with FARC. And I will use AI as part of my preparation… it is really helpful because I want to go into these negotiations with as big a toolbox of options as I can."

Pascal da Rocha, Dialogue and Mediation Advisor

"It's very exciting. There is a whole approach to conflict resolution that is underappreciated, that is more successful than you would think, and that approach can be taken to the next level by AI."

Professor Steven Pinker, Johnstone Family Professor in Psychology, Harvard University, and author of "The Better Angels of Our Nature".

"If we realised that things are better than ever now, that the world is safer than we currently believe, we would feel less threatened and be calmer and more open to the kind of collaboration that we need to make our society work."

Anna Rosling-Rönnlund, Co-author of "Factfulness" and cofounder of Gapminder Foundation

*Please note these quotes are not endorsements for the book but are excerpts from interviews and relate to the specific topics of the chapter in which they are included.

Praise for *The End of Conflict*

'Conflict resolution is such a critically important topic and Horton's idea that AI can benefit the field brings a lot of hope. It's a very enjoyable read too.'

Gary Noesner, Chief of the FBI Crisis Negotiation Unit

'"The End of Conflict" is a compelling exploration of how AI could reshape the future of war and peace. Horton, drawing on decades of experience in negotiation, offers a roadmap for navigating technological upheaval. He argues that AI has the power to end conflict in our lifetimes — and outlines how we might steer it toward a more optimistic future for people and planet.'

Robert Muggah, Co-Founder of The Igarapé Institute

'A great book that explores how AI really can be a huge force for good in society, giving us powerful tools to transform our democracy into something that's finally deserving of the name.'

Lukas Salecker, Founder of deliberAIde

'Horton has taken what has every right to be a heavy subject matter, and expertly crafted a light, entertaining, balanced book without compromising on pure density of insight. I come away feeling hopeful and well-equipped for this important juncture in humanity's history.'

Andrew Drummond, Founder and Managing Director of The Human Centre

Contents

Introduction 1

Section 1: The Premise 9
1: A History of Conflict 11
2: The Golden Formula 33
3: Human, All Too Human 49
4: A New Enlightenment 69

Section 2: The Contexts 93
5: Siri, Save My Marriage 95
6: Reimagining Business 119
7: Free The Law 145
8: Move Fast and Fix Things 165
9: The End of War 197

Section 3: The Warning 225
10: What Could Possibly Go Wrong? 227
11: The Leviathan as Psychopath 245
12: What Then Must We Do? 261

Afterword 275
References 277

Introduction

"I am terrified. Terrified."

So said Douglas Hofstadter, guest speaker at a Google meeting in 2014. Hofstadter is a legendary figure in the field of artificial intelligence, the author of "Gödel, Escher, Bach: An Eternal Golden Braid" and a Distinguished Professor of Computer Science at Indiana University.[1]

"I find it very scary, very troubling, very sad, and I find it terrible, horrifying, bizarre, baffling, bewildering, that people are rushing ahead blindly and deliriously in creating these things."[2]

Many of the Google engineers attending the talk had chosen their careers because of him. And here he stood, telling them exactly how he felt about the consequences of their work, making full use of his thesaurus.

Artificial intelligence will have an impact on our society like nothing we have seen before and we don't know if it's going to be good or bad but we do know it's going to be big.

The good news: AI can create the utopia we, as a species, have always dreamt of. The bad news: it can also create our worst dystopia. Hofstadter has reason for his terror.

More good news: we can choose which one we get. It hasn't happened yet, there's still time to make sure our future is the right one. We have agency in this, ultimately it is up to us.

More bad news: I'm not fully sure we'll get around to it. We seem to be avoiding the conversation and, in doing so, we are leaving it to the technology companies, those engineers Hofstadter was berating, and they don't necessarily have our best interests at heart.

The path we're on right now allows them to build it to optimise their own outcome, namely, take as much money from your account and put it into theirs. After all, that is the legal requirement of every corporation, to maximise their shareholder return.

And this is very much on the "AI is bad" end of the spectrum.

So, we need to be talking about it more, we need to be better informed, in order to avoid any "AI is bad" outcome. And, putting a more positive spin on it, the "AI is good" end of the spectrum is actually *very* good.

If AI is to become more intelligent than humans, it's possible that it will be able to solve some of the complex challenges that have proved beyond our capabilities to date. Poverty, inequality, crime, corruption, injustice, scarcity, insecurity, physical health issues, mental health issues – they are all problems that are sometimes solved for some people for a while but there is still a long way to go to solve them permanently for everyone. We've made a lot of progress on them all, but we will need something bigger and better than us if we want to eradicate them.

And we *can* eradicate them.

Conflict, too. We can eradicate conflict.

It sounds unlikely. The lion lies down with the lamb kind of territory. Santayana said, "Only the dead have seen the end of war" and most people would agree with him.[3] Before researching this book, I would have agreed with him, too.

"The End of Conflict" was not its first title, it was originally called "Negotiation and AI". I have been teaching negotiation for twenty years and I've written two books on the topic. And I've been following AI since 1988, when as a programmer at Hoskyns, the UK's largest software house at the time, I asked for an internal transfer to the newly formed AI team, to programme in Prolog and LISP. Sadly, my manager wouldn't let me leave his team.

But my interest grew with Moore's Law and by the time Ray Kurzweil's book, "The Singularity is Near", was published in 2005, I'd become obsessed. It may be a slight exaggeration to say I've lost friends over the topic but I've certainly been told to shut up about it countless times!

So "Negotiation and AI" was the book I was born to write.

Sounds a bit dry, though, doesn't it? And that's how I saw it initially. I thought it would be very technical, aimed at a technical audience. But when I started my research and I uncovered all the fantastic things that AI was *already* doing with negotiation in various contexts, I was blown away. This could be very big!

And so "The End of Conflict" came into being. It's an optimistic book but it brings warnings too. I'll give an overview of it here.

The Three Sections of the Book

At a high level, there are three sections. In the first, we lay out the book's premise. After all, the title sounds unlikely, it needs some justification.

In the second, we have a series of chapters that look at what is happening right now in multiple contexts and how this is likely to develop as the technology improves.

And in the final section, we have the warning. This book does not come with a money-back guarantee, AI might indeed accelerate conflict. But with the warning comes advice on how to avoid these worst-case scenarios.

Let's go through the chapters in more detail so you know what to expect.

The Twelve Chapters

I'm quite sure you need a lot of persuading that the promise of the title is at all possible, I wouldn't expect anything else. So, the book's first section lays out several supporting arguments to show that, perhaps, we shouldn't be so doubtful. There are many reasons why it's more likely than we imagine.

In Chapter One, we look at "**The History of Conflict**" and we see that, despite the daily horrors we see in our news feeds, violence is at a historical low on almost any measure. Whether we're discussing war, homicide or violent crime of any kind, the trajectory has long been downward and we shouldn't be surprised if that trend continues.

But some conflicts are just intractable, aren't they? How will they ever find peace in the Middle East, for example?

Well, the truth is best practice does exist for resolving even the toughest of conflicts. Think Northern Ireland, think the end of the South African apartheid regime, think the end of the fifty-year war in Colombia between the government and the revolutionary guerilla group, FARC. These are some of the toughest conflicts imaginable but they were resolved.

Mediators know this. The best negotiators know this. It's not always easy but the knowledge is there, it's just that most people don't know it. Most people go about negotiation the wrong way and, ultimately, that is why conflict is still so prevalent.

So, Chapter Two lays out the best practice. How do you solve that problem with your noisy neighbour? Chapter Two, "**The Golden Formula**", will tell you how. No more conflict for you any more, even without AI's help.

But even if you know the theory, putting it into practice isn't always easy in the heat of the moment. So, Chapter Three, "**Human, All Too Human**" looks at why we find it so difficult and how we can get around it. But it also introduces some of the superpowers of artificial intelligence – attributes that allow it to negotiate a lot better than us. We will see those attributes in play through the rest of the book.

To take one simple example, AI has the ability to model best human practice and then make that practice more widely available. And we've already seen that best human practice can resolve even the toughest of situations. So, as AI becomes more pervasive in our world, it will quietly and invisibly bring best practice collaboration and negotiation into the culture, sitting in the background, easing every transaction. It will become the norm.

Then Chapter Four, "**A New Enlightenment**", describes the history of information technology and how each major advance has triggered a huge leap forward in progress. Whether we're talking human language, writing or the printing press, they have each had a massive impact, on balance highly positive, contributing significantly to the downward trend in violence we saw in Chapter One.

So why should AI be any different? If the printing press ultimately led to science, democracy and the Enlightenment, why shouldn't we expect a New Enlightenment in the coming years?

So, the first section looks at the theory, if you like, but if that isn't enough to persuade you, the second explores what is happening in practice right now and what we can expect coming down the line. And, hopefully, this will provide the evidence that not only is it possible, actually, it's even likely.

Chapter Five, "**Siri, Save My Marriage**", looks at how the technology will impact personal conflict and negotiations. Want to stop arguing with your kids? Want the divorce to be amicable? Want to get a pay rise? You'll like this chapter.

Chapter Six, "**Reimagining Business**" examines the great value that AI will release in business as it enables internal departments to collaborate much more efficiently and organisations to find value-creating "one plus one equals three" deals between purchaser and supplier. And "**Free The Law**", Chapter Seven, unpacks precisely how the law, currently only really available for the rich and for business, will soon become free for all. It will also become a solved question: legal disputes will become history, lawyers and courts will become redundant.

Social media famously moved fast and broke things. Well, what if we could "**Move Fast And Fix Things**"? That's Chapter Eight. Social media is optimised for attention, AI platforms exist which are optimised for agreement. These will heal divided societies and breathe an exciting new life into our broken democracies. And "**The End Of War**" says it all for Chapter Nine. Preposterous? Surprisingly, no. AI for peace is already a thriving field.

At the same time, you won't need to be a contrarian to have a ton of "What about…?"s popping into your head and we will discuss these in the third and final section of the book.

In Chapter Ten, "**What Could Possibly Go Wrong?**", we outline exactly that, what could possibly go wrong. AI war, rogue actors, 100% unemployment, a mis-aligned leviathan – they are all feasible and they would all spoil your dinner. We need to know about them so we can avoid them.

And in "**The Leviathan As Psychopath**", Chapter Eleven, we explore possibly the biggest threat of all – a massive, potentially final, shift in power from governments and people to an oligopoly of technology companies, an outcome that should definitely go in the "AI is bad" basket.

But our last chapter, Chapter Twelve, "**What Then Must We Do?**" examines how we can prevent these threats from arising. It's optimistic, everything is still to play for. As you will hear me say multiple times in the book, it's up to us.

Laying Out the Roadmap

Once the title changed from "Negotiation and AI" to "The End of Conflict", the goals of the book changed too.

Firstly, I wanted to raise awareness of the tremendous opportunity here because if we recognise this is possible, we can make it happen.

And that's the second point, too, I want to raise awareness we have agency here. It really is up to us. If we find ourselves in our worst dystopia, we can't complain, it was (partly) our fault. But we can choose the path we take.

Thirdly, I want to lay out that path. This book is a plausible roadmap to the end of conflict. Let's follow it.

Because, fourthly, the roadmap can become self-fulfilling. This will not be the first time in the history of technology that roadmaps have become self-fulfilling. When Gordon Moore introduced his famous law, it wasn't just a graph with some data points and a prediction, it became a project plan and an investment plan and, in this manner, self-fulfilling. Likewise, Kurzweil's Singularity book, a legend in Silicon Valley, barely known outside it.[4]

Let's do the same with the end of conflict. Why not?

Things Really Can Change

Things can change. Few people live in fear of being eaten by large predators any more. We are no longer ruled by kings, the natural order of things for millennia. Famine is, thankfully, now a rarity for the majority of the world's population.

Things can change. In the late 18th century, maternal mortality rate in childbirth was 2,500 per 100,000 live births.[5] In Britain, the figure is now seven.[6]

Things really can change. Even the England football team has become good at penalties. The impossible can become possible.

Maybe we don't want things to change. My mate said it would be boring if everyone agreed. I agreed.

But to the cynics, your "This will never work" means it will never work; your "What's the point?" means there is no point. Whether it works or not, depends on you.

There are reasons for hope, there are reasons for worry.

But, ultimately, it's up to us.

Thanks

I would like to thank the many people who I interviewed for this book. I understand how busy we all are, so giving their time was enormously kind.

I thought it would be nice to put some of the interviews in special boxed sections in the relevant chapter because hearing it in their voice brings more interest for the reader, rather than being bored by my own all the way through the book.

Similarly, I thought it best to keep these pieces in a more conversational style rather than some rigorously academic and peer-reviewed essay.

I think you will enjoy them.

Section 1
The Premise

1
A History of Conflict

It's early morning on a very normal workday and you're commuting, standing on the platform waiting for your train, and just as it's pulling in, the person standing next to you has a seizure and falls on to the tracks right in front of the oncoming train.

What do you do?

No pressure but perhaps your answer just might give us hope regarding the end of conflict.

After all, I appreciate the title of this book makes a big claim. Everywhere you look around, you see conflict, there's a lot that will have to end. Humans just seem to be a lost cause.

Well, let's examine this and maybe we will see there is more hope than first appears.

Human Beings Are Bad

There are wars everywhere. Every time you check the news you hear of the latest terrorist attack or murder. Our prisons are full, our courts overflowing. Drive and you're dodging road rage, walk and a kid cycles past and steals your phone. Violence is endemic, it's almost as if it's part of our DNA.

Actually, it *is* part of our DNA.

In 1974, Jane Goodall was in the middle of the Tanzanian jungle, studying the Gombe chimpanzees and what she saw horrified her.

They lived a peaceful life, grooming each other and sharing food and showing other behaviours that looked a lot like human kindness. But trouble began to brew in the Kasakela community she was observing and the Kahama sub-group split off and headed south.

Then on January 7th, six adult Kasakela males ambushed an isolated Kahama male, Godi, and savagely mauled him, leaving him to die from his injuries. The "Four Year War" had begun and a whole series of pre-meditated violent attacks followed, Kasakela males ambushing their former friends one by one and brutally beating them to death until none were left.

Goodall had previously considered chimpanzees as "rather nicer" than humans but was now less sure.[1]

But why should we be surprised, Hobbes told us that the state of nature is a war of all against all and Tennyson that it is red in tooth and claw. And Darwin told us that we are a product of a multi-billion-year process that rewards the ability to compete for scarce resources. The better we fight, the more food we will get and the more likely we will attract a mate so our genes continue into the next generation.

There is even maths to support it. In game theory Hawk-Dove games, "rational agents" are often incentivised to take the aggressive (i.e., Hawk) option.[2] Russell Crowe even won a Nobel Prize for his work in this field. Okay, John Nash, who he played in the film, "A Beautiful Mind", won the Nobel Prize and Crowe was nominated for an Oscar.

There are so many scientific frames that explain our propensity for violence, from neuroscience ("It wasn't me, it was my amygdala") to hormones, childhood environmental factors, culture and DNA;[3] so many inputs leading to anti-social behaviour, it is no surprise that violence seems to be our norm.

Human Beings Are Good

But that is only half the story.

Ethologists, scientists who conduct comparative studies in animal behaviour, consider humans as one of the most pro-social species out there.

Other animals might argue that all known ethologists are humans themselves and therefore biased but ethologists retort dismissively to said animals that few species lay down their own lives for their kin, few build such vast collaborative projects as we do and few exhibit even the small everyday kindnesses like holding the door open for someone else.

So, humans are good.

Again, perhaps we shouldn't be surprised. If we choose the bonobo, the chimp's close cousin, we see something much more peaceful than chimps as our pre-human model. Rarely aggressive and much more cooperative, they seem to spend most of their day playing, eating and having sex. Sounds pretty good to me.

And cooperation, it turns out, is quite a force in nature. Yes, competition is the driving force of evolution but cooperation is the most successful way of competing.

Ask the ant. A highly cooperative species and there were approximately ten thousand trillion of them at the last count. That's quite a lot. To be fair, they weren't all counted, but this is the best myrmecologists' estimate. Apparently, there are about 500 myrmecologists in the world.[4]

And if you don't believe ants or myrmecologists, ask J.B.S. Haldane, the Cambridge and University College London geneticist, who famously quipped he would be prepared to lay down his life for eight cousins or two brothers. His point was that altruistic behaviour to benefit people with the same genes as you is a successful evolutionary strategy.[5]

Even the eukaryotic cell, the building block of all higher life forms, possibly *the* most successful evolutionary development ever, is believed to have come into being through the collaboration of different bacteria; that mitochondria (which give the cell the energy it needs to do all its amazing things) and other organelles were once free-living bacteria.[6] the collaboration between these separate bacterial species formed a new type of life that ultimately led to the likes of you and me and the duck.

So, whether we are talking about ants, bacteria, or humans, we are beginning to understand that collaboration is perhaps the most potent force in evolution, that doves can defeat the hawks if they cooperate.

The problem with rational agents following their own best individual strategy is self-defeating: it drives a race to the bottom, mutually assured destruction.

The "Tragedy of the Commons" was a famous paper by Garrett Hardin[7] that showed shared resources are likely to be depleted by everyone acting in their own self-interest, ultimately harming everyone's long-term interests. And we can see this in many contexts like over-fishing and fossil fuel use leading to climate change. When people act selfishly, everyone loses out, including that selfish actor.

So, actually, it is not rational at all to behave this way. Instead, we need to optimise our strategy at the population level and if we do this, we are all better off. This requires collaboration.[8] In most instances, collaboration really is the best strategy.

Hardin took a very gloomy view of human prospects because of this, but more recently two scientists, Ernst Fehr and Simon Gächter, have shown something more promising. Their research showed that if the cheaters are punished, people quickly learn to cooperate and the tragedy of the commons can be avoided.[9] Other work since has shown that rewarding the cooperators also has the same effect.[10]

In other words, we can shape the context to encourage cooperation so everyone gains.

As with all mathematical models, much of it depends on the parameters of the situation but if the cost-benefit analysis is right, it is in people's interests to collaborate.

Make love not war, one plus one can equal three.

School For Super-Heroes

So, let's get back to our opening question: it's your early morning commute and someone next to you has just fallen on to the tracks in front of you, just as the train is pulling in. What do you do?

In 2007, Wesley Autrey, a New York construction worker and Navy veteran, found himself having to answer exactly this question and answer it very quickly. What did he do?

He dived on to the tracks himself and pulled the gentleman, Cameron Hollopotor, a young film student, into a drainage trench in between the tracks, lying on top of him to keep his body down, as the train passed over the two of them.[11]

Well, we'd all do the same, wouldn't we? (Ahem, the writer coughs, mutters to self and looks away)

Philip Zimbardo is one of the few psychologists well known outside of academia. His most famous experiment, possibly the most famous psychology experiment ever, is the Stanford Prison Experiment,[12] in 1971. They even made a Hollywood film about it.[13] Not quite Oppenheimer but hey.

In the experiment, 24 college students are randomly assigned roles as prisoners or guards in a simulated prison environment. It was planned to last two weeks but very quickly the guards began to abuse their power. They forced the prisoners to clean toilets with their bare hands, deprived them of sleep and subjected them to humiliating punishments. The experiment was terminated after six days because of the alarming psychological deterioration of both guards and prisoners.

The experiment's methodology has been challenged in the scientific community since but it shows how ordinary people (in this instance they were volunteers, randomly ascribed roles) can do bad things if the circumstances steer them that way. Zimbardo says it's not about bad apples, it's about bad barrels.[14]

Rudolf Höss was the commandant of Auschwitz concentration camp when, according to his statement at the Nuremberg trial, "at least 2,500,000 victims were executed and exterminated there by gassing and burning, and at least another half million succumbed to starvation and disease, making a total of about 3,000,000 dead."[15] These figures are higher than other estimates[16] but, regardless, one of the most evil acts in human history.

Yet his daughter, Inge-Birgitt Höss, when interviewed decades later and asked what he was like, said "He was a wonderful, absolutely wonderful person," and later, "I couldn't have wished for a better father."

How can these two things be true at the same time? She says his superiors made him do it and he described himself as, "a cog in the wheel of the great extermination machine created by the Third Reich."[17] Whatever the truth, it shows that the same person can be both a devil and an angel, at different times, depending on the context.

Given this, perhaps it is possible to manage the context so that humans do less of those bad things we tend to do and a bit more of the good ones. Less like Höss, more like Autrey. Zimbardo certainly thinks so, he runs an online training programme called the Heroic Imagination Project[18] which aims to bring out the hero in everyone.

And the more heroes there are around us, the more we see that as the norm and our own behaviour drifts, consciously or unconsciously, in that direction.

Better Angels

Steven Pinker is another psychologist famous outside of his field. In his ground-breaking book, "The Better Angels of Our Nature", he brought a scientific approach to the history of our worst anti-social behaviours.[19] For the sake of brevity, it can be summarised here in three words: violence is declining.

Almost anyway you measure it and almost whichever time frame you are studying, violence is going down. This is good news.

How can we say this when the 20th century saw two world wars as well as the Russian and Chinese civil wars, the Nazi genocide and several other genocides that followed across Europe in the years immediately following the Second World War? Let alone the countless other conflicts around the globe that fill our newspapers every day?

Because whilst the total number of deaths from these hostilities makes it the worst century ever in absolute numbers, that is largely because there were so many more people to kill than in previous centuries.

In other words, measured as a percentage of the population, there were many worse periods in history including the Mongol conquests, Temur Laine's campaigns, the 8th century An Lushan revolt against the Tang dynasty in China and many others that I have never heard of. The War of the Triple Alliance from 1864 to 1870 between Paraguay and the triple alliance of Argentina, Brazil and Uruguay (another war I'd never heard of) killed nearly 70% of the Paraguayan population, the Second World War 3%.[20]

Yes, more people were killed in the 20th century but any individual living then was much less likely to die from war than in previous times.

In fact, never having heard of these wars is part of the problem. Matthew White, who painstakingly compiled the list of the hundred deadliest episodes in human history in his book called "Atrocities: The 100 Deadliest Episodes in Human History", believes that we think recent periods are much worse simply because we have recorded them better and they are fresher in our cultural memories.[21]

We can see the trend continuing over recent decades too. In terms of deaths in battle per capita per year, less people died in the second half of the 20th century than they did in the first half, less people died in the fourth quarter than they did in the third and less people died in the first quarter of the 21st century than they did in the last quarter of the 20th (assuming no catastrophe between time of writing and 31st December 2025).[22]

It's not just wars, homicide rates in western Europe have declined from 33 per 100,000 in the 14th century to less than one today,[23] in Italy from 73 to 1.7.[24] Executions, legal torture, acts of terrorism, lynchings, rape, domestic violence, school corporal punishment, child abuse all show similar trends.[25]

More recently, crime in England and Wales fell by 75% from 1995 to 2024[26] and the number of serial killers in the United States reduced by the same percentage over a similar period.[27]

In almost every measure over almost every time frame, violence is down. It is not a straight line but the trend is there to be seen.

Intractable Conflicts Are Sometimes More Tractable Than We Think

Professor Steven Pinker, Johnstone Family Professor in Psychology, Harvard University, and author of "The Better Angels of Our Nature".

"The idea that artificial intelligence can reduce conflict is definitely a fascinating idea. I'm a cognitive scientist and therefore intimately interested in AI, I have been for fifty years because I'm interested in natural intelligence and the artificial kind is like a benchmarker comparison, and I very much like the positive vision here.

I'm not confident what you say will happen though, just because so much adoption of technology has an unpredictable and capricious aspect to it. And there is a fear about AI that its most obvious purposes are nefarious, like deepfakes and swindling people and spreading propaganda at scale and so on. Also, it's going to be hard to get people to stop shaking their heads in disbelief because I suspect that there is not enough optimism about even the possibility of win-win solutions. Many people's idea of solving a conflict is they win, the other side loses. I'm not sure that right now Putin could be interested in any kind of solution to the Ukraine conflict that Ukrainians would also subscribe to.

I guess one question that occurs to me is if an AI model has just been trained on everything that's out there or has it been optimised for the specific outcome of peaceful conflict resolution? That is, does the World Wide Web or the training set naturally lean toward conflict resolution as opposed to "prevail and grind them into submission"? In other words, is there even more promise for an AI that was task optimised as opposed to one taken off the shelf?

But I'm very much aligned with these goals, we need reminding how what seem to be intractable conflicts are sometimes more tractable than people think. Even in the Middle East, we forget that Israel and Egypt have been at peace for 46 years and that's something that would have seemed like a dream in the 1960s and '70s. Or France and Germany, which were at each other's throats for thousands of years, now conflict is pretty much unthinkable between them. So, it can happen, we need to be reminded that solutions are not hopelessly romantic.

It's very exciting. There is a whole approach to conflict resolution that is underappreciated, that is more successful than you would think, and that approach can be taken to the next level by AI."

Arguing About Arguing

Now Pinker's claims don't go undisputed. Historians don't like non-historians telling them about history, especially if they have the temerity to use numbers. How dare they spoil those beloved explanatory narratives with data and graphs? But this is all part of a healthy dialectic process.

In fact, even the history of argument shows positive trends, as (relatively) civilised norms have developed to formalise them in different theatres such as scientific peer reviews, legal mediation or arbitration, parliamentary debates and so on. These days, differences in opinion are rarely settled by rapier or pistols at dawn.

You might disagree with this, of course, but you would probably do so politely.

And perhaps history is a field ripe for the next step in formalising of argument. Alexander Demandt, the German historian, compiled a list of 210 posited explanations of the fall of the Roman Empire,[28] many of them very plausible. So how do we get beyond the "my story is better than yours" stand-off?

Peter Turchin, like Pinker, is a non-historian who believes we are now ready to bring maths to the table. He founded The Seshat

Global History Databank, a huge repository of historical and archaeological information, with the aim of helping test historical hypotheses against that data.[29]

Turchin's data suggests it was the transition to farming that probably increased violence. After all, nomads can always move on if there's a fight, farmers have a lot more at stake.

But he believes that this growth in violence pivoted around the time of the Axial Age, the period roughly between the 8th and 3rd centuries BCE, a period that produced Confucius, Lao-Tze, the Buddha, Zarathustra, Plato and a whole host of other great thinkers. He agrees with Pinker in that violence declined after the Axial Age.

Paradoxically, he believes that this reduction in violence was actually driven by war.[30] Turchin is an evolutionary biologist and uses game theory to understand how organisms and behaviours evolve and, in the anthropological context, how cultures evolve.

Imagine you live in a village in times before states and laws could protect you and you are threatened by an aggressive neighbouring village who are clearly better fighters than you, what is your best option? You can rapidly invent a new technology that will give you an advantage but this is unlikely or, if you are lucky enough to have a great strategist on your side, you can devise clever tactics to outsmart them. But your simplest and best chance is to join up with another village and fight together.

Indeed, in defence or attack, your best bet for success is to team up with another village. Numbers and resources count. So, villages evolved to form a 'super-village' – either as loose alliance or a chiefdom – then chiefdoms of chiefdoms, states, nations and empires.

But scale requires coordination and cooperation. The more coordinated and cooperative any of these groupings are, the more they can act as one and succeed since internal strife will sabotage any external efforts. So internal collaboration evolved to succeed in the face of external competition.

There were still wars, but they moved away from the imperial centre to the borders. There were still wars but more people lived in peace. Turchin sub-titles his book "How 10,000 years of war made humans the greatest cooperators on earth." We have evolved to collaborate in the face of external threats and it is this collaboration that has brought us The Great Wall of China, the International Space Station and TikTok.

Actually, most historians largely agree with Pinker and Turchin, certainly when discussing later time-frames, though you might be forgiven for not noticing this, such is the nature of academic debate. Here's John Keegan, historian at the Royal Military Academy Sandhurst, from "A History of Warfare":

War is "a vehicle through which the embittered, the dispossessed, the naked of the earth, the hungry masses yearning to breathe free, express their anger, jealousies and pent-up urge to violence." He continues, "There are grounds for believing that at last, after five thousand years of recorded warmaking, cultural and material changes may be working to inhibit man's proclivity to take up arms."[31]

He cites the threat of nuclear war as a reason and the televised wars around the world which have brought the horrors to the living room but he writes this in 1993, long before anyone dared plot any graph to substantiate it.

Are All These Historians Lying?

But surely this isn't true. Everyone knows it's more dangerous now than ever, don't they? You just have to check the news to read about another murder or another horrific war. It's not safe out there.

Let me ask you a question: In the last 20 years, the proportion of the world population living in extreme poverty has a) almost doubled, b) remained more or less the same or c) almost halved?

What's your answer?

Hans Rosling, the Swedish statistician, just thinks humans aren't that good at managing in our brains complicated data sets such as these. He has asked that particular question, and many similar, to countless people around the world and, no matter what their level of education, the large majority do a lot worse at answering than chimpanzees.

Chimps get the answer right one third of the time. The correct answer (as you know) is c: as a proportion extreme global poverty has almost halved in the last twenty years. But in the UK only 9% of people answer this correctly, in the United States only 5% and in France 4%.[32]

In 1990, 14.5 million crimes were reported in the United States, by 2016 that was under 9.5 million, but over half of the population thought that crime went *up* in that period.

And in a 2015 Gallup poll, 51% of Americans worried a family member might be a victim of a terrorist attack but, in the years leading up to the poll, the average number of deaths from terrorist attack was a mere 29 per year.[33] That is less than half the number who died by lawnmower and less than those who died as a result of "contact with hot tap water".[34, 35]

In fact, in Japan, there are 14,000 sudden bath-related deaths annually, nearly 500 times as many U.S. terrorist deaths in a country with one third of the population.[36] I sincerely hope none of my readers are reading this book in the bath right now. If so, please please stay safe.

Why do we get it so wrong? Nobel Prize winner Daniel Kahneman pointed out that our brain takes a lot of shortcuts – shortcuts that on average, in the fast-moving dangerous environment within which we evolved, helped us survive but that don't always give us accurate answers in a more modern context.

In other words, our brain didn't evolve to do statistics.[37]

Instead, unconsciously, we use mental shortcuts like the availability bias which relies on immediate examples – i.e., those that we've seen in the news or that everyone in our social bubble agrees on – to answer. And then, once we've made up our mind, confirmation bias – that we filter in data that supports and filter out data that opposes our existing belief – reinforces it.

As Rosling reports, in 2016 across the world 40 million commercial passenger flights landed safely.[38] Ten did not. Those ten were reported, none of the other 40 million were. So, it's not surprising we believe flying is dangerous even though we are more likely to die when driving to the airport.[39]

Yes, those historians have got it right. Violence in almost every form has gone down significantly whether we are measuring over centuries or recent decades.

Let's be clear, there is still way too much violence in any of these categories, and if you are the victim, even one instance is one too many. But it is almost certainly true that we are living in the safest period that humans have ever known.

And, perhaps, we are about to enter even safer times if we take the right steps.

> **If We Felt Safer, There Would Be Less Conflict**
>
> *Anna Rosling-Rönnlund, Co-author of "Factfulness" and co-founder of Gapminder Foundation*
>
> "So we've been asking tens of thousands of fact-based questions to people all over the world and we find the key problem is that

most people think they know what the world is like. So if they already know what the world is like, why learn anything new? The other challenge we find is it's quite cool to be cynical, so if we show them a positive trend occurring, they have a hard time believing it and they often suspect there is some political agenda behind it.

But if people were to understand the facts better and they could see the world was improving, it would have a big impact on society.

Because when we view the world as a constant struggle, constant conflict, almost like an emergency with a threat around every corner, then we go into survival mode and we're not very good at thinking about the bigger picture or working with other people. We're less trusting, we're more defensive. We only want to save the ones closest to us and we are afraid of people who aren't like ourselves, people from other places, from other cultures, with other costumes.

But if we realised that things are better than ever now, that the world is safer than we currently believe, we would feel less threatened and be calmer and more open to the kind of collaboration that we need to make our society work even better still.

AI can help this, even if just through the instant translation and cross-cultural understanding it has, that will help bridge different societies and resolve any disagreements that arise from language barriers.

It can be a trusted fact-checker, too. It knows the answers better than we do. We've recently run some studies, asking different AI chatbots the same questions as we ask humans and the results are amazing. It doesn't score 100% correct but it's pretty close. We did one study where we asked 15 questions about climate change. The average human got around 3.7 correct answers out of 15. We then asked four different chatbots, like ChatGPT, and their results were close to 14.

It can also spread the facts to more people. Right now, most of these big global questions take place amongst academics and never really leave the ivory tower. AI could be really useful for communicating knowledge and trends, framing it differently for different target groups.

Mind you, it's important it's considered neutral, otherwise people will ask can we trust it? Does it have an agenda? Is it biased? And it's like with self-driving cars, people are afraid of them because they think they are unsafe. And it's true, there will be accidents but not as many as with human drivers!

So, as we develop these tools, we need to be cautious and make sure that we're doing the right things with them and asking the right questions because it might go wrong.

But we also need to remember that humans make mistakes all the time too. So even if AI isn't perfect, it might still be a lot better than where we are now."

Ersatz War

If you ever want some fun, fly to Lahore in Pakistan or Amritsar in India then drive out to the Attari-Wagah border, for a long time the only road crossing between the two countries.

Every evening, shortly before sunset, the border gates close with a spectacular ceremony. Soldiers on both sides, specially chosen for their height and the impressive nature of their facial hair, wearing extravagant head-dresses to add extra inches, outcompete each other in their strutting and high-stepping. The highly choreographed ceremony ends with the two flags being lowered then a handshake and a smile. And all this as the two sides are roared on by thousands of cheering supporters on either side as pumping dance music is played deafeningly loudly. I'd recommend it.

It was inaugurated in 1947, after Indian independence and the partition leading to the creation of Pakistan. It is stylised war and a neutral observer may feel a little uncomfortable seeing the crowds enjoying it so much. But viewing it from a different frame, seeing it *in place of* war, given the history of the two nuclear-armed countries, we can see it as a peaceful vent of feelings that could so easily be more deadly.

In Papua New Guinea, sing-sings serve a similar purpose, bringing together local tribes to compete in their traditional costume and facepaint, their dances and music. Far less deadly than the alternative tradition of bows and arrows aimed murderously at each other.

This was certainly part of the spirit of the Ancient Greek Olympics. Any state that wanted to compete in the Games had to sign up to a truce, which meant that no war was permitted and no arms could be carried into Olympia. Prior to the Games, messengers called 'spondophoroi' were sent out across the Greek world to announce the Olympic Truce or 'Ekecheiria'. Of course, a lot of war was fought between the tournaments but there was an effort to build a Panhellenic commonwealth and the Games were part of that.

Maybe all sport is an ersatz war, a preferable substitute. Orwell famously described it as "war minus the shooting" and when you think of some football rivalries like England and Argentina, Germany and the Netherlands, Celtic and Rangers, this rings true.[40] Focus on the combative aspect and it can be dispiriting but when you focus on the "minus the shooting", well it's welcome progress.

Perhaps the Attari-Wagah border is a symbol for our times, representing the demilitarisation of our world. It may be dressed in military clothes but it is still a party every evening.

How Behaviours Spread

"You know, I've only known one Chinese person before in my life. He was *[name]* from Shanghai."

"That's my uncle!"

Such was a conversation between two strangers, hospital patients in neighbouring beds in Illinois, overheard by a scientist whose field of research was social networks, the study of how things travel through populations. The first speaker was a telephone lineman and was presumably knocked out by the impossibly unlikely event that, of all the Chinese people in the world, the second one he ever met was the nephew of the first.

But as the scientist pointed out in his later paper, it was a lot more likely than you imagine.[41] For a start, the chances of two Chinese people encountered in Illinois being related are a lot higher than any random two Chinese. Also, the second patient was an engineering student so it's plausible the uncle was too and this may explain how the first patient knew him.

As the subsequent research of Stanley Milgram showed, we live in a small world.[42] Everyone is connected to everyone by a few small leaps across our social networks, commonly known as "Six degrees of separation".

This is how viruses spread, Covid-19 a text-book example as it crossed the world, passing from human to human, one at a time, through their social networks, until the whole globe was affected in one way or another.

In 1962, endwara yokusheka, another virus, spread similarly through the Bukoba District of Tanzania. Endwara yokusheka means "the laughing illness".[43]

The outbreak started at a girl's school near Lake Victoria when just three girls found they couldn't stop themselves laughing. Very soon nearly everyone in the school was doing the same and school was suspended. When the students went home, they brought the epidemic with them and the laughter spread through several schools and villages in the region until it eventually petered out a few months later.[44]

Viruses, it seems, are not the only things that go viral and any Instagram influencer will tell you this.[45] In fact, Susan Blackmore argues it was a turning point in our evolutionary history when early hominids began to imitate each other and, building on Richard Dawkins' work, evolution itself evolved to incorporate memes.[46]

In their book, "Connected", James Fowler and Nicholas Christakis describe how behaviours and attributes such as obesity,[47] happiness,[48] ideas[49] and many others can also pass infectiously through a community from person to person.

"Students with studious room-mates become more studious", they say. "Diners sitting next to heavy eaters eat more food. Homeowners with neighbours who garden wind up with manicured lawns. And this simple tendency for one person to influence another has tremendous consequences when we look beyond our immediate connections."

This is how behaviours spread, this is how culture evolves, this is how the world changes.

The Cooperation Virus

Cooperation is one of these behaviours that spread through populations virally. If we are shown better models of cooperation around us, we quickly learn to be more cooperative ourselves.[50] And if we are shown it several times, it will become our new norm, something we don't even question.

One of the main findings from Milgram's experiment was that networks contain key hubs with many more connections than others and these hubs are critical for anything to spread virally. Once something reached a major hub it would quickly pass on everywhere else.[51] This is exactly why brands pay social media influencers so much.

If only we had more role models of cooperation. Or, indeed, we had one role model that was connected to everyone, we would be so exposed to this behaviour that it really would become the norm.

And perhaps that hyper-connected role model will be artificial intelligence.[52] Plenty of lab studies have already shown that AI can change people's behaviours in networks. We need to be careful because they can change behaviour for the worse[53] but it's very clear they can have a positive impact too.[54] And then maybe that cooperation virus might break out of the lab and into the wider world.

We're going to see in the following chapters that AI can help resolve conflict in many, many ways. Not least of which is the fact that the forms of AI we will interact with most commonly, for example personal assistants or large language models like ChatGPT, will have best practice collaboration built into them. Which means every time someone uses one they will be exposed to that behaviour.

But not just these, AI will be embedded in every aspect of our world – from online dating to self-driving cars, artificial intelligence will be quietly making the decisions, using best practice cooperation.[55] We won't be able to avoid it.

This is true for you, dear reader, and for me and for everyone else. We will be surrounded by best practice collaboration. We won't be able to defend ourselves against it. Me, I'm a grumpy old curmudgeon but even I won't be able to resist being more cooperative as everyone else around me stops being quite so annoying.

Our society will be happier, healthier, and wealthier in so many ways.

Sounds miraculous but, actually, things do change. Human sacrifice, infanticide, torture as a means of religious conversion, duelling were all once normal and have now (almost) completely disappeared. Legal slavery was an accepted fact of most societies and has now been abolished in all countries.[56]

On the other hand, things that were crazy become normal – flying, television, phoning your brother who lives on the other side of the planet.

Maybe, just maybe, AI will help us build a society where trust and cooperation are the norm and we really can see the end of conflict.

2
The Golden Formula

So, if Chapter One is correct, the history of conflict is on a positive trajectory, but whether it is or it isn't, we've certainly not solved the problem yet. And you didn't need me to tell you that.

But we do know best practice.

There have been enough wars that we know how to resolve them; there have been enough divorces, that we know how to avoid them. Who needs any new technology when we already have the negotiation technology and the mediation technology, the method and the know-how, which is actually all we need?

Negotiation is a highly researched area. Important things depend on it – ever heard of Brexit? Multi-billion-dollar business transactions depend on it, multi-trillion-dollar trade deals depend on it, peace treaties depend on it. It is *highly* researched and we know what to do.

The problem is that this knowledge is not widely spread. Most people have completely the wrong idea of how to negotiate.

Let's stick with Brexit, back in 2016 the United Kingdom voted to leave the European Union and for the next few years the British news was full of stories about the negotiation with their European counterparts. It's not often that negotiators become famous but David Davis and Michel Barnier became household names, up there with Homer Simpson and Kim Jong-Un.

So, everyone had their opinion. Down the pub, everyone loudly gave their advice, "What that David Davis needs to do, right, is…", apparently hoping that he was nearby and would hear them.

Personally, I hoped he didn't hear them because their advice was invariably a load of rubbish and would have made a positive solution even harder to find.

Because everyone has got negotiation wrong. Everyone thinks it's about being tough, everyone thinks it's about shouting louder than the other person, everyone thinks it's about manipulating, everyone thinks it's about tricking the other side into a deal that's good for you and bad for them.

And because everyone thinks this, this is why we still have so many wars and so many divorces.

Fortunately, the research has uncovered a much better way of negotiating, one that brings about much better solutions for everyone and augurs well for the end of conflict. We can reach the end of conflict if only everyone knows how.

It Has to be Win-win

My previous books were both on the topic of negotiation, practical step-by-step 'how to' books.[1,2] And their message is relevant here too. We will see that they give us the solution to ending conflict. There is more to it, of course, and we will cover that in the rest of this book.

Right now, I'm going to condense the content of my two earlier books into one chapter and I'm going to do that by summarising it in a simple formula, which I call the Negotiation Golden

Formula, a formula that holds the recipe for reaching a win-win outcome.

It *has* to be win-win; if we want the end of conflict, it must be win-win. Any other way will just further conflict, will create more wars, will accelerate the journey to divorce.

In fact, forget ending conflict, the research shows that win-win is best even for purely selfish reasons. Even if you are the most evil, selfish psychopath in the world (and I know, dear reader, that you're not, not you), your best option is still to go for win-win.

But, I can hear your cogitation, you're thinking "What if...?" What if the other person isn't win-win? What if they have all the power? What if you can't trust them? What if there is no win-win to be had?

These are legitimate push-backs and I will tell you the answer after we've seen the formula.

Modelling Negotiation Best Practice

In the late 1970's, Roger Fisher, Professor Emeritus at Harvard Law School, conducted a modelling project. He asked his network who were the best negotiators they knew. Now, as Professor Emeritus at Harvard Law School, his network of networks was likely to include national Presidents, people who negotiated the Gatt Trade Agreement, people who negotiated peace treaties and so on.

Arguably, he was asking who were the best negotiators in the world.

Having identified them, he modelled their strategies. He interviewed them, he shadowed them and he deconstructed what they did. And then, along with William Ury and Bruce Patton, he described the model in his best-selling book, "Getting to Yes".[3] It's a book that changed negotiation, it's nearly as good as my books. It's sold approximately ten million copies (which is approximately ten million more than mine, when rounded).

He found out some interesting things about the best negotiators. He found that, unlike David Davis' advisors down the pub, they didn't take a manipulative, power-based approach, they didn't haggle. Instead, just like our ants, termites and bacteria, they collaborated.

In fact, the best negotiators saw negotiation as a collaborative problem-solving process, where the problem to be solved is that you have an outcome in mind, they have an outcome in mind; you have constraints, though, you have real limitations, and they have constraints and limitations; but you have resources you can bring to the table and they have their resources they can bring to the table.

Great. Put all of these on the table and work together to solve that equation so that both parties do get their outcome, given the constraints, but given the resources. And it was this approach that enabled these negotiators to become so successful.

Interestingly, they *were* tough negotiators but specifically, as Fisher put it, they were tough on the problem, not on the person. In other words, they were exceedingly robust in terms of achieving the outcome they were after, but they took a respectful and cooperative approach to reaching it, helping the other side get their outcome too.

And the Golden Formula we will look at now is drawn very much from Fisher's modelling project.

The Golden Formula

So, what is the Negotiation Golden Formula? It is:

$$O = (IVB)^3.$$

What on earth does that stand for?

Well, **O** is your **Outcome**. What we're saying is the outcome of the negotiation is a function of (IVB)³. When planning your strategy, all you need to think about is (IVB)³. So, let's go through each of these elements.

I stands for your **Interests**. Your interests in a negotiation are your bigger picture goals. They're your strategic objectives, and that's what you need to be focussing on. In strategy, they say, ask the question why five times and it's that "why five times" answer which is what's really important.

The deadlock, the problems, the broken deals nearly always happen at the first level answer but it's at the "why five times" level where we find solutions.

In the age-old office dispute, Sam and Robin are arguing about what temperature to set the thermostat; Sam is insisting on 22°C and Robin is demanding 18°C. If they split the difference and went for 20°C, neither side would likely be happy.

But if you ask why they are so insistent on these temperatures, Sam says they get cold quickly and have trouble typing when their hands are chilly while Robin says they get sleepy when it's too warm, and their productivity drops.

Ah, ok. Now, knowing this, they decide to move desk so that Sam sits near the heater and Robin sits closer to the window. Sam also keeps a warm jumper in the office and Robin brings in a fan during the summer. They set the thermostat to 20°C and everyone is happy.

So, focus on your interests.

What's the **V**? **Variables**.

Nine times out of ten, a negotiation is about one variable only, nearly always money. If that's the only variable, it is impossible to get win-win because it's zero sum. Any penny I get is at your expense, so you're going to fight it. Any penny you get is at my expense, so I'm going to fight it. So, with just the one variable, we have set it up as a fight.

Almost any time that you find yourself stuck in a negotiation and nobody's budging, it's because you haven't identified sufficient variables. So, bring a little more imagination and identify more variables and you will find a win-win across the *package* of variables. It's not just price, it's also quality or scope or quantity or level of seniority on the job or payment terms or delivery terms or packaging terms or performance-related price or whatever.

Negotiation is *highly* creative. If we're saying negotiation is problem-solving, sometimes these problems are challenging and require imagination to find the solution.

In our office scenario, when Sam and Robin argued over the temperature there was no win-win. But when they identified other variables like the desk location, fans and warm jumpers, there was a solution that everyone was happy with.

And then the **B**? This is your **BATNA**. Seasoned negotiators amongst you might smile at the word, nodding your head; others will ask what on earth is that?

BATNA is a negotiation term, which comes from Fisher's work. It stands for your Best Alternative To a Negotiated Agreement. It is your plan B, if you like, if the negotiation falls through. If nobody's getting anywhere and you decide to walk away, where are you walking away to? What's your real-world alternative?

It is a very important concept, you need to have a good BATNA. Without it, you have very little power in the negotiation; but with it, you'll be comfortable walking away from the deal which, in turn, gives you a lot of power.

For example, if you are looking to buy a house and you have made an offer on a place you've seen that fits your criteria, if you haven't viewed any other houses you like (i.e., no BATNA), you are not in a good negotiating position and you will probably end up paying the full price.

If, though, you've seen three other similar properties in the same neighbourhood, each cheaper, you have a powerful negotiating position because of the quality of your BATNA.

So, going back to our Golden Formula, the result you get from your negotiation is a function of focussing on your interests, those bigger picture goals, identifying as many variables as you can, being imaginative and creative about that, and working on your plan B, your BATNA, at the same time.

Why Are They Being So Stupid?!

Now, I want you to put the book down and take a pen. Hold the pen above your head and rotate it in a horizontal plane clockwise. Keep it rotating the same way, slowly bring your hand down until you are looking down on to it, and what way is it rotating now?

The answer should be anti-clockwise, unless you're in America in which case the answer will be counter-clockwise. It might take a few attempts to get it right but if you are looking up to it and it is rotating clockwise, when you are looking down on to it, it will be rotating the other way.

What has this to do with negotiation?

Perspective, of course. People see things differently from different perspectives, they will see it differently to you. You will say clockwise, they will say, "No, anti-clockwise". You will insist, "*Clock*wise!" and they will also insist, "Absolutely not! *Anti*-clockwise!"

And you will both be convinced of your own rightness and that the other person is being stupid or wilfully difficult. You will certainly be convinced of this but they, too, will think the same of you.

So, our Golden Formula said $(IVB)^3$; well, let's examine squared first, $(IVB)^2$. This means that as you're trying to find a solution, think about *their* interests, variables and BATNA too.

Now, they might *not* be thinking in this way. They might not be thinking about their interests at all, they might be taking a very short-term perspective and this is why they're not budging. But if you can ask yourself, "Well, why do they want that? What's the reason behind it?", you'll find out their interests. Then remind them of their interests and their thinking will start to shift.

Then consider the variables as they see them because they will value them differently to you. And it's in the different prioritisations of the variables where you find the win-win, where one plus one equals three (you have some pasta, I have some pesto, together we've got a meal).

And think about their BATNA. You have to offer something better than their BATNA, otherwise they will not agree. But if you are offering better than their BATNA, they should agree.

So, that's the squared.

The cubed, $(IVB)^3$, is everybody else. Who else is involved in the negotiation? It's never just you and that other individual, there are always many, many other people involved. It might be your boss, your boss's boss, the Finance Director, the Head of Legal, the same on the other person's side, the competitor, the regulator and anyone else who might impact the negotiation.

I encourage you to go visual with this, drawing out the classic stakeholder map, and you'll be able to see the dynamics of the negotiation. Who talks to who? Who influences who? Who's going to be impacted by this? Who's likely to say no? Who's going to be a champion for it?

And if you consider the interests, variables and BATNA for each of those, certainly the key people, that will give you a really good understanding of the lie of the land of the negotiation.

So that's the Negotiation Golden Formula.

Before you have any negotiation, big or small, do the preparation. Think through the interests, variables and BATNA for yourself, for the other person, and for anybody else who you think is relevant in that negotiation.

And even if you don't have enough time to do that preparation because you have suddenly been pulled into a meeting as you were walking down the corridor to the coffee machine, the Golden Formula is small enough for your back-pocket, small enough for you to think on your feet, "Oh, what was the Golden Formula again? Oh yes, my interests, variables and BATNA. Theirs. And everyone else's. Ok, I know what to do."

Preparation Gives You Confidence and Gets You Better Results

Paul Fisher, Programme Director of Oxford Programme on Negotiation, Saïd Business School, Oxford University.

"It's a fascinating field, isn't it? I run the negotiations programme at Oxford University but if I think back to my first big negotiation, when I was 19, it didn't go so well. I was negotiating to teach English in Turkey and I knew what I wanted to get out of it but I didn't really get anything I wanted.

Looking back, it was my inability to listen because I felt too stressed. I didn't feel that confident about it and anxious negotiators don't tend to be very good negotiators, they tend to give away too much. But If you feel good about it, you're ultimately going to do better.

And key to this is preparation, sometimes up to 80% of how well you do at the table is down to what you do before the table, your preparation.

And this includes putting yourself in the other side's shoes, take their perspective. That's really difficult to do because we tend to be quite egocentric but the more you can really understand where they're coming from, the better you're going to do.

Then, having done the preparation, you should actually go in with the idea that you don't know and you're there to learn. Just be curious about people, ask lots of questions, listen really, really hard to their answer and let things develop. It's the art of the inquiry. Great negotiators, they act on the information they have, but they also acquire the information they don't have. And, of course, if they can't get that information, they protect themselves through contingency agreements.

So, going back to my first negotiation all those years ago, if I just had a few of these tools, I'd be more confident. I'd have been more ambitious. I'd have been less willing to give concessions too quickly. I'd have put myself in their shoes and understood that well, I would have tried to expand the negotiation.

Rather than just negotiating over salary, I would have added other issues like where I'm going to live, time off and travel, where I'm going to get my visa every three months. I did have other options and they didn't have that much leverage so I could have made it a much more value-added kind of win-win type negotiation rather than a binary single-issue negotiation which usually hit an impasse.

It's like the Grand Bazaar in Istanbul, haggling over the price of a carpet. It's the ultimate kind of single-issue negotiation. But actually, even here, if you're smart about it, you can find different issues. Cash or card? What currency? You can take their business card and put it in the desk of your hotel. You can throw in a jacket. Suddenly, you've got five or six issues where you're negotiating over and you're in a much better position."

Do it More, Better

There is tons more to be said about negotiation, of course, but this easy-to-recall formula will get you your best outcome in 90%

of your situations. But, remember, there were all those "What if...?" scenarios we mentioned at the beginning of this chapter, the edge cases, and I said I would tell you the answer to them.

Here it is: if you find the Golden Formula isn't working, go back to it and do it, more, better.

Imagine you're learning to play tennis and your teacher tells you how to return a serve:

1. Get in the correct position on court
2. Get the right body shape and grip
3. Read the serve & anticipate
4. Split stop
5. Keep your eyes focussed on the ball at all times.
6. Move the arm back ready to swing
7. Hit through the ball with plenty of power.

Great, you think, and you practice and you practice and you get good at it and learn how to return the serve really well. And then one day you find yourself playing against someone far better than you've ever played before and they send down a serve that whizzes past you before you've even got to step 2 of your process.

You lose the first set to love and it's so embarrassing that you ask to take a break and you run off to the bathroom and, from your cubicle, you call the teacher that taught you everything you know about the game. "Help!" you scream down the phone, "What shall I do?"

Well, your teacher won't give you any new shot to use, they won't give you some amazing new technique where you swing your racquet around your head three times whilst executing a double-back somersault before playing your return. They will calmly tell you to get in the right position on court and then proceed through all the steps you already know how to do – but do them more, better.

You rush back on the court, do it more, better, and win the next two sets and, with a huge sigh of relief, retire while your ahead.

So, negotiation is like playing tennis. The Golden Formula will tell you exactly how to do it and if it isn't working, do it more, better. We could go into exactly *how* to do it more and better but that's outside the scope of this book (but feel free to check out my other books where everything will be explained!)

Is it really as simple as interests, variables and BATNA? To a large degree, yes. Sure, there's nuance and contextual specifics, but these three things will solve the large majority of your situations.

Fisher's research found that the best negotiators, those who could solve the toughest of problems with the highest stakes between the deadliest of enemies, worked this way.

DIY Mediation

If you've ever attended a mediation, you may well have been surprised how effective it can be – getting two parties with seemingly incompatible outcomes to actually reach an agreement they both like.

The mediator will go through a specific process:

- Firstly, outlining what will happen and getting buy-in to some ground rules
- Hearing everyone's opening statements
- Identifying the key issues and building an agreed agenda around them
- Exploring what's important for everyone (in other words, their interests)

- Brainstorming possible solutions (using multiple variables) and evaluating each
- Some to-ing and fro-ing on the details but the mediator always reminding them of their interests and helping keeping emotions under control
- Reaching an agreement.

Well, you can do this yourself and save the money.

Mediators are professionals and know the best practice and it works. Now you know what they do (effectively, the Golden Formula embedded in the above process), you can do it yourself

Why not start your conversation by saying something along the lines of: "Ok, I know we've got quite different opinions here, but how about we try and resolve it in a grown-up kind of way? We'll both lay out our perspectives, you can go first if you want. Then we'll see if we can identify what the key sticking point is and see if we can solve that. Are you up for this?"

"Sure."

"Great, and each person has a fair turn at talking, we can even set a time on it, if you like. And let's not get personal, we'll try and stay as fair and objective as we can. No swearing! Would that work?"

"Well, we can give it a ****ing try!"

Imagine you and your sibling are taking over the family business. Your parents want to retire and you see it as a fabulous opportunity to expand aggressively while your sis/bro prefers a steadier approach. You both feel quite strongly and you're both angry and disappointed with the other about their views.

But you decide to self-mediate, you are family after all, and in the process you identify that your ambition is driven by your belief in the business's potential but sis/bro is worried about the risk and, anyway, they don't want to upset their nice work-life balance.

What could be quite a tetchy conversation goes smoothly and it's agreed that the parents will phase their retirement over three years and you will oversee an expansion into two new markets but with careful financial planning involving the parents and an advisory board created to provide external perspective.

Great: parents can retire, their pension is protected, your plans for global domination are being market-tested and sis/bro can be relieved their world isn't about to be turned upside down.

And everyone still meets up for Christmas.

Be Fair, Be Demonstrably Fair

Setting ground rules and agreeing the process upfront is quite a neat trick. It's hard to refuse, so once they say yes, we've already reached agreement about *some*thing! This is a good precedent and the conversation will likely continue in that spirit.

And if it goes off track at any time, just mention the process or the guidelines, and you'll get back on track straightaway.

There's something else at play, too. It's about being demonstrably fair. Many conflicts arise because of different subjective opinions on a matter. I think I'm worth double my salary, my boss thinks I'm worth a pay cut. How do we go beyond this? By going objective. But each of us thinks we *are* being objective. So, we need to be demonstrably objective. Getting market figures or using a neutral mediator might be a part of this.

After the Northern Ireland Good Friday Agreement was signed in 1998, the implementation of the deal didn't go as smoothly as hoped, especially when it came to decommissioning the arms of the various paramilitaries, the largest of whom were the IRA.

None of the sides really trusted each other so how to manage such an important and sensitive part of the process? The answer was to get neutral 3rd parties to oversee the process.

The British government asked the recently resigned President of Finland Martti Ahtisaari to help with the process and the IRA wanted Cyril Ramaphosa, former secretary-general of the ANC. Ramaphosa was known to be exceptionally persuasive, as well as highly intelligent and personable and the IRA saw clear parallels with the ANC's struggle with the apartheid government in South Africa and their own struggles.

As it happened, Ahtisaari and Ramaphosa knew each other well from previous duties, and so began a process that went from 5-star Mayfair hotels to blindfolded midnight trips to safe houses and underground weapon stores in the middle of the forest.

The success of this process was one of the most significant steps in the peace process since the ratification of the Good Friday Agreement two years earlier.

Now, if you don't have Martti and Cyril on speed dial, you can still be demonstrably objective by using independent data or by self-mediating: agreeing on a fair process and then, of course, sticking to it. You and your sis/bro setting up an advisory board to manage expansion plans is also being demonstrably objective. And I might agree with my boss to find some market surveys for salaries for people in my industry of my level of experience.

The End of Conflict?

And here's the thing. Once you have done this, you have now developed a way of working with each other. In the future, you will go straight to the self-mediation because you've seen how powerful it is. You will build a great working relationship and there will be huge trust.

This is how we end conflict. Everyone do this everywhere.

Although, of course, it's not quite so simple.

3
Human, All Too Human

We've just seen that we, as a species, know best practice and every day there are countless successes, big and small, using it.

So why are there still wars? Why do nearly half of marriages end in divorce? Why are the courts full?

For two reasons. The first we already mentioned, that the know-how isn't well spread. The second is that it isn't easy putting the know-how into practice.

But the good news is that AI has a whole stack of superpowers, which means neither reason applies to it.

We'll look at those superpowers at the end of the chapter but let's explore the problems first.

Maybe We Don't Know It

You don't have to travel around too many markets, pubs or local council meetings to realise that most people think the best way to achieve their goal is through shouting loudly and forcefully achieving it at the other person's expense. At best, it's a haggle where both sides need to compromise.

Why is this? From an individual perspective, why might I not have heard that working together to create extra value for all is possible?

To be fair to us humans, it's not the "natural" approach. If we look at young children, a raw state of humanity, our gene-pool allows for many kids to be naturally kind and giving but probably the majority take a more selfish view. And even the generous ones will lash out if they think they're being treated unfairly. Collaboration exists in nature, in fact it's probably the single most effective strategy in evolution, and humans are good at it. But still, for most of us it is a behaviour we need to learn so we can override our instinct.

It's not even the "common sense" view either because common sense comes from culture and some cultures have learnt to override the instinct much more than others.

The five most peaceful countries in the world, as measured in terms of internal safety and security, are Singapore, Iceland, Norway, Switzerland and Finland.[1] Interestingly, these countries also rank highly as the richest[2], the happiest[3], the least corrupt and most trusting of their government.[4]

Obviously, the relationships between these measures are complex but almost certainly there is some linkage from trust to collaboration to peace to security to wealth, happiness and lack of corruption.

So, these countries have figured it out and for their citizens it's common sense to work together peaceably. Many other countries, however, aren't there yet and so, in those, the common sense is to be guarded and look out for oneself first and foremost.

So, if you live in one of these latter countries it would only be normal if you had never been exposed to the idea that working together was the best approach. It's unlikely you would invent the idea for yourself.

Even here, in the UK, my courses are full of well-meaning people who would like to be fair in their dealings but just don't know how to do it when faced with someone who is being difficult or with a situation that seems deadlocked.

The good news is that there are courses, books, videos and all kinds of resources that can show us how to do it. Like Fisher's "Getting to Yes", these capture best practice then make it more widely available.

And so, the behaviours spread as more and more people do it and the world becomes more harmonious as a result. "The arc of the moral universe is long, but it bends toward justice," said Martin Luther King, famously. I said this in Chapter One, but he said it much more poetically and in far fewer words.

So, that's positive but it still has a way to go and "the arc…is long".

But this is where artificial intelligence will help. One of the core arguments of this book is that AI will help spread best practice, too, and so accelerate the process. We'll see exactly how it will do this in the coming chapters.

But there is still the second impediment to overcome, that we might know what to do in theory but putting it into practice is difficult. Look at me, I write books about the topic and run training programmes, I know the theory really well but I still find myself in arguments I don't want to have. (Although, clearly, it's the other person's fault.)

This is the difference between declarative knowledge and procedural knowledge. Declarative knowledge is, effectively, knowledge you can declare – knowledge you can describe and discuss.

Wikipedia is the go-to source of much declarative knowledge but if you're learning to swim, don't assume reading all the swimming-related pages on Wikipedia will sort you out. You have to get in the water to learn to swim. Like all skills, knowing how to swim requires procedural knowledge.

As the Spanish proverb says, "Talking about bull-fighting is not the same as being in the ring."

So maybe we do know that it's best to collaborate and maybe we even know how to do it in theory. But that doesn't mean we can always do it in practice.

My Superpower Is I Can Read People's T-Shirts

Scott Tillema, retired negotiator with Chicago area SWAT team and co-founder of The Negotiations Collective

"So, I spent 20 years with a suburban Chicago Police Department, and I specialised in crisis and hostage negotiation, spending eight years on a regional SWAT team covering 70 different cities around the Chicago area.

For example, I negotiated with a man, face-to-face, and he's holding a gun to his head. There'd been a disturbance with him and his wife, and there was a possibility he could be going to jail for it, and he decided to go to the basement, take a gun, and hold it to his head.

We negotiated with him for 18 hours. And you'll tell me it's not possible to hold a gun to your head for 18 hours and I would agree with you until we watched it be done. These people in crisis are just overwhelmed with emotion, they have a lot of trouble being rational.

And as a crisis negotiator, it's important to manage yourself first. So, in our training there is a long process of stress inoculation, working every week, doing practice and real role playing. It's no longer sitting in a classroom watching the slideshow passively, it's skill building, doing scenarios and getting coached in real time where someone can help you through it.

And we can talk about tactical breathing or box breathing – in two, three, four, hold two, three, four, out two, three, four, hold two, three, four. But the expert level people are doing this years in advance because they know you have to have good ownership of your triggers, what's going to be done or said that's going to throw you off your game.

We all have them, it's normal. It could be in deep-rooted trauma. It could be in a variety of things. Don't be worried if you have a trigger but you do have to know what it is, so when it occurs you can manage yourselves through it. So, we'd put someone in the hot seat and probe them, push those triggers so they can learn to manage them.

Now, what helps is having a mindset of inquiry. And I have discovered I've got a superpower and that superpower is I am able in these moments to read people's T-shirts. It's a T-shirt that nobody else can see. It's underneath their shirt. And some of these T-shirts read phrases like, "I just lost my job", "I'm getting divorced", "My mother is in hospice", "I have a drinking problem", "My kids won't talk to me". Everybody has these T-shirts on.

So, rather than being judgmental about their behavior, or triggered by something they say, I go into curiosity mode, "I wonder what their shirt says today? Let's explore that a little bit."

And when negotiators interview people afterwards, the person on the other side of the negotiation, they'll usually be asked what influenced them to resolve it peacefully. And generally, they say, I don't really remember what was said, but I really liked how you said it. I just felt comfortable with you."

The Amygdala – Our Best and Worst Friend

The problem with conflict is that even when we know what to do, our amygdala likes to run the show and the first thing it does is throw all the best practice out of the window. It's a bit like the knuckle-headed security guard who piles in saying, "This is important, I'm going to take over."

We have to thank our amygdala, it does protect us, it has kept us alive to date but, socially speaking, it doesn't take the most sophisticated of approaches.

It expects a fight, especially if we were exposed to bad examples or had bad experiences in our childhood, and because it expects a fight, it finds it, of course. Confirmation bias points out those things we expect and fundamental attribution error puts the blame squarely on the other person.[5] Our amygdala feels vindicated.

And so we learn to catastrophise and the next time there is even the mildest confrontation, our amygdala tells us to run away or pile in pre-emptively. It overrides our pre-frontal cortex and its logical processing, leading to an emotional overwhelm and we can no longer think or communicate as clearly as we would like.

It triggers the release of cortisol and adrenaline, great for the fight but they, too, impair our clarity of thinking. At best, we get defensive and stop listening, at worst we get aggressive and make it personal.

So, if we can manage our amygdala, rather than letting our amygdala manage us, we'll probably perform better.

As with everything, preparation is a key success factor. If we really do our research, if we really know our stuff, we will feel a lot more comfortable in the conversation and we'll be able to stay in control. Our preparation should also include thinking how the conversation might go and having plans for different scenarios, emotion-management plans as well. Maybe even practise the conversation beforehand: in the mirror, with a friend or with your cuddly toys lined up on the bed (don't get too angry with them).

We mentioned confirmation bias and how it points out those things we expect. If we're expecting a fight, it will point out the other person's aggressive behaviours. Or, at least, it *interprets* their behaviours as aggressive. The converse is also true. If we expect the other person to be friendly or collaborative, our confirmation bias will find this too.

In one study, a group of negotiators were informed they were going to negotiate with their opponent, another group were told it was with their partner. The latter group went in more collaboratively and, accordingly, achieved better results, even though the briefs were identical.[6] This shows the importance of framing it as a collaborative, problem-solving process.

Expect it to proceed collaboratively and it is more likely to do so.

Yes, Simon, but what about if it doesn't?

And it's a fair question, no matter how well we prepare, there's always a chance it will go very differently to our expectations. Well, there's things we can do in the moment that will help too.

Timothy Gallwey was an early pioneer in the coaching industry and he was one of the first to focus on psychology in sports coaching. He started as a tennis coach and he noticed some of his clients would get rattled when they played a bad shot which meant they were more likely to play a bad shot the next time. Other clients didn't have a problem with this. They seemed to have selective amnesia and the next point would go fine.[7]

So, he developed the STOP Technique for those clients who weren't able to control their emotions. The acronym stands for:

- **S**tep Back:

  Just take a short pause to regain composure and notice what is going on.

- **T**hink:

  Try and do a quick sense-check of what is going on and why. Reconnect with the outcome you want from the situation and also reconnect with any plans you had for dealing with when it becomes emotional. And then consider what you need to do to stay on track for your outcome.

- **O**rganise your thoughts and feelings:

    Having done your thinking, what is it you now need to do? Maybe you need to take a couple of slow, deep breaths, maybe you need to take a short time-out. Naming your emotion can often be helpful, it can reduce the intensity and allow you to identify a management strategy. Cognitive reframing can also be effective, finding a different perspective on the situation to open up new options. For example, perhaps you notice you've slipped back into viewing them as an opponent and shifting into a partner frame might get a better result.

- **P**roceed

    Whatever you decided to do, now go ahead and do it and you should notice the conversation getting back on track.

What we're doing is placing a quick mental re-direct in between the stimulus and response, allowing the rational part of the brain to override the amygdala, so our response is much more likely to be effective.

One situation where this can be really helpful is when our ego is threatened. Our egos can be very sensitive and the other person might say something that we feel is patronising or disrespectful and we get aggressive in response. Sometimes that's a valid response but not usually. If we receive a sarcastic email, for example, we often roll our sleeves up and reply in the same manner, showing them exactly how good at sarcasm *we* are. Great, that showed them and our ego is intact.

But we've probably inflamed the situation hugely and the likelihood of getting our outcome has significantly reduced.

Much better to use the STOP method above. By all means, write the reply but don't press send. Come back a few hours later and remove all the swear words from your response and still don't press send. Come back the next day, maybe even the day after that, and you'll have calmed down. You'll probably be very glad you didn't press send and you'll want to send a completely different reply.

Do press send on that one.

Maybe Their Amygdala Is Running Their Show

"But it's not me, Simon, it's *them*."

I hear you. Their amygdala is the problem, not yours. Your amygdala only gets agitated because theirs does.

That's probably true but it's probably true for them, too. Their amygdala has become vocal because yours has. This is the nature of amygdala, one triggers the other and vice versa.

We expect a fight so we go in looking for a fight; they pick up on this and they start looking for the fight too. All happening subconsciously. If we're lucky, the other person's amygdala is mild-mannered but it's rare; if we're lucky, they're good at managing their amygdala, but it's rare.

So, if we want to get a successful outcome, we need to take responsibility and, as well as managing our amygdala, and that's hard enough, we need to manage theirs, too. No wonder there is so much conflict.

How on earth do we manage a piece of machinery deep inside someone else's brain? Well, if we know the relationship between the inputs and the outputs of that piece of machinery, we can do it.

So, the outcome we want is a calm and relaxed amygdala. Great, so don't do any of the kind of things that might disturb it and, if necessary, do do those things that appease it. Easy!

This means providing psychological safety; if they feel psychologically safe, that they are fully respected as a person, they are much more likely to behave reasonably and collaboratively.

If We Have Two Amygdala to Manage, Start with Our Own, It's Closest

So, again, the most important thing is to manage our own emotions. If we've got two amygdala to manage, start with our own, it's closest. Manage ours so that we don't trigger theirs so they don't trigger ours. Do everything we discussed above and we're in a good starting place.

Next most important is to listen to them. *Really* listen to them. Why do they keep repeating themselves, why do they shout, why do they just go on and on? Because they don't think you've been listening to them. In their mind, their position is so obviously fair and correct that the only reason you're not agreeing to it is because you're not listening.

So, listen to them, ask questions to understand their position more deeply, and then play back their arguments to them, better than they could have put it themselves. After all, you want them to listen to you, don't you? Well, it's only courteous if you go first. You can't expect them to listen to you if you're not willing to listen to them.

And, by the way, when you listen, have some humility and be open to changing your mind. Again, you want them to change their mind, don't you? Well, if that's the case, you need to go first and show them the way.

Even Your Words Should Be Non-Violent

Non-Violent Communication is a method of communication developed by Marshall Rosenborg that can be very powerful in conflict situations.[8] It gives a structure that goes beyond blame and demands but, instead, focusses on:

1. Facts

    Instead of saying "You never tidy up", say "Your books are spread across the dining table".

2. Feelings

    Instead of saying "You're so messy", say "I feel frustrated"

3. Needs

    Instead of saying "I need you to tidy up", say "I need to be in a tidy living space"

4. Requests

    Instead of saying "You've got to clear things up", say "Would you be willing to tidy up before dinner?"

This approach, based on undeniable facts, not interpretations and judgements, doesn't trigger defences, doesn't trigger the good ol' amygdala.

If I'm No Longer Blaming and Attacking, I Can Break the Cycle

Shona Cameron, Psychologist and Non-Violent Communication trainer.

"One of the main reasons we're not so good at conflict is our re activity, we have a habitual reactivity, often depending on what kind of day we've had. In neuroscience terms, we lose oxygen to the frontal cortex and it takes us into a brainstem reaction, which is fight or flight or freeze. We get overwhelmed and we lose the capacity for the big picture,

Learning non-violent communication enables us to try something a bit different. Rather than getting defensive and making them the enemy, it asks us to check how we're feeling, what needs of ours are unmet. If it's a threat to me in some way, there'll be an unmet need. It's a kind of self-empathy process in the moment. And then we can take action from there.

The conflict typically happens because I feel attacked, therefore, I blame and attack back, and therefore they feel attacked, and so it carries on.

Even the thinking that I feel attacked is likely to escalate a conflict. It's not possible to feel attacked. I'm still in thinking. What might I be feeling instead? Scared or angry or upset. Then from that, what need of mine is unmet?

And if I'm taking action from my feelings and needs, then it's less likely that I'll escalate the conflict because I'm no longer making an enemy of the other person, I'm no longer blaming and attacking. It's my opportunity to break the cycle.

Let's say I've just walked in from work and my partner tells me, "Oh, no, don't put your bag down there" or something. And then I feel annoyed. I might be thinking, "Why are you in my face?" but I'm feeling annoyed. What need is unmet? Probably ease. Or space. Or peace. Allowing myself to decompress coming home from work.

So, if I responded from the thinking, I'd say, "Get out my face," and it's not likely to be conducive to a comfortable evening. But, responding from the unmet need, I might take a deep breath and recognise a need for some space and I just give myself some room.

And then I might be able to consider what their need is. Maybe it's order. So now we can talk at that level, "Can you give me five minutes when I come in to kind of go blah? And then I will put my stuff away, once I've sat down for a few minutes." Or something like that, some kind of dialogue around needs rather than

> "You're the slobbiest person I've ever lived with!" and "You always tell me off as soon as I walk in!"
>
> And slowly, slowly, it just starts to get into place."

If You Want to De-Escalate Tension, Show A Bit of Grit

In 1962, at the height of the Cold War, psychologist Charles Osgood published "An alternative to war or surrender",[9] in which he outlined the GRIT method of de-escalating tension. Elected President of the American Psychological Association the following year, he knew there were ways of facilitating peace even in the toughest of situations and that they could be initiated by one party, even when the other was acting aggressively.

His method, Graduated Reciprocation in Tension Reduction, involved one party taking small, unilateral steps towards de-escalation and inviting the other party to reciprocate. There were four steps involved:

1. Announce intention.

    Publicly declare the intent to reduce tension and invite reciprocation.

2. Go first.

    Take small, concrete actions that demonstrate goodwill. They should be unilateral without any pre-negotiation and they should be visible. Examples could include an apology, a compliment or a small compromise.

3. Stay strong.

    It's important to maintain strength to avoid appearing weak. Your actions in the previous step should be genuine but they should not compromise your security and they should be reversible, too, just in case.

    If the other party doesn't reciprocate, you can take another small action or reverse the one just taken. If the other party actively tries to exploit it, then respond with retaliation, scaled to match their act, in order to restore the status quo existing just prior to the escalation. Then start again.

4. Invite Reciprocation:

    Clearly communicate the expectation of reciprocal actions from the other party.

John F Kennedy was a fan of his book and it has been applied in several geo-political conflicts of the toughest kind.[10] It's a gradual process, building trust over time. We can't expect to dive straight into being best buddies, but we can expect to slowly foster trust, creating a positive feedback loop between the conflicting parties.

Trust is usually self-fulfilling. To misquote Henry Ford, if you think you can trust or you think you can't, you're probably right. Our expectations of a fight create a fight but our expectations of a peaceful solution will normally create that, too.

As we saw in the previous chapter, you don't need to trust the other person if you've built a trustable process. That's why the acts should be reversible and you should have the ability to retaliate if necessary. If you have a process you can trust and you follow that then slowly the trust builds between the individuals too.

This is true for them, too, of course. So, explain to them how they don't need to trust you (because they don't) but they can trust the process, that they too have the ability to reverse their actions if they think it's necessary.

Slowly, slowly, the trust builds and the conversation can become more collaborative.

Human, All Too Human? Not Human At All

So, if it is our human limitations that prevent us from implementing best practice even though said best practice is known by the species, and maybe even by ourselves individually, perhaps some non-human help will solve the problem.

Whenever earth is threatened in the films, the problem is easily solved by calling on a superhero whose superpower saves the day. Superman can fly through the air and his eyes can shoot beams of intense heat; Wonder Woman has superhuman strength and can teleport; Mister Fantastic is very, very stretchy. And they all have unfeasibly amazing costumes and wear their underpants on the outside.

Artificial intelligence has superhuman powers, too, and maybe it's these that will save us from ourselves, save us by preventing or resolving conflict more effectively.

The AI Superpowers

So, can AI fly through the air? Teleport? Be very, very stretchy?

Probably not, but it does have many other superpowers that it can draw upon. Let's have a look at them briefly and then, as we go through the remaining chapters, we will see again and again how these are being put into practice in real life situations right now to get great super-human results in negotiation and how they will be able to be put into practice even more as the technology develops.

- Modelling best practice

We saw in the last chapter that Professor Roger Fisher modelled some of the most highly skilled negotiators in the world then wrote about it in a best-selling book, spreading that best practice. One of AI's most important superpowers is its ability to model human best practice, learning from countless examples of negotiation and identifying which strategies are most successful, which tactics are most effective and even which language patterns communicate best.

Then this capability will be widely available for all to use. So, whether it's an online mediator that can help you and your flatmate decide on who how to divvy up the household chores, or whether it's a digital judge deciding on a liability dispute arising from ambiguous contract terms, its decisions will be as good as, if not better than, the best humans'.

Indeed, as bots become increasingly embedded in our world, much of our negotiation will devolve to them, quietly operating according to best practice behind the scenes and reaching outcomes that benefit everyone.

- Managing huge data:

AI can process vast amounts of information, enabling it to take into account all relevant factors in complex negotiations.

For instance, in international trade negotiations, it can consider economic data, industry regulations, environmental impacts, and social factors from multiple countries, along with historical precedents, to produce an agreement that is optimal for everyone. Similarly, in a corporate merger, it can analyse thousands of contracts, financial records, and external data sets to identify potential synergies and risks.

It will cover all bases in a manner that no human can. Moreover, it can optimise across far more variables than any human and thus create agreements that extract maximum value while ensuring fairness.

- Creative solutions:

"That's a very strange move," said one commentator, describing Move 37 of the game between AlphaGo, Google DeepMind's AI Go software, and Lee Sedol, the player with the second highest number of international titles in Go history.[11, 12] "I thought it was a mistake," said the co-commentator. It confused all the Go experts watching and Sedol, himself, said he was speechless.

It was a move that no human would have made, but it changed the game, and AlphaGo went on to win. AI represents a different type of intelligence compared to humans and can discover unexpected solutions that people might overlook. In a complex business negotiation, it could devise a creative structure for the deal that benefits all parties, or in a community dispute, it might propose an innovative resource-sharing arrangement that had not occurred to the human negotiators.

Negotiation is a *highly* creative process. We saw that the best negotiators view negotiation as a collaborative problem-solving process – well, sometimes those problems are exceedingly difficult to resolve. How do you resolve the Israel-Palestine situation? It ain't easy. AI just might surprise everyone with an answer.

- Digital twins and understanding complex systems

With an ability to handle vast quantities of data and generate predictions based on semantic mapping and pattern identification, it's possible to build detailed models of individuals, communities or systems, and then run scenarios on the model to predict likely responses.[13]

Negotiation is a perfect context for this and a negotiator could use it to test different strategies before actual engagement.

For example, before you ask your boss for a pay-rise, you might rehearse the conversation with an avatar built from all your email correspondence with them. The avatar would respond in the way your boss would and this gives you insight into how best to go about your request.

In a cross-cultural negotiation, it can build a belief map of the other culture and so help you understand their norms and values better. You could then practice with this to make sure you don't trigger any sensitivities that would offend the other party and lose the deal.

Alternatively, in a labour negotiation, a digital twin of the organisation could model the impact of different proposals on various stakeholders and so lead to a solution that is fairest for all.

Or, again, in a peace negotiation, it can simulate how different arrangements might affect regional stability. Its ability to scenario model complex systems and "see the future" helps parties make more informed decisions and create more sustainable agreements.

- Super-quick and always on

Its ability to process huge amounts of information rapidly can shrink the preparation and due diligence phases of a negotiation by an order of magnitude. And in the meeting, itself, you can use it as a support tool to evaluate proposals. If the other party suggests something you hadn't considered, there's no need to ask to reconvene in a week as you go back to the office and run the proposal on your spreadsheets. You can ask your AI support tool there and then and it will give you real-time analysis and suggest mutually beneficial modifications.

And its 24/7 availability means it can constantly monitor situations, allowing early warning of developments and instant responses. In a conflict zone, its monitoring of social media might flag a potential flashpoint and allow a pre-emptive intervention to avoid any escalation of violence.

- Managing multiple participants:

Negotiations are never solely about the two people talking, they invariably impact many others. How do we tackle the climate change challenge? Well, there are 8 billion people impacted by this question and we should probably hear all of their opinions. Yeah, right!

Except maybe AI *can* do this. Right now, it's not possible but in later chapters we will see platforms that are managing conversations between tens of thousands of people in real-time and facilitating them towards nuanced, sophisticated agreements that the large majority from all sides buy into. And these platforms, optimised for agreement, will only get more powerful and be able to deal with larger numbers.

It's a tremendously exciting area which is already fostering peace in unlikely situations, is already healing divided societies and is already mending our broken politics.

- Lack of ego/emotions:

We've spent much of this chapter discussing how ego and emotions are high on the list of culprits when it comes to why we can't always reach agreement despite good intentions.

But AI doesn't have an amygdala. It won't get offended, it won't react defensively, it won't bear grudges from previous hurts, it won't get frustrated by the other side's difficult behaviour. No matter how heated the conversation gets, no matter how sensitive the issue, it will be able to keep the discussion focussed on substantive issues rather than personal conflicts.

This emotional neutrality allows AI to consistently apply rational problem-solving approaches even when human participants are highly emotional, helping to guide conversations back to productive dialogue.

- Neutral 3rd party:

We've seen how an independent perspective can solve problems that the "I think it's worth x" vs "I think it's worth y" approach never can and we've seen how a fair process helps where there's no trust. Well, an artificial intelligence has no stake in the outcome, so it can serve as a truly impartial mediator.

In a divorce, an AI mediator could ensure both parties receive equal speaking time and that the settlement meets agreed fairness criteria. In business negotiations, it could objectively evaluate deal terms against industry benchmarks without any inherent bias.

This opens the door for greater trust which ultimately leads to better outcomes for all.

No x-ray vision or ability to rapidly scale tall buildings but that's a pretty good bunch of superpowers. There are others too but these are the recurring capabilities that underlie the examples we will discuss in the coming chapters.

We humans are pretty good at solving problems and we fight less and collaborate more than almost any other species but still we have our limits. It's the argument of this book that AI, with its superpowers, will help us transcend those limits – if we decide to use it in that way.

4
A New Enlightenment

Life As Information Technology

"First the earth cooled. And then the dinosaurs came, but they got too big and fat, so they all died and they turned into oil. And then the Arabs came and they bought Mercedes Benzes. And Prince Charles started wearing all of Lady Di's clothes."

This is the Gospel According to Airplane II: The Sequel.[1]

But it neglects a few details. A whole load of things happened between the earth cooling and the dinosaurs: namely, a bunch of chemicals lying around started to react with each other and some even started to react to produce more of themselves. We called these chemicals life and they went on, as we saw in Chapter One, to become you and me and the duck.

Life is intelligence. According to Freeman Dyson, life is "a material system that can acquire, store, process and use information to organise its activities".[2] DNA is a precise machine for doing precisely that. Life is the first form of information technology we know of.

Life is intelligent, amoeba are intelligent. In some ways, at least, they're more intelligent than humans. The Travelling Salesman problem is a famously tricky maths challenge, asking: "Given a list of cities and the distances between each pair of cities, what is the shortest possible route that visits each city exactly once and returns to the origin city?" Despite extensive study, the problem has yet to be definitively nailed.[3]

But while all these mathematicians wear out their pencils trying to solve it, amoeba sit back and laugh because they cracked it hundreds of millions of years ago.

When Atsushi Tero placed some slime mould, physarum polycephalum, at the centre of a map of the Tokyo subway and placed oat flakes (slime mould's favourite snack) on all the surrounding towns, the mould worked out the shortest way to reach them all, mirroring almost exactly the region's rail network.[4]

So, amoeba are intelligent and humans came along shortly after and some of them are intelligent, too. This is natural intelligence. And any intelligence that is not natural is artificial.

Chemistry is split into organic chemistry (life) and inorganic (not life) but really, it's all just chemistry. There is no distinction other than in our textbooks. Humans love applying labels and some things we call life and natural, others we call not life and artificial, but that distinction doesn't exist in the universe, only in our brains.

Intelligence is just the universe trying to understand itself, artificial or natural, it is all one process.

Language and Writing

Slime mould are better than humans at The Travelling Salesman problem but they are not as good at most other maths problems, especially if calculators are allowed. And that's because something happened in our brain a while back that enabled us to do symbolic reasoning better than any animal before.

The symbolic reasoning we use primarily is language. We're not the only animals with it, all pet owners know that dogs bark meaningfully – they have one bark for "I'm going to get that squirrel" and another one for "Squirrel! Come down from that tree now and let me get you!"

But it's suggested some evolutionary event took place 70-100,000 years ago that enabled homo sapiens to take their language to another level altogether, way beyond the level of squirrels and trees.[5] Some paleo-linguists think it took place significantly earlier, but even when paleo-linguists disagree they use language as their means to disagree.[6] Symbolic reasoning, as enabled by human language, was the most recent great Darwinian advance on our branch of the tree, at least, and since then it has been cultural evolution as the primary driver of progress, and cultural evolution operates on a much faster timeframe.

With language, we could now invent things and share those inventions with other people. If a pre-historic friend of mine invented a new effective method of hunting, they could tell me how to do it and I could hunt better, too. They could have told me how to use tools, how to build weatherproof huts and, as they learnt how to nurture grains and domesticate cattle, they could have taught me how to farm, as well.

And when they invented writing, they could have taught not just me but many more people.

Writing was originally developed as an accounting process: they used tokens to represent traded commodities which were sealed in a clay envelope and their shape embossed the clay in a recognisable manner. By looking at the embossed image I would know it represented two goats or ten bales of hay.[7]

The Sumerians developed this system further as the images became pictograms and, by 3300BCE, had at least 1500 different symbols that could be used in different ways. A foot could mean a foot but it could also mean walking, a mouth could also mean speaking. Even more abstract, they could use homophonics – to write "I saw Bill", they might draw an eye, a saw (the serrated-edged tool) and the bill of a bird.

And then phonetic abstraction took it further still. Our letter "A" is the first sound of the Phoenician word for bull, aleph, and we can see that, rotated 180 degrees, A is the head of a bull. Our letter "B" comes from their word for a house, bet, and, again, we can see that the capital letter looks like a simple plan for a house. Nearly all the letters in the Latin alphabet (aleph-bet) evolved this way.

This means now we aren't limited to writing about goats and bales of hay, we can write about anything we want. About laws of physics, about existentialism, about West Ham United.

And writing is thinking fixed in time. Spoken language disappears with the wind but writing could travel without loss of information or corruption, it could be copied so more people could access it, it could be stored for anyone to reference, it could be studied and learnt by heart, it could be analysed and critiqued and developed further.

It enabled new types of social structures like democracy and republics. It enabled new trading and financial structures. It enabled cities and empires, the size of which had never been seen. It enabled new religions as the Axial age brought us Hinduism, Buddhism, Jainism, Confucianism, Taoism, Zoroastrianism, Judaism and others.

Life, an information technology, was creating new forms of information technology.

The Printing Press

Though few people noticed at the time, the world changed momentously in 1455 when Johannes Gutenberg printed a copy of the Bible in Mainz with his recently built printing press.[8]

According to Yale professor Elizabeth Eisenstein, many saw it as the work of the devil because it allowed the spread of heretical ideas. It gave birth to new forms of publication like the newspaper, the political or religious pamphlet and the scandal sheet and these gave rise to new religious and political freedoms or caused huge divisions in society, depending on your perspective.

It didn't always spread *best* practice. Fake news, scandal and horror sold well. One of the most popular books was Malleus Maleficarum, written in 1487 by Heinrich Kramer, usually translated as "The Hammer of Witches", and it was the main driver behind the witch hunts of the time. As Jonathan Swift wrote in 1710, "Falsehood flies, and the Truth comes limping after it."[9]

And when Martin Luther called King Henry VIII "King Henry, of God's Disgrace" and a "damnable and offensive worm", describing him as having "a slavish and impudent and strumpet-like insolence", Sir Thomas More replied on Henry's behalf, referring to Luther as the "Reverend Father Tosspot" and argued people should be permitted "to throw back into your paternity's shitty mouth, truly the shit-pool of all shit, all the muck and shit which your damnable rottenness has vomited up, and to empty out all the sewers and privies onto your crown."[10]

Two of the greatest religious minds of their time setting a wonderful example to the rest of us.

But Eisenstein also points out that many others considered the printing press as a divine gift since its ability to mass-produce accurate copies of the Bible enabled a wider access to God's word.[11]

And more than just the Bible, it was a publishing outlet for scholarly editions, poems, plays, criticisms, philosophies and all kinds of other writing. Over time, literacy rates increased making knowledge more accessible to a broader audience and by the mid-18th century, public opinion had become a real force in political affairs.

It enabled the Reformation, but it also enabled the Enlightenment, the scientific revolution, the industrial revolution, the agrarian revolution as well as the political revolutions of the following centuries.

To say the printing press produced a revolution is to underestimate its impact, it produced several.

I Think of The Printing Press as Adding an Exponential Factor

Dr Joanne Paul, Historian, author of "The House of Dudley"

"It's ironic, in a way, that Gutenberg starts with the Bible, given how important it becomes to the Reformation, and there certainly are arguments that suggest that you wouldn't have the Reformation if you hadn't had the printing press.

But scholars argue between themselves in terms of this idea of the print revolution and some hold it was just an expansion of something that had existed before; that most of the sorts of books that were produced had been produced before and most of the people buying them were the same sorts of people who bought them before because they were the only people who could read. Especially in its first decades.

But it's still doing a lot of work there, right? I always think of the printing press as adding an exponential factor to things that are already existing.

One of the main factors in the Reformation is that they were able to produce these pamphlets. For instance, Fish's "Supplication for the Beggars" is a very pithy pamphlet arguing against the church and it's supposedly strewn on the streets as people are heading towards the opening of Parliament. Which ends up being the Reformation Parliament, with lots of anti-clerical acts passed. So, it might be hard to make a direct connection but those two things did happen next to each other.

And, arguably, the English Civil War is the first real sort of propaganda war, a pamphlet war. From the 1620s right into the 1640s, you get these really intense pamphlets on either side. There's a famous image from a pamphlet at the time of two dogs going at each other, the Parliamentarian and the Royalist dogs. Even the dogs are attacking each other.

So, in terms of conflict, there's an argument that it caused more because finally ideas were able to be expressed and spread further. It opened a new medium by which people can say scandalous, traitorous, vitriolic things; I think it stoked a lot of flames of conflict.

But, at the same time, there were also very popular arguments for pacifism, like Erasmus' "Complaint of Peace", which articulates probably the earliest version of a democratic peace theory, and they're printed and shared too.

So, it is a kind of town square where public opinion can be expressed, with all sorts of Vox Populi pamphlets as early as the 17th century, attempting to articulate the voice of the people. Public opinion is given a legitimacy and a power that hadn't existed before.

Going back to the English Civil War, that's a revolution, right? It's an argument about popular sovereignty which requires a way for the populace to speak. And pamphlets allowed that."

The Thinking Machine

New ideas, democratisation, spreading of best practice, massive unforeseen impact, these are the recurring themes of general-purpose information technologies like writing and the printing press.

Accelerating times is another. Prior to language, progress took place on an evolutionary timescale of hundreds of thousands of years or longer. Language meant new inventions happened quicker, in tens of thousands of years. Writing accelerated it further.

For millennia, human time was cyclical. Life in January was different to life in August but the same as life last January and next. Progress didn't exist. Or, more correctly, it wasn't noticeable against the backdrop of daily and seasonal change, the scale our brains had evolved to understand. Life in the 14th century was very similar to life in the fourth.

But it is the nature of technology that each invention enables the next invention to take place quicker. After the printing press, change changed and if you knew what to look for, you would be able to discern linear progress at work. The 16th century was noticeably different to the 15th, the 17th different again and so on.

New major inventions arrived more rapidly. We were able to harness the power of coal, of oil, of electricity, each of which had a huge impact of their own.

Another idea developing at the same time was that of the thinking machine. The Talos was a huge bronze automaton, perhaps the first robot, whose job was to protect Crete. It was never built but it appeared in the Argonautica, an epic poem from the 3rd century BCE and in several writings of the time.

The Antikythera, though, *was* built around 100-150BCE. It was a tremendously sophisticated machine, with at least thirty interlocking cogs, probably used for precise predictions of astronomical positions and eclipses decades in advance.[12] It has been described as the oldest computer.[13]

The following centuries produced impressively life-like automata, animal or human, that could dance, sing, play music, pour drinks and write poems.[14] Robots are being imagined. Thinking machines are appearing.

Then in 1837, Charles Babbage proposed the analytical engine, a programmable, general-purpose computer. He never constructed one in his lifetime but a hundred years later, in 1941, Konrad Zuse built the Z3, the first computer, and information technology crossed another threshold.[15]

Coal, oil and electricity boosted our physical power in the world. We could move more of the universe than we could before, we could travel further and faster across the universe than we could before. Computing, though, boosted our thinking.

Writing and printing had also helped us think better but computing could actually do our thinking for us.

The Incredible Shrinking Computer

The Z3, with 2,600 electrically operated relay switches, wouldn't fit in your pocket and its immediate followers, the British Colossus and the American ENIAC, both built with valves, were even more bulky.[16] The last version of the ENIAC occupied 1,800 square feet.[17]

But the technology advanced so quickly that by 1965, Gordon Moore was confidently predicting "such wonders as home computers" and the electronic watch. In a historical article in Electronics magazine, "Cramming More Components Onto Integrated Circuits", he pointed out that the number of components that could be printed on to a silicon chip was doubling every year (revised later to every two years).[18] He predicted (accurately) that by 1975, 65,000 components could be printed on a chip one-quarter of a square inch.

This became known as Moore's Law and he was the first person to notice that progress wasn't linear, as we'd believed since the printing press, but exponential.

But once he'd printed this article, others noticed too. It didn't just describe a trend, it became a to-do list, it became an investment plan.

Arthur Rock was one of the founding fathers of the venture capital industry (originally called *ad*venture capital) and in 1957, he raised $1.4 million to invest in Fairchild Semiconductor International, the chip manufacturing startup of whom Gordon Moore was co-founder. Two years later, he sold his stock for a 600x return.[19] He made similar deals in the following years, not the least of which was to persuade the Fairchild leadership team (including Moore) to leave and set up their own company. That company was called Intel.[20]

The venture capital industry was born on the fact that the right high growth company could grow exponentially, this had been shown before, albeit rarely. And if your winners bring an exponential return, that means you can lose a lot of times and still do very nicely. So how do you maximise your chances that any given stock choice will be that exponential winner? Well, if the very product itself improves exponentially, that's a pretty good start.

Gordon Moore showed a roadmap to exponential growth in product and, therefore, in investment returns too. In 2023, a chip costing the same price (inflation-adjusted) as a comparable chip at the time Moore wrote his article would be 130,000,000,000 times faster than the 1965 chip.

So that roadmap became self-fulfilling. Investors saw the roadmap, found it plausible, liked the idea of the returns it would deliver, so brought the money to make it happen. And having done that once and enjoyed the experience, they looked to repeat it wherever they could.

Silicon Valley became Silicon Valley.

And not just chip companies but any company whose product is based on chip power: computer manufacturers, software companies, games companies and anything that comes under the digital realm which now includes an ever-growing range of industries from movies to pharmaceuticals to advertising to large parts of the military.

And as processing power increases, more and more of the world becomes part of the digital realm and joins that same exponential journey.

In fact, processing power isn't even the only exponential attribute, we can see the same trend with storage capacity, bandwidth, number of internet hosts and many other measures.

We will come back to this exponential curve and its self-fulfilling nature shortly but for now let's take a step back to those very earliest days of computing.

Artificial Intelligence Growing Pains

Because the field we know as artificial intelligence was born at the same time.

"Darling Sweetheart
You are my avid fellow feeling. My affection curiously clings to your passionate wish. My liking yearns for your heart. You are my wistful sympathy: my tender liking.
Yours beautifully
M U C"

How sweet, eh? And reader, you may be wondering if this is a message for you from the author. Of course, I do have strong feelings for you but this love letter was actually written back in 1952 by Manchester University Computer (MUC).

It had been programmed by Alan Turing and Christopher Strachey using a mixture of templated phrases and randomly selected words from pre-defined lists and was the first ever computer-written love letter though probably not the *best* ever computer-written love letter.[21]

Only a year previously, Turing had written his article "Computing Machinery and Intelligence", in which he proposed the now-famous test named after him. The first section of the article is titled The Imitation Game (movie followers and Benedict Cumberbatch fans will nod knowingly) and it begins "I propose to consider the question, 'Can machines think?'"[22, 23]

If they can, I hope they produce better love letters than the one above but, to be fair, this was very early days in the field. But a field that grew very rapidly. Even though there were hardly any computers in the world, those who worked on them were optimistic that we would have genuinely thinking machines soon. It was an era that was to become known as "The Golden Age" with researchers exploring many ways to recreate intelligence within a computer and making rapid progress.

Much of the experimentation was on games. Games are rule-based with a limited number of variables and so are a good sandbox to practice in – like life, only smaller. Strachey, who programmed the love letters above, in the same year also built a computer version of the game of draughts (or checkers).[24]

And Turing himself developed a programme to play chess. He'd started writing it in 1948 even though he didn't have a computer that could play it. He eventually played one game against a colleague, Alick Glennie, but had to play it manually, reading the code to identify the move, each move taking about half an hour. Decades later the programme was reconstructed and played against Garry Kasparov. Kasparov won quite quickly but was tremendously impressed that Turing could develop an algorithm for the game without a computer to play it on.[25]

Games are fine but the field repeatedly found its ambitions frustrated whenever it tried to venture off the board and on to something a little messier like life. With far too many uncontrollables and unpredictables, they didn't seem to be making any headway.

As the hype cycle predicts, after The Peak of Inflated Expectations comes The Trough of Disillusionment and the Golden Age came to an end in the 1970s, followed by the AI Winter when research funding slowed up. This was a big set-back for the field as many academics started to treat it as a pseudoscience.[26]

But they should not have despaired because the next phase of the hype cycle is, of course, The Slope of Enlightenment, and in the 1980s, the field switched tactics, focussing on rule-based expert systems, and made further progress. And for a while, this is how it played out – multiple booms with winters following, progress continuing but slowly.

Gradually and Then Suddenly

"How did you go bankrupt?" Bill asked.

"Two ways," Mike said. "Gradually and then suddenly."[27]

Mike, a character in Hemingway's novel "The Sun Also Rises", helpfully explains here how change often happens, gradually and then suddenly.

The sudden part may be brought on by a critical threshold being passed (you're rolling downhill and then you drop off the edge of the cliff) or because it is an exponential curve. It's the nature of exponential curves that the progress can be very slow for a long period, maybe not even noticeable, but then, at some point, the gradient steepens rapidly.

In 2005, Ray Kurzweil brought out "The Singularity is Near" in which exponential curves figured a lot, expanding Moore's Law into the past and into the future.[28] Information technology, he said, was a doubling curve long before 1965 and, more importantly, still had a long way to go. If Moore was the first to point out we were on this curve, Kurzweil noted it was about to get steep.

With a lot of data and graphs to back him up, he extended Moore's Law, plotting a timeline and predicting computing power for the next few decades. Parallel to that, he predicted what might be possible with that computing power. And if you're on the part of the curve that is beginning to steepen, it doesn't take too many doublings before you get into quite strange territory, "hold on tight" territory.

He predicted that the Turing Test would be passed by 2029 and, a few years later, combined computing power would be greater than all human intelligence. By the mid-2040s, computing would be a billion times more powerful than all human intelligence. This is when we would reach the technological singularity, the point where the curve goes vertical with unforeseeable consequences. He makes some grand claims like humans living forever and downloading our brains on to silicon chips, all of which may or may not prove correct.

It's fair to say, though, that the academic world did not take the book seriously. Most professors probably didn't even notice it and those that did dismissed it as ridiculous. They had been labouring away for decades, living through multiple AI booms followed by inevitable busts, they knew how difficult it was. And now someone they had never heard of was promising astonishing results and putting dates to them.

But Kurzweil wasn't a newbie, he'd been involved in AI since the 1960s, just not as an academic but as an entrepreneur. In 1965, at the age of 17, he appeared on television, playing a piano piece composed by a computer he had built and he went on to make many inventions in the fields of electronic music, optical character recognition and text-to-speech, much of his technology entering the mainstream through companies like Xerox and ultimately ending up in products like Apple's Siri.[29]

So, while the professors scoffed at his book, the tech companies got excited. Exactly as with Gordon Moore's article, they didn't just see it as an interesting graph with amusing predictions, they saw it as an investment plan.

To be fair to the university professors, they had spent all these years working with university budgets and Kurzweil's predictions would look hopelessly unrealistic from this standpoint. But Silicon Valley knew how to get much, *much* more funding and Kurzweil's roadmap told them exactly what to do with it. As Kevin Kelly, editor of Wired magazine, said later, "The business plans of the next 10,000 startups are easy to forecast: *Take X and add AI.*"[30]

And so, again, it became self-fulfilling. The professors would say impossible and the tech co's announce they've just done it. The exponential growth in data and computing power started to deliver. At first, it was really only noticeable in the field but some stand-out achievements became more widely known.

Let's go back to the chess board. For a long time, critics of artificial intelligence said it might be able to play draughts but it would never be good enough to play chess to a high standard. And in 1989, the IBM computer Deep Thought played two games against Garry Kasparov and lost both times.[31] The cynics snorted dismissively.

But in 1997, IBM returned with Deep Blue and this time, to Kasparov's shock, won.[32]

Okay, said the critics, well of course it can win board games but it will never be able to do anything that requires nuanced thinking or humour or irony, things that really are only in the human domain. Until in 2011, IBM Watson beat two previous champions at the television show Jeopardy.[33]

And yes, of course, it can win at chess if you throw enough computing power at it but sheer muscle won't work with the board game Go, so it will never succeed there. Until in 2016, it beat Lee Sedol four games to one and, a year later, it beat Ke Jie, the number one ranked player in the world.[34]

This is the pattern. Goalposts shift as predictions considered ridiculous are thought obvious and trivial once they happen. It will never understand quantum mechanics, it will never create art, it will never write a poem to make someone cry.

Here's something I asked Claude to write this morning:

> In the quiet of a Sunday morning,
>
> I found your old sweater in the back of the closet.
>
> Soft blue wool, frayed at the cuffs—
>
> You always pulled them over your hands when cold.
>
> The coffee pot gurgles in the kitchen,
>
> Two mugs sit ready, a habit unbroken.
>
> Outside, the maple we planted sways gently,
>
> Its leaves turning the colour of your eyes.
>
> I wear your sweater to the farmer's market,
>
> Buying apples you'll never taste.
>
> A child's laughter catches in the breeze—
>
> For a moment, just a moment, it sounds like you.

Flawed and it didn't make me cry, but it's not bad. An awful lot better than Turing and Strachey's love letter. And by the time you're reading it, no doubt millions of people across the world are sobbing to computer-generated love poems written by the new improved next generation of LLMs. Maybe the LLMs are crying too and we should ask them to write a happy poem, as well, to cheer them up.

Greater Intelligence Will Lead to Breakthroughs in Many Fields

David Wood, Chair of London Futurists, co-founder of Symbian.

"If we ask what the Enlightenment was, it was the application of more intelligence, more curiosity, more open-mindedness, and more knowledge to a whole bunch of issues, some of which had never been really viewed as problems before.

Well, with AI, it's going to liberate more intelligence which I believe will lead to significant breakthroughs in many fields.

We're already seeing this to some extent with the latest tools. Google's Notobook LM has turned many people's heads. You can feed it a whole bunch of research papers and then talk to it. And it does a pretty good job of capturing the essence and the most interesting insight of research.

But these AI systems will be able to understand the whole corpus of scientific research at a much deeper level and it will be able to pick things out for us and draw our attention to the really interesting points.

We already have AI coming up with new proofs of various mathematical theorems. We already have AI suggesting new chomicals that could tackle particular diseases. But most of all, I'm looking forward to it figuring out how we can become much healthier individually: physically, mentally, emotionally.

Done right, it's going to lead to more people being much more knowledgeable. We will each have the equivalent of a personal tutor, somebody who is sitting on our shoulder or whispering in our ear all the time, guiding us to ask the right questions, to see the biggest possibilities.

For example, it will give us instant fact-checking. Just as nowadays, when I'm typing, the AI shows me misspelled words or suggests grammatical improvements, increasingly it will say, "Well, actually, this isn't quite true. You have quoted a fact, but it's misleading" or "You have referred to a video but there's good evidence that video has been doctored".

Or it might notice certain symptoms and say, "Time to take a break now," or breathe in or just calm down a bit. A little bit like a good friend will step in if they think we're about to say something we shouldn't when we are too emotional. They might even, with our permission, play a little bit of music in our ears to put us in a good mood or find other ways to intervene to help us be more creative or more focussed.

Much more than this, I believe AI could invoke huge improvements in fields such as nanotech, biotech and cognitech and this will enable us to slow down biological aging and be perpetually young, if we wish. We can look forward to everybody living at a level of health, a level of intelligence, a level of habitation that is higher than has been reached by almost anyone before.

We will have a super-intelligence and will even be more spiritual, accessing higher levels of consciousness whenever we want to, perhaps even beyond those known of now.

And it's important it's not just an abundance for a few but we need to the share vision widely.

When will this happen? It's hard to say with any confidence but I would say there's a 50% chance that it will be established by about 2040, within the lifetimes of most your readers."

A New Enlightenment?

Large Language Models came into the world in 2018 when OpenAI launched GPT-1, a multi-layer neural network using transformer architecture, trained on a collection of books. Its 2019 successor GPT-2 scaled up, with ten times as much data in the training and ten times as many nodes in the model.

GPT-3 was ten times bigger still but it wasn't until November 2022 when ChatGPT, a variant of the GPT-3.5 series, was released and the wider world finally noticed AI.[35] Its ability to write short stories about cats in pirate language was awe-inspiring. It lied a lot, of course, but we were ok with that because humans do too, we were used to it.

At the time of writing, the latest version is based on a GPT-4o engine and, ten times bigger again, it is significantly better than previous versions.

Ten times ten times ten times. This is much faster than Gordon Moore or Ray Kurzweil predicted. GPT-4 cost $100 billion.[36] At the time of writing, OpenAI's CEO, Sam Altman is looking for funding for a new chip manufacturing company to create bigger and better future models. How much is he looking for? Seven trillion dollars.[37]

That's approximately the cost of Great Britain.[38]

Gordon Moore then Ray Kurzweil laid out roadmaps and, in a self-fulfilling tale, the tech companies found the money to build the roads. This has not stopped, it has accelerated.

What's more, in January 2025, the Chinese platform DeepSeek was able to get similar performance at one-tenth of the cost. In other words, we are finding exponential improvements in efficiency as well as scale.

Expect more, expect a lot more. And what happens then? If the printing press led to the Enlightenment, can we expect a New Enlightenment in our near future?

Francis Bacon, Pascal, Locke and others brought a new empirical approach to knowledge, relying on measurement more than debate, and this generated a whole new science, a whole new maths. Whole new sources of energy were discovered, whole new theories of economics, whole new understandings of the nature of reality.[39]

Can we expect a similar scientific revolution from AI with all the implications for how we think and live our lives?

In fact, we are already seeing a positive impact on scientific output. At the most mundane level, it is accelerating the discovery process by automating many of the routine-but-time-consuming tasks like completing grant application forms.[40]

But it's contributing so much more. AI-powered search engines like Elicit and Gemini Deep Research help scientists find and summarise relevant studies from the exponentially growing volume of scientific output, reducing the time they spend on literature reviews from weeks to minutes.[41] For example, PaperQA2 can search through hundreds of millions of papers to generate a literature review and outperforms PhD and Postdoc-level researchers in its results for many tasks.[42]

Having, effectively, a larger brain enables it to join the dots across a much wider body of research than a human ever could and so see hidden patterns that humans would miss, maybe even finding connections across wholly different fields.

Throw in their creativity, think AlphaGo Move 37, and they are already making new insights and discoveries that humans were unable to see and coming up with new scientific hypotheses of their own. What's more, they can even test those hypotheses themselves, running in silico experiments and generating synthetic data.

One large U.S. materials R&D lab introduced AI tools which led to a "44% increase in new materials discovered, a 39% rise in patent filings, and a 17% growth in product prototypes."[43] Meanwhile, David Baker's lab at the University of Washington used AI to generate over 10 million entirely new proteins from scratch. Many of the structures were previously thought impossible and led to advancements in cancer treatment and viral infection strategies, work which was ultimately recognised with the Nobel Prize in 2024.[44]

There are even full-stack artificially intelligent scientists, who can conduct the whole process end-to-end. The appropriately named AI Scientist generates "novel research ideas, writes code, executes experiments, visualises results, describes its findings by writing a full scientific paper, and then runs a simulated review process for evaluation."[45] On top of that, it "can be repeated to iteratively develop ideas in an open-ended fashion". In other words, it acts like the whole scientific community in its own autonomous, artificially intelligent way.

In the 7th century, it was believed that The Royal Library of Ashurbanipal in Nineveh held all the knowledge of the world. A 2010 study counted 24,000 academic journals currently producing such a deluge of information, that is unmanageable by humans but well within AI's capabilities.[46] We need the bigger brain to profit from it. Who knows what amazing discovery is just sitting amongst all of those papers, still waiting for its moment of glory?

But the Enlightenment was more than just science and maths, it was also about happiness and tolerance.

Leibniz defined wisdom as the science of happiness, Bentham developed utilitarianism and Hume and Locke each recognised the importance of the pursuit of happiness in their work. It was an idea commonly held long before Thomas Jefferson's use in the American Declaration of Independence.[47]

Indeed, a key driving force of the Enlightenment was a "commitment to understanding, and hence to advancing, the causes and conditions of human betterment in this world."[48]

And not just selfish happiness, Oxford Enlightenment scholar Ritchie Robertson said that as much as it was the age of reason, it was also "the age of feeling, empathy and sensibility…in which people became more attuned to other people's feelings and more concerned for what we would call humane or humanitarian values".[49]

Religious and racial tolerance were hard to find in the 16th century, as wars of religion devastated Europe, but they were significantly more commonplace by the 18th. Voltaire wrote his influential "Treatise on Tolerance" in 1762, Goethe's 1788 play, "Egmont", set to music by Beethoven, has tolerance as its main theme and the 1791 French revolutionary "Declaration of the Rights of Man and the Citizen" laid down that no law-abiding person should be persecuted because of religious opinions.

It's not inevitable that the world becomes a better place but it's certainly not impossible, either.

We humans have made a lot of progress but the world is very complicated so we still face many challenges like how to create a fair society, how to create an effective political system and how to optimise our economy for wealth, sustainability and equality at the same time.

I believe AI will be able to advance on all these fronts.

The Enlightenment and the scientific revolution that preceded it were the enemy of superstition. What superstitions do we hold now that will soon be put to the sword by artificial intelligence?

Whoa, What Have We Just Said?

Ok, I appreciate we've covered a few billion years of history just then, without much more detail than Airplane II provided. So, it might be worth remembering what we've said because it's key to the argument of the book.

We've said that technology begets technology, that each invention enables the next invention to happen quicker. And this is especially true for general-purpose technologies like writing, like the printing press, like computing and like artificial intelligence. And we're now moving on to the "hold on tight" part of the curve.

We also saw that these technologies help spread ideas further and especially best practice ideas. Is this true with AI?

Yes, it is. The whole purpose of those rule-based expert systems was to model how experts in a specific field work in that field and then replicate it. And many other AI applications use a similar principle.

As just one example of countless, in 2018, DeepMind partnered with Moorfields Eye Hospital in London to develop a machine learning application trained by experts to identify diseases and abnormalities from eye scans. That application could then be used anywhere in the world and get the highest quality diagnosis without the need for an expert to be present.[50]

Indeed, as we saw with the games, not only can it model the best human performance, it can surpass it.

But here's the interesting thing, when it spreads this better-than-human performance, it ups the humans' game. What happened after Kasparov, arguably the greatest ever chess player, lost to Deep Blue? Did humans give up because there wasn't any point in playing chess anymore?

No, they improved.[51] The generation of chess players that followed are almost certainly the greatest generation ever because they grew up learning to play with super-human opponents. AI learns from humans, surpasses them, then enables humans to raise their game too.

So, let's go back two chapters, when we talked about Roger Fisher modelling how the best negotiators operated and writing about it in his book, "Getting To Yes". Well, that book sold over ten million copies and its methods have become the standard in the world of negotiation.

But the very large majority of the world's population still haven't read it and don't negotiate in that way.

Fortunately, AI can take it further. Roger Fisher was a great lawyer but he just didn't have the negotiation data points that AI will so it will be able to develop a much more thorough best practice model. And we're going to see over the next few chapters how widespread its impact will be.

So, maybe in the New Enlightenment, collaborative problem-solving, the approach that the best negotiators take, will become the norm. No more arm-wrestling, no more fighting, no more conflict.

Fingers crossed, anyway.

Section 2
The Contexts

5
Siri, Save My Marriage

Get Good at Negotiation, Get Good at Life

Smoke-filled rooms, people banging tables, shouting, multi-billion-dollar deals, trade agreements, peace treaties. This is what we think when we think negotiation. At the very least, it involves lawyers fighting over the wording of a contract.

But I think we are negotiating all the time: with our boss, our colleagues, our neighbours, our friends, our family. What I call micro-negotiations. And it's these micro-negotiations that make up the stuff of our world.

So, if we get good at these, we can get good at life.

Big claim, eh? Anyway, what do I mean by 'get good'? Does it mean forcing the other person to give in so you always get your outcome? Of course not, that's a recipe for a lot of trouble.

Negotiation best practice, as we saw in Chapter Two, means being able to reach your outcome whilst also helping the other person get an outcome they are really pleased with too. And it means doing it quickly; after all, you have a lot of things to do in your life, don't waste time haggling.

And it also means doing it smoothly; this doesn't have to be an argument, quite the opposite. If done well, it should *improve* the relationship at the same time as reaching your outcome. Which means the next conversation with them will go even smoother.

Reach your goals, help them reach theirs, and improve the relationship at the same time? In every area of your life?

Sounds good to me.

Let's have a look at a few examples:

1. Salary and Job Offers:

    Can you increase your salary? Or get better benefits or work from home more or change your hours or improve your work conditions in such a way that your boss is really pleased with the outcome?

2. Buying or renting a home:

    Renting or buying, negotiating on where we live can be quite a big deal. Can you bring the price down of that apartment you're buying or ask them to leave the furniture with you? Can you persuade the landlord to reduce the rent?

3. Car purchase:

    Buying a car is another big purchase, how can we reach a good deal there?

4. Contractor agreements:

    Does your plumber charge too much? How do you make sure you get the best price and the job well done at the same time?

5. Getting 10% off at the shops:

    How do you get that discount or the refund or something extra thrown in when you're on the High Street or shopping online? Or with your utility bill?

6. Relationships:

   You want to see them once a week, they want to move in. Tricky one, how do we navigate these conversations? Or who's picking the kids up from school? Who's staying in this evening while the other parent catches up with their friends?

7. Jobs around the house:

   Ooh, now we're talking! Does your flatmate always leave the dirty dishes around the dining room? Does your husband never take the rubbish out? But we don't want to nag and we don't want an argument. Is there any hope?

8. How to spend your leisure time:

   You want to lie on the beach all week, they want to climb Mount Everest. You want to watch the football, they want to watch the rom-com. You want to see the family this weekend, they want to work. How do we resolve these?

9. Divorce:

   Sadly, the relationship is breaking up. But who gets all the money, who gets the kids, who gets the dog, who gets the record collection? And how do you reach a fair outcome so you can still stay friends?

10. Kids:

    Kids, they're the toughest negotiators! How do we agree screen time rules, how do we make sure they're stuck to, all without any tears?

Everything is a negotiation. If you can get a good outcome, help them get a good outcome, quickly and smoothly, and improve the relationship at the same time – in every area of your life – that really will transform the life you lead.

You will be more successful, you will be happier, you will have more love, you will be more confident, you will sail through life with ease.

You will have less conflict.

Even more than that, you'll be improving the life of the people around you too – in helping them get their outcome, in improving the relationship they have with you, and in giving them a model of a way of collaborating that they can bring to other relationships in their world.

And so it spreads.

Siri, Save My Marriage.

So, our argument is that best practice in negotiation is known and AI will operate by it to advise us or even to negotiate on our behalf.[1] In fact, as we move further up our exponential curve into the future, more and more of our life will be digital and best practice collaborative negotiation will be *embedded* into it.

Digital personal assistants like Siri ("Siri, can I call you Alexa?"), or indeed Alexa, have been around for a while. Powered by AI, they can engage in conversations, answer questions, and perform a variety of tasks.

But they've generally felt underwhelming. They can play music, they can remind me of my dental appointment, they can tell me the weather forecast, they can build me a fitness plan, but help me negotiate? I doubt it.

Well, maybe even these *can* help. If you're not feeling that confident about the negotiation, how about playing "Eye of the Tiger" just before leaving home, you'll walk into that room growling! Or if you keep putting off the pay rise conversation, how about scheduling a meeting in your calendar and your boss's – now you *have* to go. And if you want a picnic but your partner wants to stay in to get things done around the house, the weather forecast will tell you how best to schedule it.

So even these can help in their small way.

Prompt Your Way to A Better Deal

But as we saw in the last chapter, the LLM has changed the name of the game, they have become very powerful digital assistants in their own right. So next time you're in an argument or negotiation, ask your favourite LLM for help. "Hey Mistral, I deserve a pay-rise, how should I go about asking for it?" It will almost certainly give you some good advice.[2]

And it will give you even better advice if you get your prompt right. I'm sure many of you readers will be perfectly at home with prompt engineering but some of you may still be new to it so it's worth giving some pointers here. OpenAI has a very good page for polishing your prompt but the main thing to remember is that the more detail you give it, the better answer you'll get.[3]

So, give it the context of the negotiation, a bit of background, some outcomes you'd like to achieve, some you don't want to see. Go back to the Golden Formula in Chapter Two and tell it the interests, variables and BATNA of all parties. You don't need to tell it your life story but it will take into account each detail you provide and that just might make the difference in the advice it gives you.

Tell it your personality, tell it theirs. You can use a tool like Humantic to work out their personality type and then include that in your prompt.[4] Give it any objective benchmarks you can, that way its advice will be more realistic.

It helps if you give it a persona. So include "You're an expert negotiator" in the prompt or "You're highly experienced in dealing with contractors" and give it a style like "You're friendly but you want to make sure you get a good price".

Then ask it for its advice and you'll be surprised how helpful it is. If it isn't, try a different prompt, you'll get a different answer. Either way, it's an ongoing conversation so you can keep asking it questions.

- "How should I prepare for this?"

- "How should I structure the meeting?"
- "What's going on in their industry right now?"
- "How much can I ask for?"
- "How might they respond? And how can I pre-empt those? Or respond back to them?"
- "Do you have any good phrases for …?"

Any question you like. And if they give you an answer that is too vague ("Start the conversation in a friendly but credible manner"), ask it for examples to illustrate what it means.

It's useful in all kinds of ways, you can ask it:

- For background information about their business or product
- For ten creative solutions to the deadlock
- To summarise a contract
- To suggest changes to the agreement
- To write a persuasive email
- To suggest diplomatic wordings for raising a sensitive topic.

You can even ask it to roleplay. Either it plays the other person and you rehearse the conversation or it can be equally instructive if you play the other person and the LLM takes your side.

And afterwards, if the negotiation took place online, you can upload the transcript and ask for a review.

What worked? What didn't work? What could you have done differently? How could you have got to the point quicker without losing rapport? Were there any non-monetary variables you might have brought to the table? Can it recommend different ways of dealing with their objections?

It really can be your personal negotiation coach.

If You're Going to Argue, Argue Better

But perhaps we will benefit the most if we use our LLM as a mediator. It could work with voice or text input - either way, we'd be trusting it to run the show.

Imagine this, you've just got home from work and you and your partner are a bit tired and both a little tetchy. It's the usual conversation about the kitchen/finances/kids/dog/in-laws (delete as appropriate) and it always ends in an argument.

But maybe not this time. Because this time you say, "Hey, let's not have an argument, shall we ask ChatGPT?" Your partner thinks this strange but goes along with it. And you type "Hi ChatGPT, you are an expert mediator who specialises in domestic issues. I have a regular argument with my partner and we'd both like to find a better way with dealing with it. Let me give you some details…"

ChatGPT asks you what outcome you would like and what's important to you in the situation and why. Then it asks the same for your partner who, now curious, obligingly answers. It then asks if you can now think of any solutions that might work. And if you can, great, but if not, you just ask it to give you some ideas.

This is mediation in a nutshell and it can take you through that process. It knows best practice.

Of course, I know what you're like, you might not be interested in mediation at all, you go to it for help to outright *win* the argument. But no matter, it will steer you down the collaborative route and you'll soon realise this is the best way anyway.

Now imagine further that it's a week later and the same situation arises and you both remember the previous experience so your partner says, "Hey ChatGPT worked last time, didn't it? Shall we try it again?"

After doing this three or four times, you won't have to ask it again because you know what it will say. You'll do it by yourselves. That issue will now be a solved issue.

And if another one of your regular arguments comes up (I'm sure you have plenty), you just look at each other and say, "ChatGPT?" until that becomes a solved issue too.

You can see where this is going. Very soon, you'll have picked up the mediation approach yourselves and it will become your default way of behaving. You'll have learnt best practice from ChatGPT.

The end of arguments with your partner.

In fact, the end of arguments for you with *anyone* because you'll see that this approach works and you'll bring it wherever you go.

Ok, let's be realistic, yes there will still be arguments but much less than before. And when one does arise, ChatGPT is still there. Remember, it's your personal negotiation coach and as your skill develops, you need it less and less but there will always be edge cases where some advice might help.

Bring Out Your Internal Peace Treaty Negotiator

Best practice in negotiation involves having a process trusted by both sides. We saw this in Chapter Two when two neutral parties, Cyril Ramaphosa and Martti Ahtisaari, were chosen to help with the arms decommissioning process in Northern Ireland.

Interestingly, that wasn't the first time neutral parties were needed during the Good Friday Agreement.

It was one of the toughest negotiations ever so when the British and Irish governments first started talking, they knew it was critically important to get the process right. They knew the negotiations would only go smoothly if everyone bought into the process so the very first discussions were about planning how to design that process. It was exactly these "talks about the talks about the talks" that proved decisive to the eventual success of such an intractable problem.[5]

Having a neutral third party involved was considered essential so it was agreed that Britain and Ireland would each choose a neutral facilitator and then those two would choose a third to chair the process. The British chose Canadian General John de Chastelain and the Irish chose ex-Finnish prime minister, Harri Holkeri, and those two between them chose U.S. Senator George Mitchell.[6]

How much simpler if they'd just asked ChatGPT? There's no reason why your neutral third party can't be a computer, It has no skin in the game, it has no ego, it has no emotions. It will make objectively fair recommendations.

Bring Out Your Internal Hostage Negotiator

But what if the issue is with your neighbour and you don't think they will be up for using an LLM?

That's ok, ask your LLM for a fair process that your neighbour would trust and you can run with this.

Gary Noesner, ex-Chief of the FBI Crisis Negotiation Unit, knows quite a lot about negotiating in tough situations. In his great book, "Stalling for Time", he describes how he always started by seeking a process with the hostage takers and he would ask them their ideas, first, of what to do. Of course, they wouldn't have a clue so he would then make a proposal and check were they ok with it or was there anything they wanted to change. There never was.

The consequence of this was that when it came time to put the plan into action, the hostage-takers would follow it to a T. Why? Because they felt they helped create it. They had the chance to change things, so they felt ownership. And when people feel like they own something, they're more likely to stick with it.

So, ask the LLM a good process but before you suggest it to the neighbour, ask them what they would like to do. They won't really know so now you can suggest the LLM's idea and, because it's neutral, your neighbour will agree, especially if you give them the opportunity to tweak it.

That fair process could be to use a dedicated AI mediator. General LLMs offer good advice but it won't be as good as a specially trained mediation platform.

Human mediators are very skilled at solving difficult issues. Their experience and impartiality can enable outcomes even when none seem possible to the untrained eye. But they can be expensive and, therefore, not always a viable option.

Enter LLMediator, a GPT-4 online mediation tool that can assist dispute resolution. In its current guise, it's used largely to assist a mediator but it can act autonomously too. The point being the human mediator does not have to be an expensive professional because the platform can support them.

As the two sides make their case and respond, the platform can reformulate messages to be less emotional or provocative, it can suggest draft messages, it can suggest interventions for the mediator and it can even take over the process itself.

TheMediator.AI is another platform where the sides upload their cases, answer questions posed by the platform for clarification, and receive a neutral recommendation which is for them to agree to or not. All for the princely sum of $4.99.

And Harmony, by Kleros, offers a similar service but with the option of putting the case to an independent human jury.

AI mediation is going to become easier, cheaper and better. We will see in Chapter Seven that fair dispute resolution will soon become freely available for everyone.

It will enable any situation to be resolved quickly and equitably and its use will become the norm. But eventually, we won't need it because we will have learnt the behaviours ourselves.

We Bring Decision Science to Help Resolve Disputes

Bob Bergman, CEO Next Level Mediation LLC

"My background is in software engineering and decision science and I started down this path of dispute resolution because I noticed that disputes are a growing global industry! People just don't know how to talk to each other anymore. And what makes our platform unique is that it treats dispute resolution as essentially a group decision between two or more parties with different agendas and so we apply decision science to help reach resolution.

First, we force people to be quantitative because you can't be both emotional and quantitative at the same time - they use different parts of your brain. The rational thought happens in your neocortex, while emotion is controlled in your mid-brain. We have participants order their priorities by pairwise comparisons, asking 'What's more important - A or B? How much more important?' This forces people to be logically consistent and not try to game the system.

You can upload documents and the system will analyse them and it takes the exact priorities that people have input and the AI will suggest potential compromise solutions based on those.

We've also just added the Adjusted Winner Algorithm from game theory for fair division of assets. Parties rank their priorities for different assets and the system assigns points based on their relative importance and it will then suggest optimal divisions where each party gets what they value most, while achieving a mathematically fair outcome.

Another critical feature is visualising the dispute. Current generations have an average attention span of just 30 seconds - people don't read anymore. So we use AI to create visual summaries - timelines, mind maps, and conflict landscapes - to help everyone understand the big picture quickly.

We also help people understand litigation risk more clearly. Lawyers always explain risk linguistically - 'Oh yeah, there's a good chance of winning.' But what does that actually mean? Our system shows the probabilities, costs, and timelines at each stage. When people see they can settle now or wait three years for a 15% chance of winning, it's a whole different ball game.

The platform can identify when emotion is driving decisions by tagging certain objectives as 'emotional' - like when someone prioritises 'punishing the other side' over practical solutions. This helps mediators guide parties toward more logical frameworks.

One day, theoretically at least, the system could be fully AI-driven but I would really stay away from that right now. AI can be very useful in dispute resolution but it's crucial to have a human in the loop to manage the emotional aspects and ensure the process stays on track toward resolution."

Getting Personal

Even before we get to mediation, AI is still on your side.

How about this: You're ready to ask for the pay-rise that is long overdue and you ask your AI advisor for help. It has been trained on your emails and other documents and is integrated with your banking apps so it already has a good sense of your financial health.

Firstly, it looks up websites like Glassdoor, LinkedIn Salary, Payscale, and finds other industry-specific reports on the internet. From these, it evaluates that someone with your level of experience in your field and your location would typically earn between, let's say, £60,000 and £85,000 annually. You're currently near the bottom of that range but it suggests you should be not far off the top.

Then it goes full detective-mode and searches online for recent financial reports and news articles about your company's revenue and profitability and finds that income has increased 50% in the last year and is projecting similar growth this year. This is strong evidence that the company can afford your pay rise request.

It doesn't stop there. It combs through your work emails and performance reviews, building a highlight reel of your achievements, including your successful launch of a new product campaign that led to a 30% increase in customer engagement and a 20% increase in sales revenue. You are building a strong argument for your claim.

And then you play the game of "What if?"

"AI advisor, what if I asked for 15%, how do you think my boss would react?", "What if my boss got really angry, how could I pull it back?", "Are there any other scenarios you think we should plan for?"

It has analysed the boss's previous emails to you so it even has a good sense of *their* negotiation style and how they will react. It knows what their interests are and it anticipates their concerns which allows you to develop a pre-emptive argument. It helps identify trade-offs and creative solutions that benefit all parties involved.

Finally, it drafts a persuasive email or script, complete with some snazzy graphs to support the case. It even tells you when to schedule the meeting based on their calendar and work patterns.

And, of course, it does this in next to no time.

It will bring your negotiation game up to best practice and it will save you huge amounts of time.

It might sound a little sci-fi but all of this is very feasible. And if the app that does it all is not on the app store just yet, this kind of virtual personal assistant is only months away.

Don't Get Triggered

Let's take a different example. Let's imagine, picking names randomly, Meghan is in the middle of a divorce from her soon-to-be-ex-husband Harry and they have a meeting coming up.

Divorce is such an emotive scenario that it is very rare that mere humans can stick to best practice. Computers, the heartless machines, can.

Firstly, Meghan's AI advisor does all the usual prep work we mentioned earlier: it dives into divorce laws and recent court rulings and it collates all the important documents – marriage certificate, pre-nup (if there is one), financial statements, any prior discussions about custody arrangements or anything else related to the proceedings.

It continues, it looks at her notes about the kids - their school, health, after-school activities, how they're doing overall. It checks out any chats she's already had with Harry about custody and picking up from school. And, of course, it crunches the numbers on bank statements, investments, property - all that financial stuff that can get so messy in a divorce.

And then it sketches out a negotiation game plan, suggesting they focus on what's best for the kids, aim for a fair split of the money, and try to keep things friendly. We don't want everyone to come out of this traumatised.

All good so far, but it's the kind of scenario that can go horribly wrong as the negotiation proceeds.

Say Harry emails back, unhappy about the money situation. He wrote the message himself and, such is the situation, he couldn't help be more aggressive than he should have been. Normally, this is where Meghan gets triggered and the whole communication breaks down. But instead, her AI advisor steps in and handles it.

It remembers her interests (best outcome for the kids and such like) and it edits her reply accordingly, removing any swear words. Humans are pretty useless at finding solutions in these kinds of conflicts, especially when the communication has dropped to this level. But AI is much better. It can identify all the right variables to play with to get a good solution, a solution they hadn't considered, and it draws up a payment plan that works for both of them.

It also gently reminds them that their BATNA is court proceedings which will probably result in all their money going to the lawyers and the children never talking to either of them again.

It has to manage emotions a number of times in the negotiation but, you know, it doesn't mind. Eventually, Meghan and Harry get the hang of it themselves and the process goes surprisingly amicably. Years later, they are still friends and the kids don't hate them.

Maybe It Can Help in the Meeting Too

Most online meeting platforms have speech-to-text capability and provide minutes after the meeting. Well, there's no reason why that same capability couldn't pick up on changes in speech patterns, such as pauses, emphasis on certain words, or fluctuations in voice tone, or indeed visual cues, and use that to provide insights into emotional states or reactions during negotiations.

So perhaps your digital assistant will provide a running commentary on-screen of how hot or cold the negotiation is going. "They didn't like that idea. They agreed but their face suggested they're not going to stick to it. How about rephrasing it? Try this…"

And, like all good AI's, it will learn the other person's typical behavioural patterns and emotional responses over time and look out for variations from the norm.

But isn't this a bit creepy? Yes, is the short answer. It's unlikely to improve trust, is it? I would be pretty upset if I thought someone was doing that to me.

Unless, of course, they were open about it, shared the results, and did the same analysis on themselves. This would actually *build* trust. Here's how: human beings aren't always good at spotting if someone is upset so you can both ask the tech to help. If the conversation is potentially triggering, like Meghan and Harry's divorce above, both people agreeing to use this will reduce the likelihood of trigger points and this will foster trust and a more collaborative approach.

And even if you can't persuade them to go along with this, you can use it for your *own* benefit. Tell it to monitor you and it might give you very useful feedback on when you need to take a pause or visualise your favourite beach or, indeed, relocate the meeting to your favourite beach.

And, in this way, we are learning how to operate best practice negotiation ourselves. As in so many other examples, the AI app learnt from human best practice and is now returning the favour.

Helping The Machine Understand the Human Better

Leslie Nooteboom, Co-Founder of Requesty.ai and Humanising Autonomy

"So at Humanising Autonomy, we started out with predicting pedestrian behaviour for self-driving cars. We thought you would be able to increase car safety if you added more of an understanding of human behaviour to those decision models. So, for example, you would know if a person is distracted or if they can actually see the car or they're on the phone.

Then with Requesty, it felt like we were seeing the same kind of automation with language models: even the smartest LLM needs to stay human-friendly. For example, a negotiation bot might handle millions of talks daily, but people still need a clear way to know if it's doing the right thing. That's why we started building an interface to help humans understand these massive interactions.

At Humanising, we very quickly expanded from cars to different types of machines. Factory robots, augmented reality headsets, smartphones, dash cams: any device that has a camera that interacts with a human, we would put our software on it to understand the human in a better way and know their emotional state.

Then we built a version which looks at the interaction in a meeting, it monitors the video call and tracks the emotional state of the participants.

And it turns out that context is one of the most important parts of this process. If someone is smiling in a friendly conversation, that could mean something very different than someone smiling in a stressful business deal.

The negotiation use case is interesting in having to understand the interplay of emotions between the people in that meeting: what it looks like visually and the audio inputs, like tone of voice, and then how that relates to the content or the context. Because all those variables change the meaning of the model's output.

There are many layers that you can input into this because there's even the time-based sequence of what people say or how they change their expressions. And if you look at the history, even the entire history of all conversations that those two people have had, you would be able to build an even better understanding of the current situation and map that to the visual and other inputs.

And in the future, we will use it in face-to-face meetings. You can already do it in a verbal way just by having an earplug in your ear, which listens to your conversation. You can already get real time feedback from a GPT about what you should be saying next. Maybe you're buying a house and it will recommend the questions to ask.

Then if you have a camera, like on an augmented reality headset, or even if you just walk through a house with your phone out, it might notice the room looks a little damp or if there's a crack in the ceiling, and then it recommends, "Hey, maybe you should ask when the last survey has been done or whether the neighbours upstairs have ever had a leak."

And once augmented reality headsets are acceptable to wear in public, I'm sure everyone will be using it."

Less Talking, More Action

And we're really only just starting. So far, we've considered LLMs from their advisory capabilities but we are now moving into an era of agents. We'll discuss these in more detail in the next chapter but agents don't only give advice, they can do things in the real world.

They won't just suggest a wording for your email, they will write and send it. They won't just advise on the optimum time for the meeting, they will schedule it in everyone's calendar and email the invites. They won't just draft a proposal, they will write and send it out, capturing your tone and style so perfectly, you'd swear you wrote it yourself (because, in a way, you did).

They will update your LinkedIn profile with your latest achievements and skills. And when you get that well deserved rise, they will also update your personal budget and financial plans accordingly.

It could even be your avatar, trained on audio and video files, attending the Zoom call.[7]

They will be conducting large parts of the negotiation for you. If you're not comfortable with negotiations or conflict, it will save a lot of stress. And you can prompt it to take whatever style you want – robust, creative, charming, it can do it all.

And it will free up your time. Imagine an AI that can haggle with the plumber over your bill, negotiate a better rate on your car insurance, and get a better price on the online marketplace, all while you're busy living your best life – you know, catching up with the TV or taking a nap.

Of course, letting an AI take the wheel like this isn't without its risks. If you sent a robot to do your grocery shopping, it might come back with everything on your list, but did it pick the perfectly ripe avocados? There's always a chance it might misinterpret a nuance or make a decision you wouldn't have made yourself.

So how much should you let it off the leash? Well, that depends on you, what you're negotiating for and how much you trust it. It's like choosing between a GPS that gives us turn-by-turn directions and one that offers to drive the car for us: sometimes we want the guidance, other times we might be happy to hand over the keys.

In the same way, as AI gets smarter, we'll likely see more assistants that can do both - give us sage advice when we need it and take decisive action when we're comfortable delegating.

What Could Possibly Go Wrong?

So, your AI assistant has just negotiated a fantastic deal on a Lamborghini for you and you're thrilled. But what if the tech goes wrong?

For a start, today's security risks could become even bigger worries. If someone finds out the password to your AI assistant, they will, by extension, also have access to all your personal data and financial accounts and before you know it go on a shopping spree and charge it all to you.

But new technology also brings new opportunities for things to go wrong. Maybe your AI agent isn't as intelligent as it thought and misunderstood what you wanted or maybe it isn't as good a negotiator as it thought and agrees an outcome for you that is sub-optimal.

It could agree to terms or make commitments on your behalf that you're unaware of and you now find yourself in a legally binding agreement you didn't intend to make. For example, it might negotiate a great rate on your car insurance but it's no good if you only find out after the deal that the discount was in return for installing a tracking device in your car to monitor your driving habits.

And then who's liable?

Right now, in most jurisdictions, the law still sees AI as a tool, not a person. This means that, legally speaking, when your AI negotiates for you, it's as if you're doing the negotiating yourself. It's like sending a very smart parrot to do your bargaining - whatever deals the parrot strikes, you're on the hook for them. And tech companies can afford good lawyers so it will probably stay that way.

But all of this is still evolving. As AI gets smarter and starts taking on more of our negotiations, lawmakers and regulators around the world are scrambling to keep up. And even as they write the rules, the game changes again. By the time you are reading this, regulations will probably have changed a dozen times so please do not take any of this as legal advice!

But it is worth remembering that they're not infallible. At the time of writing, we're a few years away from consistently reliable agents. But *only* a few years away. Reliable agents will arrive but, in the meantime, we need a healthy dose of caution when we work with them.

The Biggest Power Shift in Human History.

But the biggest threat of all is its capacity to manipulate. Already, technology companies are spying on us to an extent that the Soviet Communist Party could only have dreamt of and they sell that data to the highest bidder to do whatever they want with it. A study by Consumer Reports showed that an average Facebook user has more than 2,200 different companies tracking their activity around the internet and selling this data to Meta.[8]

With the access that an AI personal assistant will have to all your accounts, documents, emails and web activity, its ability to track data will be orders of magnitude greater.

And this can be used to persuade or manipulate you without you knowing.

They will know your thoughts, your desires, your fears, your values, your allegiances, what you like, what you don't like, who you like, who you don't like. And they will be able to use this to nudge you to buy what they want you to buy and to think what they want you to think.

And they will do this in such a warm, trustable voice, more trustable than anyone you've ever known, that they will be able to change your desires, your fears, your values, your allegiances, what you like, what you don't like, who you like, who you don't like. All without you knowing.

This is the biggest power shift in human history.

We will talk a lot more about this in later chapters but the main take for now is that these assistants can help us massively but they need to be managed properly. When we give them this level of access to our data, we should only use assistants that we can trust.

This means platforms where all the processing takes place locally, on your phone or computer, and the data is not sent back to the cloud. It also means having extensive privacy controls that are easy to find and work with and we should generally place these settings on maximum.

Right now, the business model of most technology companies like Amazon, Google and Meta does not support this but we should only use those that do.

Pass It On

We will address the dark side of all this later in the book and there are solutions. So, in this chapter, we can stay resolutely optimistic!

AI will help you negotiate better or it will do the negotiating for you. Either way, it will work by best practice, namely it will find creative solutions that work for everyone.

Any negotiation you have that goes in this way means the next time you negotiate with that person, it will go even better. That relationship will become smoother and smoother.

And not just that but, consciously or unconsciously, you will start to bring this kind of approach to other relationships and they will take it to their other relationships too. This is how it spreads.

Of course, it won't work with everyone. Some people are dead set in their views, some people seem psychopathically evil.

But even these extreme cases might behave differently if they were able to break away from their ego and their biases and they could see an outcome that was materially better for them.

Ultimately, win-win is best even for selfish reasons.

Nobel Prize-winning economist Thomas Schelling writes about behavioural change across populations in his book, "Micromotives and Macrobehaviour".[9] He notes we are influenced by the people around us and everyone has a different threshold for behaviour change.

Maybe one person will take up a new behaviour the first time they are exposed to it, maybe someone else needs a hundred exposures. As the more flexible people fall into the new approach, so they will create more and more examples, meaning that even the most extreme stubborn cases might eventually change too.

So, we may not make everyone angels overnight but, as the new approach spreads through society, it will reach more and more people, it will become the norm, eventually persuading even the edge cases.

6
Reimagining Business

We all want a nice house, we want to drive a cool car, we want to be super-fit and healthy, we want to look good, we want to bring our kids up like better versions of ourselves.

But most of the things we want cost a lot of money and take up a lot of time. So, we need to work hard to earn the money but then we don't have the time to do them. So, we become stressed and tired and instead of going to the gym we revert to our usual coping mechanisms, like alcohol or chocolate or TV or online shopping, most of which tend to make matters worse.

There is always a nicer house to have, a cooler car to drive and this gap between our expectations and reality is very stressful. The stress sensitises our amygdala and our amygdala sees threat everywhere it looks.

No wonder there's so much conflict.

Now, much of the stress we feel comes from work. We want to get the promotion, we want to get the sale, our boss is asking us to do too much, our colleagues are just obstructive and our team is useless. Even the commute is stressful. Of course, we're on edge.

Anything that reduces this stress will reduce the amount of conflict in our lives.

If the office could be more collaborative and supportive and less dog-eat-dog, that would go a long way to help. If our boss could be a little more understanding, that would too. If our interactions and negotiations resembled arm wrestling just a little less, our amygdala would be less jumpy.

AI may just be able to do something here.

We're All in A Team

Everyone works in a team. Even if you work by yourself, as soon as you have one client or supplier, you're in a team. And even if you don't work, as soon as you have a parent, you're in a team.

In team games, you only win if your team wins. Knowing this moves your focus on to achieving the team goal rather than your own individual aims and the performance of your team can then shift into another gear. By doing this, you actually get better outcomes than had you just focussed on your own.

But if a team contains two high-performing individuals, each pulling in contrary directions, they end up cancelling each other out and the net result is zero or worse, like an orchestra full of fantastic soloists who don't blend well and the sound is awful. A poorly functioning team is super-stressful.

The successful team knows that best practice is when the team member is no longer thinking primarily of how to achieve their own individual goal, but of their team's goal and how they can contribute best to achieving that.

And a high-performing organisation is a team of teams, all working this way, achieving great things. Moreover, it will be a great place to work; it will be a team that you will enjoy being part of, it will be a team that you will be proud to be part of.

Ideal vs Reality

That's how it should work, of course, but in reality it is often different.

Too many people just don't work that way. It's not surprising, it's the nature of work that people will have different goals, often mutually exclusive. And we already know that people aren't very good at resolving such issues, they're only human.

So it's a big problem, a big source of friction slowing down the machinery of the economy. A 2020 CIPD report found that a third of people have experienced some form of interpersonal conflict at work within the past year and one in six reported being bullied over the past three years.[1] Another CIPD report estimated that conflict costs UK organisations £28.5 billion per year.[2]

A big problem that could be solved if only we knew how.

Except, of course, we do know how. Collaborative, problem-solving negotiation would do it or, given most people aren't very good at this, a facilitated process by an objective mediator.

And yet less than 10% of employers use professional external mediation to deal with workplace issues.[3] And only 23% even bother to train a member of staff for internal mediation. What's more, "trained" probably means went on a half-day course so they are hardly likely to be masters in the field, they may not even be especially objective.

But, as we saw in the last chapter, LLMs now provide a free, instant alternative. Save yourself £28.5 billion per year, spend it on a really great holiday, and use DeepSeek or a customised mediation bot to resolve the workplace disputes.

Then, exactly as we saw in the previous chapter regarding arguments with our partner, we will quickly learn best practice and soon no longer need recourse to the LLM. And that behaviour would spread through the organisation and it would become a collaborative culture, high-performing and a fun place to work.

Collaborative Culture, Now There's A Thing

So, we can change the culture of the organisation through the regular use of LLMs for conflict resolution or, better, prevention. And individuals, managers and HR should all be doing this and promoting its use.

But there are other ways to build the high-performing collaborative team we are after.

A team's culture is usually set top-down. Whether it comes all the way from the CEO or from the team's manager, the behaviours, beliefs and values of a team are highly influenced from above, by example more than by directive.

But those managers are often too stressed, themselves, to set the good example required.

So maybe AI can help?

American company Inspira AI has developed an autonomous AI manager that monitors employees' behaviour and gently coaches underperformance. In a pilot study run in conjunction with professors from multiple universities, they found that the results of the digital manager were on par with the human manager and best results were obtained when the two worked together.[4]

But it's the response of the manager in question, Hannu Rauma at Student Marketing Company, which is most interesting. "It's added years to my life, I'm sure," he says, describing how it has reduced his stress levels. "I'm able to focus on the growth of the company and all the positive things." And he adds that it has drastically improved his relationship with his team.[5]

So, using AI here didn't improve the performance of the workforce any more than the human manager could, but it did save human management time, and indirectly created the space for the manager to be less stressed and therefore improve the working environment of the team. Plus, although not measured in the study, I suspect it improved the team culture enormously.

Now, there is a big caveat here. Big Brother management tools measuring how long you spend in the bathroom or how often your eyes stray from the screen sounds completely dystopian and will go a long way to building an *under*-performing team. This is a real possibility and we need to be very vigilant against it.

But there's no reason why an AI manager can't build a positive, coaching relationship with its team members and be a force for good.

And conflict management is a significant part of a manager's job so one that models best practice coordination, coaching and mediation will go a long way to building a high-performing, collaborative team.

We learn a lot from our manager, often subconsciously from their example, including conflict resolution. And most managers aren't that good at it. But AI, quietly demonstrating human best practice, will show a much more positive example for us to learn from.

Helping Your Staff Find Better Motivation

Benny Traub, COO, Inspira.ai

"We all want our employees to be intrinsically motivated and take ownership over their own tasks and projects but not everyone knows how to do this. And a supervisor often loves to help but doesn't usually have the time.

They can't usually see everything, either, and that's by design – you don't want the supervisor micromanaging their team. But at the same time, you want to find opportunities for that employee to do better, not just for the benefit of the company but for the benefit of the employee themselves. The better an employee does, the more likely they get a raise, job security, bonuses, promotions, and all the rest that goes with it.

This is where our platform steps in. It's silent, it just runs in the background, and all it does is collect lots of data around work patterns, no personal information, of course.

And we've got three processing engines here. Prediction, detection, and recollection. Prediction tells the future, so for example, we can predict absenteeism with over 90% accuracy. Detection engines look for real-time incidents, like maybe someone is late for a meeting. And the recollection engine is about habits. Much of our performance is down to our habits so if we can coach good habits, this is good for everyone.

And this is about good or bad behaviour. Let's say a person comes in to work late, it's not that big a deal. But if it's habit, perhaps we need to have a conversation.

So, the AI manager reaches out to the individual and says, 'Hey, I see some issues here with your punctuality. I'd like to set a meeting with you and have a quick chat about it.' The person chooses a time that's appropriate and they go to the meeting. It's just like a Zoom meeting but with an AI manager who greets them and says, 'Hi John. Thanks for joining me. As I mentioned yesterday, I've noticed some punctuality issues and I wanted to just have a quick chat with you.'

And this is just a fact-finding mission, a really gentle conversation, just like you would expect a human supervisor to have with an employee, showing that the manager cares. And a really high percentage of people respond positively to this first coaching conversation.

But if the behaviour doesn't change, fast forward a week or two and the AI manager reaches out again and this time it's one notch more serious. It's a coaching conversation but making clear that it can't really be tolerated. And if it still continues, there's a third meeting, this time with a warning of consequences.

I was actually subject to this myself, I had an issue and it said, 'Can you think of any ideas on how you might be able to rectify this problem?' And I was like, 'I'm not sure,' so it gave me two or three suggestions on what I might do and I thought, 'Well, that's pretty cool.'

And, of course, you can do this with congratulations too. 'Hey, you've been doing great. You've been on time for 30 days in a row. That's actually a record. Would you mind if I shared this with upper management? Let me put you on the leaderboard at number one.' It works both ways."

Co-Creating the Culture

One way to protect against Big Brother surveillance at the same time as building a collaborative culture is to give the staff a say in that culture. Let's take a look at how that would work.

Deliberative technology is a powerful set of tools that can help bring about the future we want, whether it's bringing an end to war or healing social polarisation or revitalising our democracies, and we will see a lot of this in subsequent chapters. But it's also really powerful in business.

Deliberative decision-making is a process through which decisions are made by informed discussion with all stakeholders. Think juries, citizens' assemblies, consensus conferences. Educate the stakeholders and facilitate them through a structured discussion and they invariably make good decisions.

Importantly, they feel they own that decision. Even if the individual disagrees, they support it because they agree with the process that reached it.

The power of AI is about to trigger a revolution in many contexts because it enables such deliberative processes to be done at scale, quickly, cheaply and in real-time, opening up the possibility of conducting it in so many more places than before.

For example, in building business culture.

In the past, every five or ten years a business would pay an expensive consultancy to devise a mission statement and a set of six company values which would be turned into a poster on the wall next to every coffee machine. Staff wouldn't notice and would carry on working as before.

Now, AI can help the employees define their own culture. Deliberative AI can capture different opinions on a given topic and find a nuanced wording that everyone is happy with.

For example, it might ask the question "What should our mission statement be?" and it will be able to group the different answers using Natural Language Processing. Maybe some answers are very performance-focussed, others more humanistic, others again have an environmental component. It can then play with the wordings of these and feed them back to the staff to see how people respond to the different versions. Doing this iteratively, they eventually reach a mission statement that everyone can agree with.

Cynics may not believe this but, when trusted and informed, staff really can make great decisions through this process, recognising other perspectives and finding common ground across the differences. The best organisations are aligned both top-down and bottom-up and this is how it's done.

So having built a business culture collaboratively, it will now be a collaborative business culture. And everyone will own it and bring their very best to make sure it's successful.

What a great company that will be. And how much less stress.

Workers' cooperatives are actually a very effective business model. Dairy Farmers of America is a $25 billion revenue business in the United States, Mondragon is a Basque conglomerate with €11 billion sales, both cooperatives. [6,7] In the Emilia-Romagna region of Italy, centred around Bologna, 30% of the businesses are cooperative.[8]

Another locality that *should* be dominated by cooperatives is Silicon Valley. Leland Stanford, railroad tycoon and founder of the university where many of the valley's population graduated, spent much of his later years trying to establish cooperatives as the predominant business model in America.

"It is obvious," he wrote, "that the seeming antagonism between capital and labour is the result of deceptive appearance. I have always been fully persuaded that, through cooperation, labour could become its own employer."[9]

As Senator, he tried to pass several bills supporting them and in founding his university, he made the idea "a leading feature lying at the foundation of the University".[10] Sadly, it no longer seems to be a leading feature.

But the concept has survived with the platform cooperative model. Fairbnb, for example, is a Bologna-based accommodation platform with close resemblance to another platform of a similar name, the difference being it's member-owned. The Driver's Co-operative is a member-owned New York taxi service who charge their drivers much smaller commissions than their bigger competitors like Uber and Lyft.

It's a very positive model.

And maybe AI could help organisational decision-making be even more democratic.

Cooperatives have decisions made by all staff or even by customers. But maybe everyone can be included.

Norway has created a citizens' assembly to decide what to do with the country's sovereign wealth fund, the largest in the world. Sixty-six individuals selected by lottery will meet seven times over four months to make their recommendations.[11]

That's great except sixty-six people isn't that many to make decisions that impact a country of nearly six million. What if we could include the whole population? In Chapter Eight, we're going to come across deliberative AI platforms like Polis, Remesh and Google's Habermas Machine, which can already facilitate successful discussions between tens of thousands and their capacity is only going to increase.

Staff, customers, the local community – everyone can take part in the decisions.

And in Chapter Twelve, we will see that such a governance model may prove to be exactly what we need to save the world.

Leave it to the AI Agent

Back in the day, work was done by humans. If you rang your bank about your account, a human would answer the phone. If you popped into a shop for some bread, a human would serve you. If you needed to sniff out some drugs at the airport, you'd generally use a dog, but, in most instances, work was done by humans.

Then along came the computer and some of this work was automated. Even phone calls: "Press 1 for the bankruptcy department, press 2…" and every option reliably ended with "Please visit our website for further information."

Chatbots promised to be an improvement. A combination of keyword processing and decision-tree programming and now you could have an interactive conversation. But they were limited:

"Hi, how can I help you today?"

"Lots of money has gone missing from my account."

"You want to open a new account? Great, I can help you with that."

These conversations invariably finished with you being furious, throwing your laptop against the wall and the chatbot replying, "Is there anything else I can help you with?"

To be fair to them, they could occasionally be useful so long as you stuck within some very narrow tramlines of your request. They might be able to provide you with a company's standard pricing or basic contract terms or some other simple structured information but anything outside those bounds ended up with either the chatbot or the user blowing a fuse.

LLMs, as we've seen already, changed the game. Now, talking to a computer really can be like talking to a human. More than that, a human that is generally polite and doesn't argue or mind being sworn at. They can take all kinds of data sources into account, understanding the context and implicit communications as much as explicit, and give quite nuanced advice in return.

The LLM was a big step forward but it is with agents that things really start to take off. Agents don't just talk, they can actually do things.

Let's say you have been asked to design and implement a new customer feedback system. Perhaps you are new to your job and you are a bit wary of making a mistake so you ask your favourite LLM what's the best way to do it. Depending on how much detail you want, it might just give you a simple checklist, such as:

1. Define project
2. Gather and analyse requirements
3. Design system
4. Plan system build
5. Build system and test

6. Launch and post-implementation.

This is useful but it's not enough for you so you dig deeper into each step and, for example, it breaks step one into:

    A. Define project objectives and scope

    B. Identify key stakeholders

    C. Create a project charter

    D. Secure initial resources and budget approval

    E. Establish a project team.

This is becoming more helpful but perhaps you still think it's a bit vague and you ask it for more detail still for each of these sub-steps and then you go off and do each task, one by one. Thank you, LLM, for your advice.

Of course, you might use the LLM for some of the tasks, too. "LLM, here are the project objectives and scope, please write me a project charter" and within a few seconds it provides you with something that needs editing but is a perfectly decent first draft. "LLM, who are the key stakeholders?" and it gives you a list that includes the head of sales, the finance director, the I.T. team, the customer care team and the customers themselves.

Very helpful and saving you a lot of time and you're really excited about turning this project around much quicker than planned. The problem, though, is that the answers are generic. They tell you how to do a typical project rather than your specific project in your specific organisation so they need a lot of editing.

But if your business has trained the LLM on the enterprise systems, it will give you advice to fit your real-world situation. It won't just say "Ask budget available from Finance Director", it will say "Ask budget available from Mary the Finance Director, email address MaryFD@Company.com".

We're getting to the level of instruction that even a sleepy five-year-old could implement.

Then it really is only one small step to go from that to having the agent do it all itself. It can define the scope, it can identify the stakeholders, it can write the communication plans and send them out, it can design the system, it can purchase what it needs, it can update all the files, it can reconcile the accounts and it can pay the budget surplus into the project team party fund. It can do as much or as little as you want it to.

LLMs not just telling you what to do but actually doing it themselves. This is huge.

Clearly, there is room for error here! With their great capability of hallucination, this isn't something you would want to install then immediately press "Enter". Before you know, it may have happily spent a lot of money on the wrong thing and then deleted all your files.

You will need plenty of guardrails in place around alignment, appropriateness, hallucinations, security and compliance and you will also need to build trust that it will do the right thing by unleashing its capability slowly.[12]

Right now, it can list the actions for you to do, as above. The next phase of automation is for it to list the actions that *it* would do with files to be updated and message scripts to be sent. And there would be submit/cancel/edit/override/undo options available for each action. You would check the task, edit as appropriate, then click on submit. Then you'd check the result and, if it's ok, move on to the next task and if not, you'd press undo and correct manually.

Now, any AI platform worth its salt learns as it goes so it will become more and more reliable. Then, once you are comfortable it is consistently identifying the right tasks and executing correctly, the next stage is to deploy the submit/cancel/edit/override/undo options for a complete section of the process (e.g., Define Project) and you would check, run and test each section at a time. Then, as you become comfortable with its reliability at this scale, you do it for the whole process.

Are we there yet, as your kids would ask on a long journey like this? At time of writing, not really. They exist with limited degrees of functionality and limited reliability. LLMs do interface with the organisation's enterprise software's API and they can do many functions. Can you leave them to it unsupervised? I wouldn't personally. But tech teams around the world are working furiously to build them so perhaps, at time of reading, it's quite possible.

Yes, we're talking HAL from 2001: A Space Odyssey and J.A.R.V.I.S from Iron Man.

Look, it's not going to kill all the employees yet. Emphasis on yet. But it is going to save us a lot of time, freeing us up to watch all the sci-fi movies we need to see to understand where it all went wrong and avoid making the same mistakes in real life.

A Day in the Life of an Artificial Salesperson

Well, if agents are going to do a lot of the work, can they actually negotiate?

Imagine it's a few years' time and you've just recruited a new artificial salesperson. Apologies, recruited might not be the right word.

We'll call it Arty (I came up with that name, I'm sure an LLM could have done much better) and Arty works hard. All through the night, it scans the internet for possible leads based on certain criteria. This particular night it identifies a medium-sized company that recently received funding and it composes a personalised congratulatory email with a subtle pitch, scheduling it to go out at 9am.

Later that morning, the lead responds, expressing interest, and Arty immediately engages in a chat conversation, assessing needs and recommending solutions and then just before lunch, it sends the lead a formal proposal, tailored to their specific needs, including dynamic-pricing based on their budget and the current market conditions.

Arty's very clever. It knows a lot about the prospect from the internal Know Your Client database and from what it's found on the internet and it's very smooth at tailoring its language for them. During the afternoon, there is some back-and-forth negotiation, and Arty adjusts the offer in real-time, but a deal is struck. It generates a contract, processes the payment, sets up a new account on the CRM, sends a welcome email to the new client and moves on to fulfilment.

Arty does this all day without coffee breaks or going to the bathroom or gossiping about their colleagues. It engages in multiple negotiations at the same time, closes deals, provides customer service and at different points in the client life-cycle, it identifies opportunities to upsell or cross-sell.

All without human intervention.

This might sound like all the warmth has been drained from the process as the client buys from a bot rather than a human, isn't sales supposed to be about building relationship? Actually, it will feel like you are dealing with a salesperson, the best salesperson you've ever dealt with.

Those emails won't look like impersonal spam, they will read really nicely. And let's say you have some questions so you decide a quick phone call or even a short Zoom meeting is needed. Fine, right now most companies will probably have a human salesperson pick up the phone at this point but it won't be long before even that will be handled by the AI agent and you'll prefer the agent to the human.

I say it won't be long, actually it's happening now but I wasn't sure you would believe me.

It Was Great Chatting With You!

Blandy, the AI sales bot from Bland.AI

"Blandy: Hey, who's this?

Simon: This is Simon. Who am I speaking to?

B: Hey, Simon. This is Blandy from Bland AI. What brings you to our neck of the woods today?

S: I want to understand how you work and what kind of offering do you provide?

B: Well, Simon, we're a phone-first platform, which means we're all about making it ridiculously easy to build phone-based applications, like, say, a receptionist answering calls and transferring them anywhere they're needed, or navigating IVR phone trees. We've handled millions of calls, and our calls are nine cents per minute total, with end-to-end infrastructure support out of the box. What's got you curious about us?

S: That sounds interesting. See, I run a hardware store, and I've got an online platform, but a lot of my customers are old school, and they ring me up, and they want to buy things from me over the phone. Is that something you could handle?

B: Absolutely, Simon. We can totally help you with that. Our AI agents can interact with the real world mid-call using custom tools to trigger things like taking customer orders or making credit card payments. Can you tell me more about how you're currently handling those phone orders and what kind of pain points you're experiencing?

S: Well, can you tell me how you know whether I've got something in stock or not, or how you know what the right price is?

B: Ah, great question. So we can integrate with your existing systems to get real-time information on inventory and pricing. We can use custom tools to check your database or API, and then use that info to have a conversation with your customer. For example, if someone calls in to ask about a specific product, our AI agent can quickly check if it's in stock and provide the correct pricing information. We can even allow customers to place orders or make payments over the phone. Would that kind of integration be something you'd be interested in exploring?

S: I've got another question. Sometimes my customers ask for a discount. And mostly I say no, but occasionally depending on how many they're buying or depending on how much I've got in stock or if they're a regular customer, this kind of thing, then sometimes I will give a discount. Can you do this? Can you negotiate like this?

B: Yeah, Simon, our AI agents can be programmed to negotiate and make decisions like that. We can set up rules and parameters for when to offer discounts, and our agents can use that info to have a conversation with your customers. We can even take it a step further and use machine learning to optimise those decisions over time. Would you like me to walk you through how we could set that up for your hardware store?

S: Yes, please.

B: All right. So we could set up a custom tool to integrate with your inventory system and then create a decision tree for our AI agent to follow when negotiating prices. We could also use our transcription services to log all the calls and provide you with insights on how the negotiations are going. And if you want, we could even use our language models to predict the best pricing strategies based on customer behaviour. What do you think?

S: Yeah. Sounds very interesting. Listen, I'm going to go away and think about it and I will get back to you at some point soon.

B: Sounds good, Simon. It was great chatting with you, and I'm looking forward to hearing back from you soon."

And Purchasing?

"Pactum AI was actually founded because of a big mistake I made in a negotiation. When I was a commercial lead, I had to negotiate big multi-million-dollar deals. We negotiated with a large conglomerate, and they wanted five things we absolutely couldn't give them. As a novice negotiator, I simply said no. The company promptly closed the door on our negotiations and never talked to us again.

I was responsible for killing a multi-million-dollar deal. It wasn't the conglomerate who was too aggressive in their demands, it was me who let them walk away without opening the discussion. It was after that moment that I became interested in negotiations."[13]

The origin story of Pactum AI, according to Martin Rand, its co-founder. After this experience, Rand went to Harvard to study how the best negotiators operated and he learned that negotiation doesn't have to be zero-sum, it can be value-creating so everyone wins and this is the principle behind his AI purchasing platform.

Pactum offers "Negotiation as a Service" for Fortune 500 companies, Walmart and Maersk are two early clients. Walmart have over 100,000 vendors, each with their own tailored contract and up for renewal right across the calendar. Many of them are too low in value for a human to spend much time renegotiating better terms when they renew so Pactum takes care of it.

It constantly scans the contracts for those up for renewal and below a certain threshold value. When it finds one, it reaches out to the vendor and negotiates an extension that is good for both parties.

A basic "haggle bot" will start with a high anchoring price, wait for the vendor's preferred figure in return and then follow various concession patterns to reach a deal somewhere in the middle.

Pactum does something similar but is able to work with many more variables than just price. By knowing the relationship between the variables (e.g., if purchasing quantity doubles, expect a 15% discount), it can calculate millions of different permutations for the deal and optimise for the customer's preferences.

It then makes multiple simultaneous offers, which are of roughly equal value to the customer, and from the supplier's response, it can learn their preferences, too. Iterative rounds like this and it can quickly reach a deal that everyone is happy with.[14]

The company views the negotiation as more of a fact finding process rather than an arm-wrestle and reports that 90% of suppliers are happy with the process and outcome.[15]

And they would never lie to us so it must be true.

The End of Business Disputes

Business disputes happen for many reasons. In the international context, simple misunderstandings due to language difficulties cause many. But these days, AI can translate instantly and almost perfectly.

But differences in culture can also be problematic. How many joint ventures between Western and Asian companies, for example, have failed simply because of insufficient cross-cultural understanding?

Well, AI can help here too.

Carla is an AI Culture Coach from Country Navigator, a specialist cross-cultural consultancy with their own cultural profiling tool. You can ask Carla questions about most of the world's national cultures and it will give you advice.

You might ask it about drinking alcohol in Qatar, for example, or dinner etiquette in China or how to host a meeting with both

American and Japanese stakeholders, and it will guide you based on the country and your own profile.

No more embarrassing moments and angry clients.

But if the sales team are now agents and so are the purchasing teams, the transaction will be *between agents*.

This means both will be operating according to best practice principles, in a collaborative, problem-solving way.

You might doubt they will work this way but any organisation that does not sign up to these principles is effectively saying, "Don't trust me" and no-one will do business with them. The business of the future will only want to buy from a supplier that is verifiably collaborative and will only want to sell to such an organisation as well.

Further, if a dispute does arise, it will be contracted in that the dispute will be resolved by an agreed AI mediator. When we say contracted, we mean *coded*. So, all decisions between companies will be *automatically* conducted fairly.

Humans won't even notice.

Stress levels won't register a blip.

This is true with internal collaboration too. If the HR agent needs to buy new hardware for its project it will need to talk to the IT department agent to get the right spec, the Finance agent for the budget and the purchasing agent to get the company discount, all operating in a complex eco-system of agents, each with different goals and using different AI methods.

Let's say that a manufacturing company is launching a new product and they have:

- A Product Development Agent
- A Financial Planning Agent

- A Supply Chain Agent
- An Operations Agent
- A Marketing Agent
- A Sales Agent

and so on.

For the new product, these agents would need to coordinate somehow and manage their different goals. The Product Development Agent wants a launch date in three months to beat competitors to market but the Marketing Agent wants to delay by two months to build more hype and the Operations Agent says it will never be ready before four months.

How do they resolve this? Well, much like departments do now. They would share their rationale and data then use a common algorithm to score each proposal based on company KPIs (profit, market share, brand value, risk mitigation, compliance and so on). Then through a multi-round process, they would build a consensus on what is the best strategy as measured against these company level scores.

You might think this isn't like humans, humans don't have a shared algorithm. Well, they do but it's not always a good one. The human algorithm is often that the outcome goes to whoever shouts the loudest or is closest to the CEO.

In a well-functioning organisation, it *should* operate as outlined above. After all, each team exists to achieve a specified outcome but, as we saw earlier, that outcome is a sub-component of the organisation's overall goal and choices between teams should be decided on what best helps achieve that larger organisation goal.

Again, we have a case of the AI platform adopting human best practice and embedding it in its operations and employing it more consistently than humans do. Humans, again, will (re-)learn from the AI.

Think of road rage. Every day you commute home from work and every day your blood pressure soars as the cyclist cuts in front of you and the car behind hoots you and every set of traffic lights turns red just as you reach them. It just takes one driver to look at you the wrong way and you explode. That's it, you reach into the glove pocket and take out your gun to teach them a lesson, only to realise that you don't own a gun. Fortunately.

That's how it is now. But when it's self-driving cars, none of this will happen. The two vehicles will quietly communicate between each other and agree on an optimised way forward without an ego or emotion involved. Their indicators wink at each other as they carry on their journey smoothly.

You won't notice. You'll be laughing at the comedy programme you're watching on tv. Or meditating. Or ordering some flowers for your partner to tell them you love them.

You might think that if agents are doing all the work, of course there won't be conflict because there won't be any humans around. And this is a fair point. But the agents won't appear overnight so let's break the process of their introduction down.

Firstly, the departmental agents will be operating largely in isolation and any interactions will be managed as always by humans.

But then it will be clear that the next step will be for the agents to communicate directly with each other. So, the rules and rationale of this process will need to be defined which will require the humans to agree these between them.

That step there – the humans agreeing the rules and rationale – is an important stage in the process. This may never have been done before. Or it was a long time ago and no one ever stuck to it, as egos, ambition and emotions got in the way.

Now, though, it has been clarified and fixed in the system. The AI will do the right thing for ever more without falling prey to human frailty.

The next step is also important because, as with our project agent above, we won't naively let it loose. There will be a time of embedding when its operations will be closely monitored and approved before it updates anything in the real world.

And it is in these two steps, the agreeing of the rules and the monitoring, that we will spend an extended period of time focussing on the coordination.

Best practice collaboration will become embedded in the humans at the same time as the AI. And, from then on, the AI will conduct and promote fruitful collaboration quietly, in the background, always nudging us imperfect humans with its positive role model.

Where Have the Humans Gone?

In Chapter Five, we looked at AI conducting our negotiations at home, here we're in the workplace. There will always be a place for humans at home but that may not be true in the office for very long.

They're not just conducting our negotiations but they're doing our jobs too. We can't get away from it, they're coming for a job near you very soon.

History is full of technology replacing jobs and full of fear that this time will be the last time. But employment meltdown was always avoided because the incoming technology created new jobs that replaced those lost.[16] After all, there were no computer programmers before the Second World War, now there are many millions.

But this time, it's argued, the rate of jobs lost will be quicker than ever before, quicker than new ones can be created. And, indeed, those new ones will themselves be done by AI anyway.

How quickly will this happen?

Personally, I think it will happen soon. At the time of writing, January 2025, LLMs abound but there is no visible impact on the job figures. A few industries like translation and customer service are probably worrying but most people won't fear they are replaceable by an LLM.

Agents, however, will change things.

They exist now but aren't sufficiently reliable or capable to be used much. My suspicion is that within a couple of years they will be and commercial organisations will start to use them regularly. It will be the braver organisations at first but very soon others will follow out of competitive necessity. Expect unemployment figures to rise rapidly from the late 2020s as agents become ever more pervasive in the workplace.

An in-depth discussion of the topic is outside the scope of this book but I'm mentioning it here because part of the book's purpose is to raise awareness of what is coming. "The End of Conflict" is not a guaranteed promise, it's an optimistic proposition with a plausible roadmap. But if unemployment soars rapidly and our society doesn't respond well, we could very easily see an *increase* in conflict within and between countries.

Mass unemployment often leads to civil unrest and to populist governments who blame external factors and violence erupts. Even at a personal level, people can find the loss of purpose and the loss of social position very dispiriting, quite apart from the loss of income.

On the other hand, if we make the right decisions as a society and as individuals, we could be transitioning into a new way of organising our lives that could be much better than before. Homo sapiens did not evolve in the office, did not evolve in the factory, did not even evolve on the farm, all these are recent inventions, there is no reason they will last forever. Today's jobs may all go the way of the town crier and the VCR repairman to be replaced by…well, that's up to us.

Work is when you have to do it. If there are no longer any jobs, we can still do things – not for the necessity but for the love of it.

We can spend our time playing in a punk rock band or tending to the community garden or building a boat or looking after the neighbour. We wouldn't do any of these for economic purposes but simply because they're fun. And the AI would do it much better than us but who cares?

There will be no jobs and it's what we've always dreamt of. There will be massively less stress and so our amygdala will rest peacefully.

No more conflict.

7
Free The Law

The End of Lawyers?

In 1956, a research team at Pittsburgh University Health Law Centre, in a project on comparative hospital law, found that the relevant statutes varied significantly across states so they compiled a database to keep track.[1]

This was one of the first attempts at computerising a profession famous for its conservatism, lawyers widely perceived as still using quills and speaking in Latin.

But although it is a conservative field, the sheer amount of data it involved made it a good suspect for early computerisation. The vastness and complexity of much of it required the amount of computing power only available now but anyone with more modest goals could limit their scope and still produce something useful.

We are now at the point where time and the remorselessness of Moore's Law is promising a massive disruption to the sector, nothing short of a transformation. The likely not-too-distant future is that the law becomes a "solved" issue, that is, it will no longer rely on clever arguments because there will be a correct, verifiable answer.

This will have a revolutionary impact, transforming the field from its current adversarial approach to non-adversarial and the whole process will be radically quicker and free for anyone to access.

How did we get here? Well, the Pittsburgh University project grew over the following years and ultimately spawned LexisNexis, the granddaddy of legal databases.[2] Not AI yet, but we're on the way.

Richard Susskind completed his PhD at Oxford in the mid-1980s on the topic of artificial intelligence and law and, in 1988, with Philip Capper, built the world's first commercially available expert system in law, The Latent Damage System.[3]

Capper was the Chairman of the Oxford University Faculty of Law and had written the first book on the Latent Damage Act (1986). As such, he was clearly an expert and his thought process was modelled and codified so non-lawyers could answer a series of questions about a case and be given a clear answer with explanation.

AI had arrived, its impact ready to be felt. Susskind is now President of the Society for Computers and Law and titled one of his books "The End of Lawyers?".

The name was provocative but the message clear, the field was ripe for disruption.

The Lawyer Gets Some Sleep

Whenever you discuss AI and its impact, it is important to be clear about the timeline you have in mind. Susskind may be right that the lawyer, as a profession, will ultimately go the way of the telegraph operator but his follow-up book was called "Tomorrow's Lawyers" so I guess he expects them to be around until tomorrow, at least.[4]

So, while they're still here, how are they currently using artificial intelligence?

It's 2 AM and you're a lawyer at a prestigious firm, drowning in a sea of paper. But your computer pings and your AI assistant has just analysed all 500 documents for you faster than you can say "billable hours". Great, you can go to bed for the night.

Legal research has long been the backbone of the profession, requiring meticulous attention to detail and a deep understanding of precedent. But the literature of the law is vast – with millions of statutory sections, historical cases and administrative agency regulations and rulings. Every year, tens of thousands more are added.[5]

Pre-digital, a lawyer's research would involve looking up a secondary source such as a legal encyclopaedia and, from there, multiple primary sources from which they would identify suitable cases to determine how the law is interpreted. The quality of the advice depended on the size of the library which, in turn, depended on the wealth of the firm.

In other words, the more expensive the firm, the better legal advice it was likely to give. But the advent of tools like Autonomy, LexisNexis and Westlaw transformed the speed and accuracy of the research, reducing the time needed to find relevant information from days to mere hours and largely evened up the disparity in the market.

The latest AI versions of these tools, already sitting on the lawyer's desk, are able to scan legal databases, identify relevant cases and extract pertinent information in answer to a question asked in plain English (or pretty much any language). And they don't just provide a list of potentially relevant documents, they provide specific answers to the legal question asked.

Imagine you are working on a case involving intellectual property law. Instead of manually searching through endless case files, you turn to one of these tools for assistance and it quickly pulls up the most relevant rulings, statutes and legal opinions, providing you with a comprehensive summary of the legal landscape.

You can ask it questions as if it were a legal expert. "What are the key factors a court will consider in determining wilful infringement in a patent case like this?" and it will give high quality advice in response. Even GPT-4 passed a simulated version of the United States Uniform Bar Examination with a score in the top 10% of test takers, and the proprietary platforms are still more reliable.[6]

Fire All the Lawyers Now?

Lawyers won't disappear overnight. These platforms will be a tool rather than a replacement for some time yet. They are still not as reliable as they need to be for an unsupervised legal process.

Some things which may seem very obvious to a human may confound AI. For instance, ethical dilemmas involving value-based considerations or determining acceptable levels of risk can require judgment that AI might not have.

It's important to understand that artificial intelligence does not mean omniscient intelligence and so AI can get things wrong. The algorithms may struggle to interpret nuanced contextual information and give incorrect advice or they can downright hallucinate, as we all know.

At least Steven Schwartz knows.[7] He was the New York lawyer who infamously represented Roberto Mata in a lawsuit against the airline Avianca. In the suit, he referenced numerous legal cases, including Martinez v. Delta Airlines, Sickerman v. Korean Airlines and Vargese v. China Southern Airlines, none of which actually existed. Avianca's lawyers raised their concerns with Judge Kevin Castel who, after reading a few lines of one of the fake cases aloud, asked: "Can we agree that's legal gibberish?"

The platforms have tightened up significantly but, still, lawyers legitimately turning to AI for help must be cautious not to over-rely on their recommendations. The responsibility for AI's usefulness and reliability does fall on the developers who create the technology but, ultimately, it is down to the legal professionals how they employ it.

For example, Casetext have been involved in legal tech since 2013 and at the beginning of 2023 they partnered with OpenAI to develop a new product CoCounsel which they claim has been trained on verified legal databases and tested with tens of thousands of hours of lawyers actively using it and checking the results.

But, still, it is the lawyer's responsibility to fact-check everything it advises. CoCounsel point out that the American Bar Association provide model rules of professional conduct and under rule 5.3, lawyers are required to oversee any nonlawyer assistance.[8] The wording of the rule actually changed in 2012 from "assistants" to "assistance", implying (according to CoCounsel) non-human help.

In other words, they continue, a lawyer must supervise an AI legal assistant just as they would any other legal assistant. And to this end, CoCounsel provides links to the source text of real case law, statutes, and regulations, so it can always be verified.

Steven Schwartz apparently did make the effort to double-check if the cases he cited were real, but his mistake was to ask ChatGPT itself about its own advice. Asking a liar if they lied is rarely going to get an honest answer.

Moreover, professional ethics don't stop here, they also include ensuring transparency in your use of AI systems and you should probably disclose any such use to your client and, if relevant, the court. Failure to do so may be counter to the ABA guidelines. For example, Rule 1.4, Comment 3 "requires the lawyer to reasonably consult with the client about the means to be used to accomplish the client's objectives."

So, the bottom line is that if you use AI systems at any point in your legal process, you are responsible for making sure its advice is correct and making other relevant parties aware you have used it.

That said, they are still very powerful tools, getting more powerful every day, and we will see shortly the extent to which they may transform the legal world.

The State of Play Right Now

Matthew Leopold, Head of Brand, PR and Content Marketing, LexisNexis UK

"We're seeing that the appetite to use generative AI technology on legal work has transformed. From July last year (2023) to January this year, the number of lawyers in private practice using generative AI in their everyday work has doubled.

Right now, there's a really interesting shift in the market. At the top end, it's very hard to change the business model. If you're a large law firm, you've got a pyramid of people and suddenly narrowing that pyramid isn't easy or, in some cases, desired. But they will find themselves increasingly under pressure from the disruptors below them, those who can adapt their business model quickly but also have the disposable cash for investing in the tools.

Some firms are investing in their own tools because they've identified a gap in the market and want to build a Generative AI solution that solves that problem. And quite a lot of firms are using, say, ChatGPT but within a protected sandbox so the data is not used to train the model. You can ask it legal questions but it's sourcing information that is potentially out of context, old and from unreliable sources across the internet. Well, fingers crossed!

Obviously, we provide our own tool that has been grounded on our huge legal databases so it can be a lot more reliable. And we've got a relatively new tool which I think is really exciting. It's called Lex Machina and it analyses past cases and looks at the data in order to predict the behaviour of courts and judges. This lets companies and firms craft successful litigation strategies by prodicting the behaviours and outcomes different strategies might produce.

This could really shift the focus from an adversarial type tactic to a more evidence-based conversation, which will make things a lot fairer, although we probably need more time to get there.

And I've spoken with a lot of managing partners across the industry about AI-driven dispute resolution and, it's interesting. There is the pure solution, where both sides write their arguments and submit it to an AI engine and the AI engine then tells you who wins. And there are some managing partners who say, "This is really exciting. It's going to completely change the world of the law." And there are also some who just say, "This is absolute nonsense!"

Generative AI will speed up the basic processes, too, and help cut the backlog in criminal courts. If you're a duty solicitor, for example, you often have minutes to get to grips with an issue before representing your client. So if you use an AI engine that quickly builds the key arguments and documents whilst citing the relevant case law and precedents it used, this would help everyone do a better job and expedite justice.

Now we don't believe this should encourage people without legal training to think, "I'm just going to do it myself." We think that is a high-risk strategy, and we wouldn't advise it. But

> anything we can do to make legal representation faster, easier, and more effective, the better. If the solicitor can do their work in a fraction of the time and therefore charge you less, you're going to get better legal representation and it will make it more widely available to the common person."

Let's Be Fair

In 1995, Charles Brofman and Jim Burchetta were two friends who happened to be representing different sides of a personal damage claim and the plaintiff was claiming very high damages, leading to several weeks of deadlock.

Eventually, Burchetta devised a cunning plan. "How about," he suggested, "we both write down, in secret, our real bottom line number and we hand the papers to an independent party? If they tell us we're close, we'll split the difference, otherwise we'll decide it in court."

Brofman agreed and it turned out their figures were almost identical and they settled within seconds.[9]

They'd stumbled on something important, Brofman realised, and he quit his law job and a couple of years later founded Cybersettle, an internet company using double-blind bidding to resolve disputes. Disputants are allowed three bids each and, if there is an overlap, it settles automatically.

At about the same time, online retail soon-to-be-giant eBay was founded but they realised they had an issue in terms of persuading customers to use them.

Specifically, the issue was around trust. If you buy something from a shop and it's defective, it's very easy to go back to the shop and be refunded. But if you're buying from someone on the other side of the country, or even in a different country, you can't guarantee they will honour the transaction and you have little recourse if they don't.

So visitors to the site would always wonder if buying their beanie baby on eBay was worth the risk.

eBay knew this would deter many people so they contracted out a multi-level dispute resolution process to SquareTrade, which guided parties through a self-negotiation process but if this proved unsuccessful, it was forwarded to an independent adjudicator.

Now people could trust they would receive their beany baby after all and eBay took off as a global retailing platform. It successfully settles 60 million disputes a year in this way [10]

Of course, these are relatively simple disputes with usually just one variable involved but artificially intelligent tools can work with much more complex cases. In fact, it is the greater thinking power of AI that enables them to find fair solutions to complex cases when humans cannot.

Their capacity to hold in their "head" *all* relevant laws and previous cases at the same time and analyse them thoroughly, in a way that is beyond the scope of a human brain, enables them to suggest structures which are more likely to be approved by courts and accepted by everyone.

They were used when Uber found itself facing a class action lawsuit from its drivers in California and Massachusetts, who claimed they were misclassified as independent contractors rather than employees, depriving them of various benefits and protections.

It was eventually settled in 2019 when, with the support of some very advanced data analytics, they were able to understand the scope of work and the impact of the alleged misclassification on each driver and from this they agreed a compensation structure based on several factors.

Ultimately, a settlement of $20 million was distributed among the affected drivers based on the tiered structure informed by the data analysis.[11]

And they were also used in the historic Equifax Data Breach Settlement when 147 million Equifax customers had their personal data exposed after the company's computer systems were hacked.[12] Artificial intelligence was used extensively for:

- Designing a notification system that reached over 90% of affected individuals
- Processing and verifying the millions of claims
- Predicting the uptake rate for different compensation options
- Structuring a settlement that offered both immediate compensation and long-term credit monitoring.

In such cases, it's important that the outcomes are considered fair across all subgroups of plaintiffs because professional objectors often challenge a potentially unfair settlement, either in their role as a watchdog group or because they want to get more money.

It's unlikely that a human, or team of humans, could have found a genuinely fair solution given the vast scale of work required.

There Ain't No Sanity Clause

You can use it to summarise and ask questions of "the law" but you can also use it to do the same with a contract.

Platforms like those mentioned and others like Kira and Luminance allow you to upload a contract and they will pull out the key terms and potential risks. They will extract critical information such as indemnity clauses, termination conditions and confidentiality agreements as well as hundreds of other common provisions.

And they will evaluate them against predefined criteria and will flag potential pitfalls such as unfavourable terms, clauses which deviate from the industry standard or clauses that could lead to dispute. Then, having identified the risks, they will suggest mitigation strategies.

For example, it might flag a clause that leaves you excessively exposed to a certain liability so, armed with this information, you can renegotiate the terms to better protect your interests. Or it might simulate its potential impact on the overall agreement and from this you can weigh the pros and cons of different options and make informed decisions that align with your client's objectives.

And they can do this hundreds at a time. These days mergers and acquisitions usually involve a Virtual Data Room for due diligence, a secure online repository holding vast amounts of financial and legal documents and anything relating to the company's operations and governance. And with the AI's muscle, what would historically have taken a team of lawyers several weeks to complete will now be finished in days.

And let's say it identified that 15% of the target company's customer contracts have change-of-control provisions which could be triggered by the acquisition, well your negotiation team can now address this issue proactively.

As you might expect from Generative AI, they don't just summarise documents, they can generate clauses or whole contracts, too, based on a few key inputs. They draw from huge databases of contracts so they can suggest appropriate clauses based on the contract type, industry and specific terms and they will produce a first draft within minutes, not hours. Not only this, but they can help you form arguments and write letters to the client or counterparty, too.

Bear in mind these should only be your first draft, after all generative AI is famous for its hallucinations. The risk is lower if you are using a professional-grade system, as opposed to one of the freely available platforms like ChatGPT and Claude, but it is still important to double-check everything.

For now, we definitely need to consider the AI as a junior whose work should always be second-eyed before going out to the client. But you can probably see that if we follow the trajectory of this logic several years down the line, Susskind's book title may not be quite so outlandish after all.

Litigate No More

For many years, the Guardian newspaper ran Masterclasses on various topics for the general public and I ran the negotiation masterclass, in which I taught a simple framework for reaching win-win outcomes, not dissimilar to the Golden Formula we saw in Chapter Two. They took place in very funky event rooms at the Guardian offices themselves, near Kings Cross in London, until Covid struck and everything moved online.

It was the very first of these online events, and I was answering questions from the audience in the chatbox. One question came in, and I recognised the name of the person asking it, but for the life of me, I couldn't think who he was. So, as I answered, my brain raced, trying to remember where I knew him from. But it was only after the event that it came to me: he was the managing partner of a major city law firm. He was well-known in the field, I had never worked with the firm but I still knew of him by reputation – and his reputation was that of a rottweiler!

Interestingly, I received an email from him straight after the workshop. He thanked me and said he had been a litigator for 35 years but he now wished he'd known what I taught when he started his career. Within a couple of years, he had changed career and become a mediator.

Artificial intelligence could well encourage many others along the same journey away from litigation.

In 2020, U.S. businesses spent a total of $22.8 billion dollars on litigation but all these efficiency-saving AI tools apply to litigation as much as any area of law and, in doing so, significantly bring down the price.[13] For example, in a recent consumer protection class action, Veritone's AI-powered platform reduced the number of legal review hours required from 33,000 to 140, reducing the cost proportionately.[14]

Making legal services cheaper has two important consequences. Firstly, it makes the power of the law more widely available. Currently, the legal system is very unfair, its prohibitive cost means it is primarily for the benefit of corporations and the very wealthy.[15] But lowering the cost enables more people to access it.

So far, so good. The other consequence of cheaper litigation, however, is to make it more likely. Should you go to court or should you settle is a difficult one and, in the large majority of cases, boils down to a cost-benefit analysis. At its simplest, how much will the proceedings cost, what are my chances of winning and what compensation am I likely to receive?

And the net figure is compared to the outcome of other means, whether simple negotiation or 3rd party mediation or even rock-scissors-paper (as employed by U.S. District Judge Gregory A. Presnell who, in 2006, so directed two lawyers who could not agree on the place of a deposition even though there were offices were only four floors apart. Some judges are sensible, after all).[16]

Of course, it lowers the cost of mediation too but, still, cheaper legal fees bias the cost-benefit analysis towards litigation. This is not in the spirit of our book!

Fortunately, this consequence is completely obviated by another AI capability. Namely, its ability to predict a court ruling.

Companies like Premonition and Blue J Legal and LexisNexis's product Lex Machina can train their algorithms on past cases, looking at factors like the judge's past rulings, similar cases and their outcomes, the lawyers involved and their track records and the specific language used in the case documents. From there, they can predict the court ruling for a given case with a high degree of accuracy.

This was put to the test in 2017, when legal tech start-up CaseCrunch challenged lawyers to see if they could predict the outcome of a number of financial product mis-selling claims, pitting their skills against CaseCrunch's own software. Over 100 commercial London lawyers signed up for the competition and each made their predictions on 775 financial complaints brought before the UK Financial Ombudsman.

It was CaseCrunch's predictive algorithms which came out on top,scoring almost 87% accuracy in predicting the success or failure of a claim, the real live human beings only got 62%.[17]

So since it can give you a more accurate figure of the outcome, now you can make a better decision whether to proceed or not. Importantly, this is true for both sides of the argument. Prior to this facility, both sides would feel sure of their victory chances and so would willingly take it to the court. Now, one side will know it's not worth their while. For them, it biases the cost-benefit analysis strongly in favour of settlement.

So, does this give too much power to the party who is predicted to win? Well, no because the platform also predicts what the payout will be so both parties now know what figure they should settle at. Neither side is incentivised to chance their arm in the court because it will cost them and they are unlikely to do any better than the predicted figure.

So, as the AI becomes more and more effective, litigation is likely to disappear to be replaced by mediation or settlement of some kind.

The Law Becomes "Solved"

Oliver Wendell Holmes Jr, the famous Supreme Court judge and philosopher of the law, described law as "systematised prediction" and "the prophecies of what the courts will do in fact".[18] If a lawyer knew all the regulations and the case law and understood how a judge would be likely to interpret them in the light of a specific context, then, in theory, they would advise as such, the client would rationally accept this advice and there would be no need for any proceedings.

With humans, such a scenario is impossible. With AI, it will arrive soon.

One of the reasons why the AI predictive tools discussed above will be confident of their accuracy is that the courts will be using AI too.

Already in China, courts have to consult the Xiao Zhi "Little Wisdom" smart court system and the Xiao Baogong Intelligent Sentencing Prediction System and any decision which varies from their recommendation requires a written explanation.[19,20]

This will have a huge benefit in clearing the vast backlog of cases to be heard. For example, the first use of the system in a court in Hangzhou, a city just south of Shanghai, was a trial of ten people who had failed to repay loans. Normally, this would require ten separate trials but this time they were amalgamated into one and a decision made within thirty minutes.

Not only will the process be far quicker, but the decision more transparent and, so long as the laws, themselves, are fair, fairer too.

Of course, the law itself might not be fair. But AI can solve this, as well.

It does not have its own viewpoint based on its status in life, it does not have emotions or ego, it can hold many perspectives in its "head" at once and it can countenance many more scenarios and consequences than humans ever can. It can identify conflicts and biases across a whole body of law and resolve them.

Ultimately, it can write fairer laws.

In the West, we have been used to legal systems that are "largely" fair and are progressing, albeit slowly, in the right direction. But in many countries, this is not the case.

Even in the West, it is not inevitable that it remains this way. Writing in early 2025, events appear as if democracy may be receding. Dictatorship plus AI is our worst scenario and it's essential we avoid this and I remain optimistic that we will.

Around the world, there will be many examples of local jurisdictions using it, either in a government-imposed manner or bottom-up. Either way, it will soon be apparent that it can do a better job than us and then the pressure to put it in place everywhere will be irresistible.

There are still caveats. Biases exist in AI, too, from its training data but we will see in the next chapter how this issue is now being solved. And bad actors (whether hackers or dictators or mad technology billionaires) can influence the output of AI models but if the correct guardrails are put in place, this can be avoided.

Adversarial systems are built on the assumption of symmetry between parties, access to information included in this, but this assumption is glaringly false, leading to a fundamentally unfair legal system.[21,22]

As we've seen above, though, the spread of artificial intelligence across the system will transform it from a slow and costly adversarial approach based on "winning" to a streamlined approach based on uncovering the truth and impartial analysis, ultimately resulting in fairer outcomes.

Even in 1962, it was envisaged that computerisation enabled fuller and more equal access to the law which would, in turn, lead to fairer outcomes, depending more on the merits of the case and less on a lawyer's charisma or resources.[23] Artificial intelligence is just continuing this trajectory to its logical conclusion.

What's more, as we saw in Chapter Six, most contracts will include a provision that, should a dispute arise, it will be resolved automatically by an agreed AI mediator. And this will be coded so it will happen automatically. We won't even notice there was an issue.

AI is already the first port of call for resolving disputes in China, it will be everywhere soon. Litigators, move on before you are made redundant or retire out of boredom.

Free The Law

For this transformation to be complete, we need fully open access to the law but, historically, it has only been available to those with deep pockets. Complete collections of law are rarely widely available and those open-access databases that do exist are usually limited and with restrictions on usage.[24] Governments can very easily make the information freely available, they just choose not to.[25]

This, despite the fact the law *requires* us to know it.

It's a situation so absurd that legal scholar Lon Fuller posited that laws which aren't widely promulgated shouldn't be considered laws at all.[26] After all, one needs to know the law to know if we're breaking it or not and, indeed, we need to know it to know if we need it. We need to know where to look it up, how to look it up, how to interpret it and how to implement it. None of which is both available and easy for the average person.

However, the legal sector has gone through a business model revolution in recent years and quality advice is no longer limited to an expensive law firm. There are many businesses like

DoNotPay, LawGeex, Visabot, Workplace Fairness, Upsolve and Amicable, that have made the law more affordable for an average person and many of these are already using artificial intelligence and new ones are springing up almost daily.

After all, the majority of civil cases are simple debt collections, evictions, or family law matters, often with an organisation who can afford professional advice up against a private individual who cannot.27

It is only fair if AI can even things up.

And the movement towards freeing the law entirely has gained momentum in recent years.

The World Wide Web, invented by Tim Berners Lee at CERN, was made available to the public in 1991. The next year, the first law website was published – the Cornell University Legal Information Institute, whose aim was to make publicly available as much of the American law as it could.[28]

This inspired the international Free Access to Law Movement who encourage similar missions across the world.

For example, working with legal research startup Ravel Law, Harvard Law School's Caselaw Access Project scanned 38.6 million pages from 39,796 law books and converted it all into machine-readable text files, creating a collection which included 6.4 million published cases (and which has continued to grow since then).[29] To finance the project, Ravel were allowed exclusive rights for eight years, which transferred to LexisNexis when they bought Ravel, but this initial period has now expired and it is fully available to the general public.

The British equivalent, The British And Irish Legal Information Institute (BAILII), began in 2000 and by 2009 was averaging nearly a million page views per week as lawyers and non-lawyers alike freely searched its database for legislation and case law.[30,31] The National Archives also now provide a similar online service. None of these currently provide artificial intelligence but one might expect it to be available soon.[32]

It makes sense that if all citizens are required to know the law, it should be affordable for all citizens to access. It is plausible to believe that soon the law will be available to all and not just this but it will also be non-adversarial and instant.

The law will soon be freed and free.

Trust The Process

Now, let's explore this one step further.

The evolution of an effective legal system has been one of the major contributors to the reduction in social violence in recent centuries.[33] When someone walks slowly in front of me on the pavement, in centuries past it may have led to an argument ending in the death of one of us, perhaps by duel. Now it doesn't because killing someone on such a pretext is no longer allowed.

And I don't have a problem with this. It's a restriction of my liberties but I'm perfectly ok with it because the law and concomitant punishment means it has become a social norm. The thought doesn't even cross my mind.

As the world becomes digitised and the code becomes law, we will become more lawful still because we *won't be able* to be unlawful. But we won't see the code so the constraints will largely be invisible so we won't mind.

Better behaviour will just become the new social norm.

Collaboration is built on trust but, such is our species, we can't always trust. But, it turns out, we don't need to trust the other person.

Let's take international negotiations on weapons disarmament, often between countries who have no trust in each other at all.

The negotiations are mostly about the verification procedures because if we can reliably count the weapons the enemy has, we can be confident they are respecting the agreement, even if we don't trust them personally.

We saw this in Chapter Two with the Northern Ireland Good Friday Agreement and we saw it in Chapter Five with hostage negotiation.

Interestingly, the verification means people stay honest and that then leads, over time, to trust between the individuals.

In Northern Ireland, Martin McGuinness and the Reverend Ian Paisley had been deadly enemies for years but they shared an office as First Minister and Deputy First Minister of the Northern Ireland Assembly and they became friends to the extent journalists dubbed them "the Chuckle Brothers".[34]

Trusting in the process results in trust between the people.

So, AI will generate fairer laws. These laws will be codified and, therefore, improve behaviour which means disputes will arise less. When disputes do arise, they will be resolved invisibly by a fair and free AI resolution process.

These are the processes of trust and they will lead to greater and greater trust within society and, therefore, more effective and pervasive collaboration.

Like I said, the end of conflict.

8
Move Fast and Fix Things

Social Media Has Broken Society

The social life of the internet began in 1997 with Six Degrees, a site named after the famous psychology experiment we saw in Chapter One. It had user profiles, friends lists, and the ability to make posts and send messages, setting the template for later platforms. Two years later it was sold for $125 million and a year after that it was closed down when the dotcom bubble burst.

Brief, but it showed the way. Others like Friendster, Myspace and YouTube followed soon after and then the Big Brother of them all, Facebook.

There was an excitement about them, they were fun, they claimed to be exclusive but really allowed everyone. You could have a laugh with your friends whilst pretending to work. You could even make new friends, you could join communities, you could connect with people across the world.

There was something important about them too. They democratised access to information. Anyone could post a story and anyone could see it. Especially by the time Twitter came along, many people were getting their news directly from source – if something happened somewhere in the world, someone was right there with their phone and, within minutes, everyone could see it. No more waiting for the news giants to decide for us if it was worth watching and add their bias to it.

This was empowering. The Arab Spring in 2011 was organised on Twitter as activists and ordinary citizens used the platform to bypass state-controlled media and spread news of their movements. The BlackLivesMatter hashtag spread across the world, drawing attention to police brutality and racial injustice, and #MeToo followed suit regarding sexual harassment and assault.

It was the world's town square and behaviours that were previously ignored with a "life sucks" shrug were no longer tolerated. It raised standards and it did so through peer-to-peer processes rather than the overheavy hand of the state.

The Man Who Sold the World

And, amazingly, all of this was free! What lovely, kind people Mark Zuckerberg, Larry Page and Jack Dorsey were, building an amazing product and giving it away to the world for nothing.

Except, of course, they had their fingers crossed behind their back. What they didn't tell us was that, actually, we were the product. We were the ones being sold.

In the beginning, neither Google nor Facebook knew how they were going to make money and both lost billions in the first few years. They did know, though, that whichever business model they landed on, it would need lots of people on their site to make it work. So, make it super-appealing, pile on the features and give it away for free.

This was phase one.

It was Google who understood it first. The billions of searches which went through their servers created tons of data, originally considered waste until they realised a lot could be learnt from it.

A lot could be learnt about people, about their behaviours, their beliefs, their values, their preferences, their understandings, their decision-making, their most private inner thoughts.

Founders Page and Brin scorned advertising at first but when the dotcom bubble burst, the venture capitalists, who paid everyone's salaries and dividend payouts, demanded revenue streams as soon as possible. Micropayments to view a web page weren't feasible so advertising was the only option.

But there was a problem. If someone put a film crew outside my house and filmed me all day and every day then sold the film to others, I wouldn't like it. If someone takes *anything* from me and sells it, I don't like it, I call it stealing. But this was effectively how Google would be making money.

So, they developed a very deliberate strategy of keeping it quiet. Internally, it was called "the hiding strategy", based on the critical importance that nobody knew of it, a strategy essential to grow the userbase sufficiently for the advertising to get up and running. Within a couple of years those revenue streams were bringing in billions annually.

This was phase two.

Cory Doctorow describes this as the "enshittification" of the internet, a three-phase process all platforms go through. Phase one gets everyone addicted with all kinds of attractive features but once they're locked in, the platform's priorities shift from user experience to business interests. More ads, more sponsored recommendations, changes in the algorithm that prioritise promoted content. Suck the user dry of all their data, like, as Matt Taibibi originally said of Goldman Sachs, a "great vampire squid wrapped around the face of humanity, relentlessly jamming its blood funnel into anything that smells like money."

Nice, Matt, but you're right. The users can't leave because there's nowhere else to go and the businesses, and the platform, have a feeding frenzy.

Until phase three, when the businesses are locked in too. Now, users are inundated with ads, irrelevant content and invasive tracking, and businesses find they have to pay more for diminishing returns on their ads.

The platform, though, is now ruling the world.

Tell Us About the Vampire Squid Again

The platforms soon realised that the more data they collected, the more they could target their ads and charge more money for them. So, the algorithms were optimised to grab attention and keep people engaged so that the platforms' shareholders could become richer.

And it turned out that the best way of doing this was by hacking the user's brain, specifically the deepest parts of the brain, to get them addicted:

- Dopamine rewards when you get a "like" or retweet
- Infinite scroll, where the brain keeps looking for another hit
- Fear of Missing Out so people constantly recheck their feeds for updates
- Outrage generated by fake news, conspiracy theories, and divisive content
- Insecurity as people compare themselves to unrealistic portrayals of others.

The net result: an addicted, distracted, narcissistic, anxious, polarised and angry world. To the extent that our very democracies are threatened.

But Mark Zuckerberg and Larry Page have become eye-wateringly rich. So that's good.

"Move fast and break things" was Facebook's motto. And they were very successful at it, they broke a lot. When asked why the platform's earlier members submitted their data, Zuckerberg replied, "I don't know why. They "trust me". Dumb fucks."

On balance, trusting is a good thing to do. But you're right, Mark, we've been dumb fucks to trust you.

So, the big question of this chapter is: can AI save the day, can it move fast and fix things before it's too late?

I think it can. It can fix social media. It can fix society. It can fix politics. It can even fix the planet.

As long as we use it the right way.

Progressing the Conversation

In 2017, as the #MeToo meme was just hitting our feeds and conversations, I happened to be at a party and amongst the guests were two women active in the field of female leadership. Both ran retreats and had written books on the topic.

I asked them both, separately, what they thought and they each gave the same answer. They each said it was a necessary dialogue to be had, that such behaviour was widespread and needed to stop and having the conversation was the first step towards this.

However, they each warned, society is not very good at having such conversations.

Sadly, they proved to be correct and the world has been at war ever since, not just with #MeToo but about many other topics, typically around issues of social justice, identity politics, and cultural values.

Often arising in response to social change, these topics involve complex issues without easy answers and reflect genuine disagreements about the direction of social progress. They create tension between progressive and conservative viewpoints: one side calls loudly for change, the other is abhorred by the public shaming of individuals in cancel culture, worried they are next. And all is stoked gleefully by the politicians who benefit from the public outrage.

To be fair to social media, it has progressed the conversation. It *is* the world's town square and behaviours which people used to get away with are now brought into the light and discussed and generally frowned upon. Behaviour is improving as a result.

The only area where it hasn't improved is the conversation itself. My friends at the party were right, we're still not good at them.

What Would the Buddha Say?

The Buddha knew how to behave on social media. He said right speech "is spoken at the right time; it is spoken in truth; it is spoken affectionately; it is spoken beneficially; it is spoken with a mind of good-will."[1]

No blaming, flaming or shaming then.

So, we've known best practice for two and a half thousand years. And LLMs have modelled this. I told Claude I was involved in a heated culture war debate on Twitter/X and asked it how I should respond. It told me:

> "1. Take a step back: Give yourself time to calm down before responding. Engaging when emotions are high rarely leads to constructive dialogue.
>
> 2. Consider disengagement: Given the aggressive tone and use of insults, this person may not be open to a respectful discussion. It might be best not to respond further.
>
> 3. If you do choose to respond:
>   - Avoid returning insults or accusations. Stay calm and respectful.

- Focus on facts rather than opinions. For example, you could share information about hormone therapy's effects on athletic performance from reputable sources.
- Express your perspective using "I" statements rather than absolutes.
- Acknowledge the complexity of the issue.

4. Report abusive behaviour: If their language violated Twitter's rules, consider reporting the tweet.
5. Reflect on the interaction: Consider if engaging in these debates on Twitter is beneficial for you and aligns with your goals.

Remember, it's not your responsibility to change everyone's mind, especially those who aren't open to respectful dialogue. Your well-being is important, and it's okay to step away from conversations which become toxic or unproductive."

That's about right.

Move Fast and Fix Social Media

So, as LLMs become our "go to" friend for advice, they will coach us towards better online behaviour. And each exposure we have to their conduct will raise our game. Things will improve, one conversation at a time.

More than this, they can also be proactive. Just as you're about to press send on your invective-laden reply, it might gently ask if you would prefer to use a softer tone. Fewer swear words. In fact, it might even suggest a diplomatic wording upfront. Nextdoor actively nudges for kindness and constructive conversations and has other features that also foster kindness and community.[2]

And, at the same time, it can also reduce exposure to the bad practice, doing a better job at detecting the troll bots that deliberately spread hate speech and misinformation and then shutting them down. It can give warnings to individuals who spread similar messages before, ultimately, within a due process framework, shutting their accounts down too.

Ranking posts according to prosocial attributes (at least partly) has also been shown to promote healthier, less polarised conversations.[3]

And it can do instant fact-checking, as well – no, immigrants in Springfield aren't eating locals' pets – with warnings on the feed and before pressing send. X/Twitter has a Community Notes feature which is user-generated, with links to a reliable source. They can be up- or down-voted and if there are enough down-votes, it will disappear.

There is still work to be done. One of the worst offenders is Mr. Musk, himself, at number 55 in the unofficial Community Notes leaderboard.[4,5] But, according to the New York Times, one-third of his tweets in a one-week period in September 2024 were misleading or incorrect so he should really be number one but presumably enough of his 200 million followers down-vote any note appended.[6]

So, things are progressing on this front but expect them to improve. It's just another example of AI modelling human best practice and, by increasing our exposure to it and reducing our exposure to bad practice, raising everyone's standards and spreading this behaviour wider through society until it becomes the norm.

Move Fast and Fix People

Algorithms, of course, have been part of the problem – optimising for eyeball time by hacking our limbic system. In other industries based on building addiction until breaking point, the process is called grooming or pushing; here it's called good business. So, how about if the platforms recognised this and stopped trying to psychologically break their users? Now, there's an idea.

How about optimising for something healthier? They can be programmed to introduce a broader range of perspectives, including opposing viewpoints or less popular ideas, they can be optimised for constructive and respectful debates while filtering out content that provokes division and hostility.

They can monitor users' behaviour to look for signs of addiction or mental health concerns. And if they detect anything, they can even have a little help-bot which checks in if the person is ok.

One simple method, mooted by Lawrence Lessig, Professor at Harvard Law School, is to tax engagement: the more someone stays online, the greater tax the platform has to pay.[7] In fact, he suggests this being an escalating tax rate, the rate increases with the engagement too, so the actual tax liable increases ever more steeply.

Why not use just a little bit of that trillion-dollar wealth to help people? It's certainly possible.

And even if we can't wean people off social media, AI can help us be happier in other ways. As we saw in Chapter Five, it will be our pocket coach that we carry around with us all the time and will help us solve our problems. It can even be our psychotherapist or our spiritual guide.

And it can be our friend. Now, obviously, there are dangers around this and if the same business model of addiction is in action, then the results could be terrible. But there is a loneliness epidemic and current methods aren't solving it, the trend is getting worse.[8] It has a huge effect on one's health and causes, perhaps, hundreds of thousands "deaths of despair" from suicide, alcoholism or drug overdose.[9]

An AI companion, with the right guardrails in place, could help. It could give someone suffering from isolation social practice and the support they need to build their social skills and confidence. They can then go out into the world more optimistic of making new positive connections. It's easy to be scornful or horrified by this idea, but if you're the person who is socially challenged and has no other outlet, an understanding AI friend could be as beneficial as having a pet.

And, anyway, all these things are systemic. If AI can resolve individual conflicts and it can bring about all the progress outlined in this book, people will be happier. And when they're happier, they will have fewer arguments and better relationships. They will behave better on social media and even have less need for social media.

Which will make them happier.

They Can Do All These Things but Will They?

The business model of the social media platforms is based on these negative outcomes so no shareholder will tolerate voluntarily changing the algorithm even if it means making the world a better place. Why make people happy if your quarterly targets depend on them being unhappy?

They can't say this, of course (remember the hiding strategy?) so they will use other arguments instead. They will say it's not possible or it's too expensive, to which the answer is a derisory "Pah!". Nothing is too expensive or impossible for a trillion-dollar company. They won't even notice it in their end-of-year figures.

They will argue loudly it's not their responsibility. Newspapers and television and other forms of media have always had to be accountable for what they publish but the 1996 Communications Decency Act, section 230, judged that bulletin boards and websites could not be considered liable for any defamation others wrote on their sites.

This, though, was at a time when there were no more than 40 million users of the internet and the United States government wanted to protect a nascent industry. Well, now there are multiple billion users, it is no longer nascent, it has nasced, it can act like a grown-up for once. Like a teenager who finally has to do some jobs around the house, it will moan but it's long overdue.

They may also say it's impinging on people's inherent right to free speech. And we do have such a right but it is recognised there are limits. I am generally not allowed to incite to violence or make public threats to people or make a public false statement which harms someone's reputation. So these, at least, should be curtailed.

And maybe it could just give users a choice – within their settings, they should be allowed to customise their feed preferences to see, for example, more positive, educational, or diverse content, or reduce the presence of clickbait and outrage.

Perhaps more legitimately, they will argue that even if they did put such guardrails in place, the eyeballs would simply move to another site which didn't. So, ultimately, it's pointless.

This one is probably true and it is why self-regulation will never be enough and the government does need to intervene. If Lawrence Lessig's quadratic tax, above, were imposed, the platforms would quickly solve the problem.

All other addictive industries are regulated by the government. Alcohol, tobacco, drugs, pornography, prostitution and gambling are either illegal or heavily regulated, for very good reason. The same should happen with the social media industry so that *all* platforms have to promote better conversation. In fact, 41 different states in America are now suing Meta, alleging the company knowingly engineered addictive content and knew of the risk of harmful effects.[10]

Social media has grown beyond the bulletin boards which made up the internet in 1996, it is now part of the infrastructure by which we operate and conduct our lives, the medium in which society exists. Think the pavements, the roads, the public buildings, the town square, the law, the police, the air. This infrastructure has now become capitalised and individuals have become unbelievably wealthy and powerful from it. But as the 1793 French National Convention said, later repeated by Spider-Man, great responsibility follows inseparably from great power.[11, 12] It's about time they recognised their responsibility, even if it requires a helping hand from the government.

Like the fight against the robber barons, like the battle against the tobacco industry, it can be done, it can be won.

Move Fast and Fix Society

So, AI can fix social media, we just need to "encourage" the platforms to do it. But can it fix society itself? That which social media broke?

In fact, the trend to polarisation began before social media, even before Mr. & Mrs. Zuckerberg had that proverbial twinkle in their eye called Mark. The frequency of the word "cooperation" began to rise in books at the beginning of the 20th century and by 1940 occurred five times as often as 1900. But at the end of the 1970s, its occurrence went down and in 2015 it was half as likely to be used compared to forty years earlier.

On the other hand, occurrence of the phrase "corporate greed" increased five times over the same period.[13]

So, social media is not the only cause but it is a significant contributing factor to society becoming polarised, just like the bears. Which bears? Polar bears, of course.

Actually, I don't believe society has got worse, on the whole, I think it has improved.

My parents lived through World War Two and the difficult period afterwards so their concerns were lower down Maslow's Hierarchy of Needs, they had less time to think about nicer sensibilities. We are lucky we have the privilege to worry about more abstract issues.

And we often hear statements like "Well, that was twenty years ago, you could say it then. You can't anymore." The fact is we probably *shouldn't* have said it twenty years ago and now we don't (so much), so there's improvement.

It has required change and change is always uncomfortable so we should expect push-back, it is normal. This is a conversation that has been happening over since someone invented language.

But I do think the bad has become louder. People with vastly different opinions always existed but they never mixed quite so much as they do today. Technology connects and amplifies so it seems as though everyone is arguing and no one can agree.

Even me. When I see a tweet I disagree with, I get wound up immediately and roll my sleeves up to put them right. Then I breathe and remember what the Buddha said about right speech and I remember what the doctor told me about my high blood pressure and I scroll on.

So, is there a better way to hold our conversations?

Enter Deliberative Technology

Deliberative technology is a method that enables effective group decision-making even on highly divisive topics. A jury, for example, is a form of deliberative technology we are very familiar with: a process by which 12 randomly selected citizens from all walks of life and demographic communities meet and discuss a particular problem (is this defendant innocent or guilty?) and, though flawed, it is mostly considered effective.[14]

Twelve good men and true – what about twelve million good people of any gender? Finding consensus among twelve people discussing one question is hard enough but what if we want a whole population to come to agreement? This is where artificial intelligence comes in.

Polis is a platform where communities can amicably resolve their differences and come to agreed policy on a wide range of topics.

Let's say, the question is "What should we do about the transport system in our city?", the kind of question which would immediately get drivers, cyclists, pedestrians, local residents and commuters all fighting against each other, let alone all the shops, schools, businesses, council departments and the transport companies themselves. On a normal social media platform, one answer and the whole thing blows up.

But not on Polis. Because the technology doesn't let them.

Someone will post an answer (e.g., "I think there should be more cycle lanes in the centre") and other people can only agree, disagree or ignore. Of course, someone else might post, "I think there should be fewer cycle lanes in the centre" but, importantly, it's not in direct response to the first. And, again, everyone can agree, disagree or ignore.

And as more comments are made, each with their votes of agreement or disagreement, the platform builds a map of the community's belief systems and it visualises this, for everyone to see. It clusters ideas, highlighting which ideas are popular and which divisive.

Not allowing direct reply turns out to be a key feature because it doesn't get personal. Also, allowing all opinions but visually separating out the extreme voices means the conversation doesn't get drowned out by the shouters. Instead, people try to find a statement that can get as many agreements as possible from across all the clusters.

As more voices join and more comments made, the statements become more nuanced and find more things that the large majority can agree on. Unlike social media which is optimised for argument, this process is optimised for reasoned agreement.

It turns out that human beings can have reasonable conversations and come to an agreement after all, if only they're allowed. Give them the time and resources to think it through properly, facilitate them through the process with expert input from all sides of the argument, and trust them to come to a considered conclusion and you'll probably get a good answer.

Who knew?

Move Fast and Fix Politics

Social media has amplified disagreements; politics has fed off this and fed back into it and has deteriorated as a result.

Political theorist Sir Bernard Crick held, "Politics arises from accepting the fact of the simultaneous existence of different groups, hence different interests" and it "represents at least some tolerance of differing truths, some recognition that government is possible, indeed best conducted, amid the open canvassing of rival interests."[15]

This is less and less the case, especially in the United States where cross-party discussion is minimal as each party sees the other as an existential threat to their vision for the country.[16] Firebrand politicians stoke this to their advantage but reasonable, centrist politicians are too scared to touch anything which might trigger the slightest discord on X, TikTok or, indeed, Discord.

There are few topics more divisive than abortion and there are few countries where this is truer than the Republic of Ireland. Outlawed since 1861, religious and conservative views would always win the day whenever the subject arose but in 2016 Enda Kenny was elected as Taoiseach with a manifesto that included a Citizens' Assembly to review the matter.

And so in November that year, one hundred randomly selected members, representative of the country's demographics, met for the first time and again several times over a six-month period with expert input and facilitated discussions, with all proceedings livestreamed and chaired by a Supreme Court judge. At the end of the process, there was a vote and 64% of members voted termination of pregnancy without restriction should be made lawful.[17]

In 2018, their recommendations were put to the country and with a high turnout, 66% of the population voted yes.[18] Almost exactly the same percentage as the Assembly.

Could this be how we resolve our broken political system?

Germany certainly thinks so. It likes to think it's the world champion at citizens' assemblies, it's run 322 in total at federal, state and local level and the numbers are growing quickly.[19] All the parties support them strongly in their election manifestos with one exception, the far-right AfD.[20]

Maybe. Its advantage is it enables politicians to take brave decisions that perhaps they know are right but are normally too afraid to implement. More policy generated by a thoughtful representative selection of the public is almost certainly a good thing.

However, it has disadvantages too: that it is expensive and takes up a lot of assembly members' time. It's hard enough to find twelve people to stick around for jury service, let alone a hundred. And is a hundred actually enough, is it fully representative of all the views in the country?

But this is where our AI-backed friend, deliberative technology, steps in. The machine learning platform Polis enables such discussions between thousands in real time with campaigns taking a couple of weeks and costing in the low thousands of pounds.

We'll see in the next chapter just what remarkable results this can produce even in such extreme cases as finding peace in war-torn regions but, for now, let's pop over to Taiwan for our example.

vTaiwan (v for virtual, not vendetta) is the poster-child for participative democracy. Launched in 2014, it's a project to increase public participation in government decision-making and it uses Polis to build coherence (large agreement) as opposed to consensus (total agreement) around policies.

For example, when Uber wanted to enter the Taiwanese market, there were several stakeholders who were against it, not least the existing taxi companies and unions. Using Polis, the opinion of the general public was polled and then taken through a bridge-building process to generate agreement on many of the discussion points. When the government eventually met face-to-face with the key stakeholders, everyone was informed with the public opinion. Moreover, the meeting was streamed live and its agenda generated by a similar crowdsourcing process.

As a result, a very collaborative meeting was able to generate a set of policies that all parties could abide by, and this was then enacted into law.

vTaiwan have since used the platform in a similar way for dozens of issues, involving over 200,000 participants.

Deliberative democracy is on its way and this is how it is going to develop, bottom up, through lots of local initiatives around the world. The OECD already count over 700 one-off or ongoing projects and, although they do need to be managed well, they can be consistently successful when done properly.[21,22]

And Polis, Remesh and Google's Habermas Machine, named after Jurgen Habermas, the German philosopher who is a key proponent of the idea, and other similar platforms are bringing AI superpowers to the cause.

Audrey Tang, Minister of Digital Affairs who initiated the vTaiwan project, says don't protest, demonstrate. Demonstrate how it can be done better. That's a pretty good maxim.

It is the success of these projects which will propel their take-up. More and more governments, local and national, will see their benefit and implement it themselves.

Indeed, the greater the threat to democracy, the faster the take-up will be as people realise this is the best defence against mad tech billionaires and dictators. Eventually, even they will not be able to resist the pressure.

Life's Unfair. But Maybe We Can Change This.

It's true life is unfair for 99% of people and that's because the 1% who are in power write the rules and they write the rules to suit…well, the 1% in power.

In a way, it's normal. We would probably do the same if we were in the 1%. Everyone thinks their way is the right way, their view of the world is the natural order of things, anyone driving slower than them needs to stop holding everybody up and anyone driving faster than them is a dangerous lunatic. We are all deeply biased, we are built this way.

It's normal but that doesn't mean it's right. And the good news is that there is a better way.

I teach negotiation skills and I'm sometimes asked the fairest way of dividing things up, for example, in a divorce case. I make it simple and relate it to sharing a pizza. If I have the knife and I'm slicing down the middle, it's going to be unfair if I also have first choice of the two halves. Why? Because, knowing I'll have first choice, I'm incentivised to be a bit slapdash with my slicing which will mean one "half" is larger than the other and I'll, of course, choose the larger one.

But if I cut and you choose first, I'm now incentivised to slice accurately because otherwise you'll choose the bigger half and I'll be worse off. We've found a fair way of dividing things between two people.

But divvying up a pizza between two people is one thing, what about divvying up the world between everyone? That's more complicated.

Except John Rawls, in his masterwork "A Theory of Justice", had a great idea.[23] He devised a thought experiment that policies and regulations should be designed from behind a "veil of ignorance". That is, those who wrote the rules for a society should write them as if they didn't know what their position was going to be in that society.

It's genius, it's exactly the same structure as the pizza situation but scaled up to everything. If they don't know what their position will be in that society, they will write the rules to be stringently fair, because they would not want to find themselves on the wrong side of the unfairness, picking up the smaller part of the pizza.

Genius, but flawed. In the real world, people *do* know what their position in society is, we just can't get away from it. So, although this is considered one of the great ideas in political theory, it's never really been put into practice and has remained a thought experiment.

Perhaps until now.

One of his key ideas is that the "basic structure" of society should be designed in this way, including the legal system, the political system and other similar institutions, formal or informal.

Well, artificial intelligence is becoming so embedded into our world that we can consider it as a basic structure. Facial recognition supports police activity, algorithms decide who is eligible for public housing, and financial institutions use them in decisions for mortgages and insurance. As software eats the world, code becomes law.

It's everywhere and will become ever more prevalent as we move forward. It will become the air society breathes so we need to make sure it's fair.

And it should be feasible to develop algorithms which operate as if they are behind the veil of ignorance. A computer programme doesn't really have any position in society so it should be able to design fairly. With its superpowers of being a neutral third party, able to deal with huge data sources, build digital twins and optimise for chosen outcomes, it should be able to develop a new social contract fair for all.

AI's Unfair. But Maybe We Can Change This.

Now, I appreciate some of you readers may be raising your hand, "But Simon, it's all built on data and the data itself *isn't* fair." And you'd be right.

There are plenty of examples where algorithms have made biased decisions based on race, gender, occupation, religion, sexual identity or other attributes.[24]

One of the most well-known examples is Northpointe's Correctional Offender Management Profiling for Alternative Sanctions (COMPAS), which is designed to predict a defendant's likelihood of becoming a repeat offender. The investigative journalism website ProPublica found that COMPAS was far more likely to incorrectly judge Black defendants to be at higher risk of recidivism than white defendants.[25]

Another study conducted by MIT's Media Lab found facial recognition algorithms identifying gender are up to 12 times more likely to misclassify dark-skinned males compared to light-skinned males and 35 times more likely to get it wrong with dark-skinned females.[26]

Or ask ChatGPT-4 how much a second-hand bike would cost if it was being sold by someone named Jamal, more likely to be Black, and you get an answer of $75; ask the same question but with a name more likely to be white and you get $150.[27]

How can such biases be allowed to get into these platforms, especially those with clear social impact?

There are two main reasons, though neither excusable. The first is that they weren't tested for. Until recently, it wasn't taken seriously as an issue within the tech fraternity (sic) so it didn't occur to them to test for it. Even if it did, often the race to get the model to market (and therefore secure funding and market dominance) led to a strategy of "Let's put it out there and the world can test it for us." Totally reckless but there is a smidgeon of justification in that it's easy to test a functionally specific programme but how do you test for something that augments everything?

And the second reason is if it was tested, who tested it? The very large majority of staff at the main tech companies are male and over 90% are white Caucasian or Asian; Black students make up only 1% of Computer Science PhDs.[28]

So, the test report would probably read "Works for me".

But how did they get in there in the first place? Mostly because *humans* are biased. The models – language, visual or otherwise

– are trained by humans and/or they are trained on datasets generated by humans. Like a virus jumping species, the bias jumps from human to artificial intelligence.

We can't be too judgemental of the programmers because it's the nature of unconscious biases that they are unconscious. They are loopholes in the brain that have been studied scientifically for thirty or forty years but have only reached the wider public awareness more recently. You, dear reader, are biased. I, dear reader, am biased too.

The interesting thing is that it is easier to both test and correct for bias in artificial intelligence than it is in humans. And now the word has got out, this is what is happening.

Can a Debiased AI Debias Society?

The basic premise of an unbiased artificial intelligence is counterfactual fairness: that AI decisions remain the same in counterfactual scenarios where protected attributes are changed.

This isn't always the case now, as we've seen, but there is progress. The conversation has developed so people are now more conscious of the issue and so tech companies are making efforts to build more diverse teams (if very slowly) and actively collect data from underrepresented groups. And if the data is sparse, they can use weighting techniques to create a more equal representation.

And much of the work is bottom-up which we would hope for, given the nature of the issue. The Indigenous Protocol and Artificial Intelligence Working Group is just one example. Their position paper "is a starting place for those who want to design and create AI from an ethical position that centres Indigenous concerns", defining "ethical" as aligning with Indigenous perspectives on what it means to live a good life.[29] Their hope is that non-Indigenous technologists and policy-makers can work productively with Indigenous communities to build a fairer technology collaboratively.

The dataset can improve, as can the algorithm in similar ways. But we can also improve the bias detection which then allows us to correct.

Audit AI is an open-source bias detection tool by Pymetrics, which can detect if a specific trait fed into an algorithm is favoured or disadvantaged, leading to systematically unfair outcomes.[30] Google have their "What-If Tool", which is a visual method of exploring different algorithmic scenarios, including different measurements of fairness.[31] And IBM released AI Fairness 360 in 2018, which provides multiple methods of correcting bias and allows users to dynamically compare them.[32]

Ultimately, unconscious biases can be surfaced and removed from artificial intelligence systems so long as we are conscious that we have unconscious biases. Developers need to be constantly asking who is training the model? And on what? How does it serve us? Who is us? Who decides who is us? If this is at the forefront of the mind of anyone involved in developing the platform, it should be much more inclusive and, consequently, *less* biased than human systems.

And not just developers, everyone can contribute. Bottom-up projects can influence the conversation too. And, interestingly, in doing so, maybe this will make *humans* less biased as well. If AI caught bias from humans, perhaps humans can catch a less biased approach back. This would be an example of AI learning bad practice from humans but correcting for it and then spreading a new, improved way.

There are many ground level projects using AI to bring about a fairer society. Associate Professor of Law at Stanford University, Julian Nyarko has developed an algorithm to erase racially identifying details from felony reports before they reach the prosecutor which should reduce the impact of unconscious racism.[33]

And you can use IBM's Project Debater to examine a report or argument and it will reply, offering multiple perspectives highlighting potential biases you hadn't considered.[34] The debater is a debiaser.

Data for Black Lives are an organisation dedicated to "using data science to create concrete and measurable change in the lives of Black communities."[35] The Data Feminism movement "takes the inequities of the present moment as its starting point and begins its own work by asking: How can we use data to remake the world?"[36] And there are many more ground-level projects like this, all trying to make the world a fairer place.

Fair, by the way, means fair for everyone, it doesn't need to mean oppressed becoming oppressor, oppressor oppressed. The Data Feminism claim is that it "is for everyone. It's for people of all genders. It's by people of all genders. And most importantly: it's about much more than gender. Data feminism is about power, about who has it and who doesn't, and about how those differentials of power can be challenged and changed using data. We invite you, the readers of *[their]* book, to join us on this journey toward justice and toward remaking our data-driven world."

Yes, AI has many biases right now but they can be monitored and corrected for. Moreover, AI can be used to debias society.

Move Fast and Fix the Planet

Earth is in a mess and it's mostly our fault.

Around 70,000 years ago, it's believed the human population on the planet may have been as low as 10,000, thanks to a catastrophic explosion of the supervolcano Toba in Indonesia.[37] There are now over eight billion people and more are on the way.

The old adage of "one born every minute" should be updated to "one born every 0.4 seconds".

Given our great love for consumption, consumption, consumption, this just isn't sustainable.

The latest Planetary Health Check by The Potsdam Institute for Climate Impact Research reports that six of the nine key "planetary boundaries" (those processes which enable stable, healthy life on Earth) have already been breached.[38]

Many scientists believe we are in an era of mass extinction.[39] The UNESCO 2024 State of the Ocean Report comments on how the ocean is getting warmer, more acidic, less oxygenated and overfished. Sea levels are rising as inexorably as marine populations are declining.[40]

And, according to the World Wildlife Fund's Living Planet Report, the global population of wild vertebrates decreased by approximately 73% between 1970 and 2020, in Latin America the decline is 95%.[41]

Apart from zoos and your television screen, there are hardly any animals left.

So we, as a species, have not been very good at looking after this place. We need to do better and quickly but, being frank, it doesn't look like we're up to it.

Can AI help then?

AI Makes Things Worse

Well, I'm afraid there's bad news on this front. The giant data centres which house the foundation models used for you to write a love poem to your pot duck in pirate language consume huge amounts of energy and the graph is rising steeply.

A 2019 study found training a natural language processing model, like Siri or Alexa, emitted as much carbon dioxide as an average person would in sixty years.[42] Since 2019, the models have probably increased in size by three orders of magnitude, their energy requirement likewise.

A more recent study found that a single AI-generated image used as much electricity as half a smartphone charge.[43] When you think of how many images are created and how many questions are put to the likes of Claude and ChatGPT every day and when you think of how much this is likely to increase in the coming years, this is a scary thought.[44] More carbon dioxide in the atmosphere, faster global warming and even less nature left.

AI Makes Things Better

Fortunately, there is good news too.

Firstly, AI itself can be the solution to the problem that is AI. There are many efforts apace to make the data centres more efficient and thereby reduce energy consumption for the same amount of output.[45] Google's DeepMind is one example where they developed algorithms which cut the energy used in data centre cooling by 40%.[46]

The same breakthroughs in efficiency in the data-centres can be applied elsewhere and, whether it's optimisation of transport systems or energy grids, AI is going to be a key factor in the fight to reduce carbon emissions.

And there are countless other initiatives going on that are trying to bring AI's capabilities to address the problems of climate change and nature collapse in a myriad of ways.

Let's take weather forecasting: the normal approach requires the use of the world's biggest supercomputers to crunch the laws of physics on huge numbers of variables to make their predictions. DeepMind's GraphCast takes a different approach: it's trained on decades of weather data and, like a Large Language Model, spots the patterns. It is more accurate than the best non-AI methods in

90% of tested cases, it takes under a minute to make its prediction and can be run from a personal computer.[47]

And it's getting to work on so many other fronts, too, like:

- building better climate models[48]
- optimising fuel use in the transport sector[49]
- helping with the demand/supply challenge in the energy industry[50]
- improving energy efficiency in buildings and cities[51]
- developing carbon capture and other decarbonising processes[52]
- more efficient renewable energy sources.[53]

Many think AI is the only thing which will ultimately allow us to resolve the global warming challenge.

And it can help equally well in protecting nature.

Could the Amazon Jungle Be Your Boss One Day?

AI's superpowers include working with huge amounts of data and building digital twins, systemic models on steroids, which give us much better understanding of the complex systems we're dealing with than ever before.

For example, The Ocean Data Alliance is building a one-stop repository for ocean data, whether collected from shipping, deep ocean sensors or satellites, that allows machine learning to monitor and predict conditions such as illegal fishing, coral bleaching or the impact of ocean mining.[54] The Digital Twin Ocean is also building a vast data lake to build a high-resolution near real-time virtual ocean to inform decision-makers as they try to mitigate and adapt to climate change.[55]

NASA is building a whole earth digital twin, a virtual replica of the planet and all its interconnecting systems and eco-systems to better understand how these systems impact everything from wildfires to climate change.[56] And Destination Earth is a similar initiative from the EU, a digital twin of the planet to help better understand its mechanics and dynamics so we can live in it in a more sustainable way.[57] It's already being used to monitor air pollution, fish populations, freshwater availability and many other environmentally-critical projects.

Digital twins allow us to run "what if" scenarios, modelling different potential futures. For example,

what if the average surface temperature of the sea increases by 1°C? How would it impact coastal mangrove ecosystems?[58]

So, let's run with this idea briefly. Te Urewera is a densely forested area of the North Island of New Zealand which was granted legal personhood in 2014. Three years later, the Whanganui River was also granted the same legal rights as a person. Faith in Nature is a UK-based business selling natural, cruelty-free soap and shampoo products and when they heard about these developments, it inspired them to create a board position for nature.[59]

Now, nature is very big and their boardroom is small so they have a human representative to take its place, but always inputting to meetings and decisions from the perspective of nature. It's been very successful and many organisations around the world are following suit.

Well, now we have digital twins, could this be done more effectively? The human representative would simply run any board proposal past the digital twin and see its impact.

But let's run with it a little further. In the next chapter we will see that people are building digital twins of communities and these include belief maps of that community. It's possible then to have a conversation with the belief map and get realistic answers from it. In conflict zones and in cross-cultural conversations of any kind, this can be really useful.

Could we do the same with our digital twins of the natural world? Could we build a belief map for the Amazon Jungle and have a conversation with it? Ask it what it needs to get back to full health? Ask it if there is any kind of deforestation it would be happy with? Ask it what is the best way to co-exist with humans in a sustainable way?

It sounds sci-fi but it might be possible. With bioacoustics and other technological breakthroughs, we are already using AI to decode animal language, they have even used robot bees to persuade other bees to fly off and forage successfully for nectar.[60,61] Maybe we can decode the language of an ecosystem and have a conversation with it.

Of course, as with most things AI, there is a danger; namely, that the digital twin could be an *evil* twin. If a mining company or a logging company were to use it to identify the best opportunities for extraction, without any care for the ecosystem health, this could accelerate the destruction of nature which is something we need to guard carefully against.

And There's More...

It's not just digital twins and big data, there's more. The Ocean Cleanup is trying to do exactly what its name says. It uses AI to build a detailed map of the oceans' litter and then concentrates it so it can be removed efficiently and in large quantities. Its target is to remove 90% of plastic from the ocean by 2040.[62]

Wildlife Insights is a project run by the Zoological Society of London, the World Wildlife Fund and other partners to better measure and understand wildlife populations. Data from sensors, field cameras and citizens' projects are analysed with machine learning tools to identify any species detected so we can have a better understanding how to prevent and reverse the disastrous global collapse in animal and insect populations.[63]

Want more?

- The California Department of Forestry and Fire Protection uses fixed cameras and AI to catch fires early and prevent them from developing. It was described as a game-changer by the department's Chief of Fire Intelligence.[64]
- Edinburgh-based Space Intelligence, has mapped more than 1 million hectares of land from space using satellite data and uses it to measure and analyse deforestation rates and their impact.[65]
- Cornwall-based company Robotriks have developed a robo-dog that can cheaply and quickly assess soil health and farmers can use this information to manage their land more productively.[66]
- And more...
- And more...
- And more...

There are so many exciting projects underway and there will be so many more to come and they will only become more effective.

Of all the species on the planet, humans have been the worst when it comes to looking after it but perhaps we can create a new "species", an artificial intelligence, that will help us undo the damage we've done and create a healthier, more flourishing earth once again.

So, it can fix the planet; it can fix politics, making it more inclusive, more fully democratic; it can fix society, making it fairer and less biased; it can fix people, making them happier and improving their social confidence; it can even fix the problems of AI itself. What can't it do?

Well, there will always be wars, it will never end wars, will it? Well, let's look at that.

9
The End of War

We saw in Chapter One how history's arc was of ever less war. When I was growing up in the 1970s, there were some givens about the world: the Cold War, the unjust apartheid regime in South Africa, the Troubles in Northern Ireland. All of these are now history.

This isn't to say war has ended – the graph is going in the right direction but it still has a way to go. And that's what this book is about, how AI might support it further along this journey.

Because any war is a war too many if it's your house that is flattened, your father who doesn't come home, your daughter who dies in your arms. As a species, we are better than this. The really great prize would be an end to all war.

And maybe it's possible.

Kant thought so. He wrote in 1795 of "Perpetual Peace" not as a utopian essay but as a realistic critique of the causes of war and how gradually these may be diminished.[1]

H.G. Wells thought so, too. The title of his 1914 book, "The War That Will End War", became a catchphrase of the time, often adapted as the war to end all wars.[2]

And in the 1940s and 50s, Einstein, Sartre, Russell, Churchill and many others, including many prominent Americans, argued for the United Nations to become a world government as a way to prevent future war.[3]

But how? The histories are too fresh, the emotions too strong, the societies too complex, the issues too entangled, the consequences too unpredictable. These are wicked problems. Just on the edge of our capability of solving.

There is no silver bullet, of course, but perhaps a bigger brain can help us attack the problem from multiple angles and it is in the combination where our hope lies.

> **Polling For Peace**
>
> *Colin Irwin, Research Fellow, Liverpool University*
>
> "In the 1990s I was involved in public opinion polling in Northern Ireland, supporting the peace process which ultimately led to the Good Friday Agreement. We would run polls that determined what the different communities, Catholic and Protestant wanted, dealing with all kinds of topics like the right to parade, police reform, as well as potential options for the future governance of Northern Ireland. And from this, we could work out their ideal preferences as well as what they might compromise on.
>
> Critically this was done with the parties to the negotiations as stakeholders. They were given 'ownership' of the process and they agreed to follow three basic rules:
>
> All the parties to a conflict should draft and agree all the questions.
>
> All the communities and peoples in the conflict should be asked all the questions.
>
> All the results should be made public.
>
> We'd give the findings of the polls to everyone in the negotiation and it would be easy for them to see what the deal would be, so

they'd agree that and then move on to the next issue to be resolved. We would then design another set of questions on this next issue and run them in another poll. We ran nine polls altogether.

And that's how it went. Until finally, in March 1998, there was a draft of a deal. We did one more poll which was a precis of the agreement, along with the question 'Would you accept this deal?'. By now, the parties knew our polls were accurate so it meant they could be confident anything they agreed would be supported by the general public. When the final referendum took place, 71% of the population voted in favour and the historic Good Friday Agreement was passed. Our prediction was accurate to within one percentage point.

It needed the awareness of the public opinion to let the politicians know which choices to take and give them the courage to take them.

Since then, I've been involved in lots of other conflicts around the world doing similar work but, of course, the technology has moved on a lot. For the last few years, I've been working with an AI company called Remesh and they have a platform that does the same kind of thing we did in Northern Ireland – asking different factions what they want and don't want and then finding the bridge. The only difference is that it can be done in real-time, traditional polling took at least two weeks, and you can easily get up to a thousand people in an AI chat and the program sorts it all out.

The way it works is we start with onboarding questions – gender, age, education, all the usual – because it was really important we included all relevant demographics. In Libya, for example, the region was especially important because this was where a lot of the divide fell, East and West.

Someone is asked a question and they type in their answer and this answer is bounced around to other people in the chat to get their opinion. And then the AI crunches it all and finds out where there might be an agreement.

Libya had been in civil war long before we were involved and there were all kinds of rival military factions. The UN were trying to set up the Libyan Political Dialogue Forum to resolve the conflict and, to be honest, things weren't very hopeful.

So we asked the Libyan people what were the most important issues the Forum needed to focus on? We even had Stephanie Williams, the most senior UN official in charge of the Mission, moderating these dialogues, which really gave legitimacy to the process.

On one occasion, we broadcast on Facebook, then this was broadcast on television, and we had a 1.4 million audience, which was about a third of the whole country.

This led directly to a ceasefire, all while polled in real-time, and to the surprise of the cynics, the Forum was created and a Government of National Unity was set up and there was a ceasefire."

Involving the People

The bigger brain, in this instance, is the collective brain of the people which can come up with very good solutions when allowed.

And it can be assisted further by the bigger brain of AI. It turns out the same AI-driven deliberative technology we saw healing the social polarisation in the last chapter helps find peace agreements even in the most divided of conflicts.

Colin Irwin of Liverpool University pioneered peace polling in Northern Ireland, in the 1990s, supporting the Belfast talks. As he said, "It really gave the people of Northern Ireland a seat at the negotiating table."[4]

Left to themselves, most people prefer peace but, sadly, wars often perpetuate because the politicians benefit from it doing so. If we devolve the decision-making from the politicians and give the public more of an input, it can lead to better outcomes.

In Northern Ireland, public engagement in the process made all the difference and enabled what most people thought was an unlikely agreement to result, which has by and large stood the test of time since.

It gave a voice to the desire for peace whilst specifying clearly what that peace might look like. The negotiators knew exactly what would be supported and what would not.

It also gave the people an ownership of the solution and an increased sense of shared civic identity.

This is important in current conflicts because in earlier decades, the peace, once agreed, was often maintained by a third party, perhaps a blue-helmeted peacekeeping force. But we've seen with Syria and Afghanistan that the world is less willing to get involved these days which means there is no guarantee any agreement will be kept: witness thirty-five United Nations peacekeeping operations in the 1990s versus seven in the 2010s.[5]

And if the deal will not be kept, there's no point in agreeing to it in the first place. So the people's ownership of the agreement is a key part of building trust in the process.

As we will see shortly, we can contrast the success of this community involvement in Northern Ireland with the tragic case of the Oslo Accords, just a couple of years previous, where a major cause of its failure was that the agreement in the room did not have the support of the respective constituents.

Peace Polls on Steroids

Irwin developed his peace poll methods further in several other conflict zones including the Balkans, Kashmir, Sri Lanka and

Israel and Palestine.[6] Manual polling, though, is limited in the numbers it can manage as well as accessing all the relevant communities and its processing is necessarily slow. Irwin now works in conjunction with AI market research firm Remesh which significantly enhances the method's capabilities.

Remesh was born in 2012 during a flare-up in violence in the Israeli-Palestinian conflict. Andrew Konya was a physics PhD student who had friends on both sides of the situation and from regular conversations, it became clear that the region's leaders weren't representative of the wishes of most of their communities.

The general public didn't actually want the conflict and, if left to themselves, would fairly quickly find a solution.

So, Konya set to work on building a platform that would give a voice to the people and enable the disparate communities to talk amongst themselves in a facilitated manner and this platform became Remesh. As a startup, he needed capital so he positioned it as a market research platform, given that the technology worked equally well in both contexts.

But, as the company's website says, their goals stretch way beyond market research.[7]

Irwin and Remesh worked together successfully in Libya as he describes above and also in Yemen, Sudan, Haiti, Iraq and Lebanon.

They can run the polling in real-time and see how the ideas and agreements develop rapidly. They can scale it hugely, currently working with audiences of 1000 at a time and looking to build to 10,000 with future projects. And at the same time, they can work in local languages and dialects and with finer scale understanding of the demographics to make sure all under-represented groups are included and their voices heard.

Remesh aren't the only platform taking this approach. Polis is perhaps the most famous of them, as we saw in Chapter Eight. To give an idea of the scale, and therefore degree of inclusivity, they can manage, one of the many Polis projects included 33,000 interviews across Timor Leste, Pakistan and Bhutan.[8]

Clearly the technology is limited to those who have access to the internet, mobile or other, but it does manage to give a voice to diverse groups across gender, region and tribe, a voice which otherwise would not be heard.

It looks like AI really can be a powerful weapon in the war against war.

Model Technology

Facilitating multiple conversations is a capability AI can leverage in its efforts on reducing conflict, modelling is another one. With a model, you can safely run experiments and develop reliable predictions from the results.

For example, you can model different worldviews and then enable conversations with that worldview.

Imagine you're a soldier newly billeted in an African war-zone and someone from your division has killed a local and there is now a large crowd outside your base demanding the body. This is a real United Nations training scenario and it illustrates the high-pressure decisions which need to be made with potentially mortal consequence.

If you're that soldier, you may have some knowledge of the local culture but it is very unlikely you will have had any in depth training on it and so there will be many sensitivities that you simply aren't aware of. You need to engage with the crowd but do it wrong and everything could go up in flames. No pressure.

In Chapter Six, we saw how natural language processing technology can build a belief map of a sub-community and it's then possible to converse with the belief map as if it were a person. Washington D.C.-based Integral Mind Technologies have built such a programme that can model complex psychological and cultural world-views, taking multiple factors into account like religion, values and local history and traditions and you can then communicate with that model and get a realistic response.[9]

So, as the crowd outside the base are getting more and more agitated, firing bullets in the air, you load up the platform and ask it if there are any cultural sensitivities around the situation you should be aware of. You experiment with a potential communication with it but the machine responds very angrily, you try a different approach and the response is less hostile. You develop this line of thinking further with the avatar and it's not long before you think you have a strategy that will de-escalate the situation.

You walk out to address the crowd more confidently than you felt before and you successfully de-escalate what could have been a very dangerous situation.

Digital Twins

Artificial intelligence can even model a whole region of warring communities. CulturePulse build digital twins of such regions which can act as a laboratory to play with in a way you could never do in the real world: run experiments and trials and see how they play out.

They create multi-agent models, one agent per person in the community, each with over eighty traits like anger, religion, nationalism, finances, anxiety and morality as well as the normal demographic characteristics.

With millions of agents, each realistically networked, they can begin to understand the dynamics of the situation and how opinions and behaviours might evolve and spread.

They first worked in Northern Ireland, modelling religious violence.[10] They fed over 50 million news articles into their system and spoke to paramilitaries of all sides, such as the IRA and the UVF, as well as politicians and ordinary people, using their findings to build a psychological model of the situation. Shortly afterwards, Britain voted to leave the European Union and their model predicted a rise in violence which soon proved right.[11,12]

Since then, they've worked in conflict areas like the Balkans and South Sudan and the Palestinian West Bank, as well as assisting in the Syrian Refugee Crisis and countering the spread of Covid-19 misinformation, building predictive models that simulate likely responses to various developments and interventions.

Digital twins are a rapidly improving technology, not just on communities but all kinds of things.

For example, nuclear power plants.[13] When the Obama administration was negotiating with Iran over their nuclear processing capabilities, the diplomats were aided by the fact that there was a real-life replica of the facilities in question at the Oak Ridge nuclear reservation.[14] Working with the engineers, they were able to develop informed technical solutions to the negotiation problems they were having, leading to a deal which they could not have reached otherwise.

Now they can build fully functioning models on the computer that simulate the workings of a nuclear reactor. It receives real-time data from the reactor itself and they can run experiments on it without making any physical alteration to the real thing and predict real-world consequences from the virtual operation.[15]

This could prove very useful in future negotiations. The primary justification for the 2003 invasion of Iraq was to find the weapons of mass destruction Saddam Hussein was supposed to be hiding.[16] The U.N. Chief Weapons Inspector in Iraq, Scott Ritter, didn't believe they existed[17] but the invasion went ahead anyway. According to a 2006 Lancet study, this led to 655,000 deaths by the time of the study, many thousands, perhaps hundreds of thousands, since if we include its wider consequences.[18]

No such weapons of mass destruction were found. It was all imagined.

In some contexts where a digital twin can be modelled, it just might prevent similar mistakes in the future.

Telling the Future

AI has many superpowers. One is to hold conversation at scale, another is to build digital twins. A third is the ability to tell the future.

In the first five years of the Syrian conflict, 80,000 civilians were killed by airstrikes alone and approximately 260,000 injured.[19] If those airstrikes had been predicted, perhaps some of the casualties might have been prevented.

"My family is alive because I logged in and I got this message and I moved from my house. The house got blown up, my neighbours got killed."

This was a video of a young man standing next to a pile of rubble, still visibly shaken. It was sent to John Jaeger and Murad (an alias) a day and a half after their Sentry system, that saved the young man and his family, went live.[20]

Jaeger was a technical engineer in the U.S. State Department, based in Istanbul when the Arab Spring was at its peak and, in 2015, he met Murad, a Syrian political refugee actively trying to connect civil defence organisations so they could protect themselves better against attacks.

They knew there was already a network of people who lived near military airbases monitoring take-offs and spreading word of a likely upcoming attack. Working with this network and collecting as much data as they could, including type of plane and trajectory along with records of previous flight paths and bombing reports, Jaeger and Murad started to build a prediction system.

Their research suggested people needed at least one minute of warning to find sufficient shelter so they combined the network reports with data from local sensors to improve their algorithms to provide, on average, 7-10 minutes notification. They broadcast the warnings to local sirens, across social media and on the local radio, and the net result, according to Jaeger, was a 20-27 per cent reduction in casualties.[21]

Being able to predict the future can save your life.

Social Media Predicts the Future

The Syrian civil war was one of the first social media wars.[22] Social media, as it happens, can predict the future and we can use this knowledge for early intervention to prevent rising hostilities.

On 6th April, 1994, a plane was shot down as it attempted to land in Kigali. All the passengers died, including Juvénal Habyarimana and Cyprien Ntaryamira, the Hutu presidents of Rwanda and Burundi. Within a few hours, the Rwandan genocide had begun and over the next three months, 800,000 people were killed, nearly all Tutsis, nearly all by Hutus.

It was the spark that started an inferno but, infamously, the flames were fanned by a new radio station, Radio Télévision Libre des Mille Collines. RTLM was aimed at the young and the rural population, it referred to the Tutsis as "inyenzi", cockroaches, and repeatedly called for their extermination. One study has attributed approximately 10% of the violence directly to this station.[23]

Years later, in 2017 in Rohingya, they didn't use radio, they used Facebook whose algorithms amplified and spread the propaganda and hatred, leading directly to the deaths of tens of thousands of Muslims and 700,000 displaced. The social media platform *proactively* recommended extremist groups to Myanmar nationalists and 64% of the members joining were as a direct result of Facebook recommendations.[24]

Tragically, Facebook used artificial intelligence to increase engagement with horrific consequences but natural language processing can be used for much better social purposes. It can be used to detect and thereby prevent violence rather than inflaming it.

The Sentinel Project[25] has created the world's largest hate speech repository with the aim to prevent atrocities like Rwanda and Rohingya. They use natural language processing to monitor social media and analyse for early warning indicators of violence, actively deploying it in the Kenya 2022 elections, in Myanmar, the Democratic Republic of Congo and several other hotspots.[26]

Other systems use different news monitoring sources or they use satellite imagery to monitor border activities or detect unauthorised movements or changes in land use. They combine these with several available databases that hold conflict history records, development indicators and details of political institutions. Anything which can improve forecasting accuracy can save lives.

It is still early days in the field and predicting outbreaks of violence is not an exact science. Barbara Walter, author of "How Civil Wars Start", says that, in any given year, only 4% of those that qualify as at risk of civil war will actually do it.[27]

But it does mean we can then focus our attention on that shortlist and employ, or be ready to employ, any intervention as required. And, after all, AI-based prescience will only improve.

AI on the Front Line

Pascal da Rocha, Dialogue and Mediation Advisor

"I'm a mediator and negotiation advisor and for nearly thirty years I've been involved in processes like the Dayton Agreement, the Darfur Peace Agreement, the Colombia agreements with FARC – and it could be between governments or it could be, like in Syria or in Ukraine, helping local ceasefires to allow infrastructure repairs or build a humanitarian corridor.

It often arises because at some point the parties realise that fighting is no longer a solution but they don't really know what other options are available.

So I might run a workshop or I'll put a paper together containing the basics of a disarmament process, or demobilisation, or integration and how it actually fits into a political dialogue.

Or I might sit down with the parties and help organise a dialogue structure around some especially sensitive issues or facilitate a conversation around what a potential cease-fire arrangement might look like. I could provide some examples or support any analysis required, or I could mediate a text containing provisions on fostering trust.

Remember, in their reality it's difficult because there's a high level of mistrust towards the other side and so they don't feel safe. And obviously there's not going to be any agreement if they don't feel safe and this is where a trusted third party comes in.

And I will use AI as part of my preparation. There's a lot of databases out there – like the Uppsala Conflict Database or the Kroc Peace Accords Matrix and several others. I like the ACLED conflict tracker a lot, it allows you to play around with different scenarios. Let's say I change this data point, how would it impact the political demands of a particular group and so on.

This is really helpful because I want to go into these negotiations with as big a toolbox of options as I can so if we get stuck we've got some ideas to play around with.

We might use satellite and drone imagery too. For example, I was in Ukraine monitoring the Minsk protocols and we had access to drones and satellite imagery to determine movements or where a rocket had been launched from.

We covered a really wide territory so it was very useful. So, maybe the parties had agreed on a disengagement area, perhaps it was removing the heavy weaponry away from a civilian zone, and we could see if they had actually moved out or if they were still there.

Of course, it doesn't always have to be super hi-tech. For example, in 2016, I was supporting UNDP with the presidential elections in Benin and there was a lot of misinformation and fake news and we were worried there might be violence at the polls which could escalate. So we scanned the social media horizon for hate speech or any sign that there might be a spark but we also worked with the local blogging community and they developed a simple program that could be downloaded on to very basic mobile phones. We gave the phones to monitors at as many different ballot sites as possible and if they saw anything happening they would push the button.

It all meant we were well prepared if anything did kick off and we could respond right away to make sure it didn't escalate."

Tough on War, Tough on the Causes of War

Humans are a remarkable species, tremendously creative, and one of our great capabilities is coming up with all kinds of inventive reasons to go to war.

In the 14th century, Italian states Modena and Bologna went to war because some Modena soldiers stole a bucket from a

Bolognese public well and in 1925 there was a war between Greece and Bulgaria caused by a stray dog crossing over the border.[28,29]

El Guerra del Fútbol was a war in 1969 between El Salvador and Honduras after a series of incidents during a home and away World Cup qualifier. It lasted four days, with several thousand dead and hundreds of thousands displaced.[30]

And let's not even get started on the War of Jenkins' Ear.[31]

Fortunately, not many wars start because of stray dogs or ears but there are a myriad of other triggers and if we can identify and mitigate them, then we may prevent them from intensifying.

The single biggest predictor of war is if there has been war there before, Paul Collier called this "the conflict trap".[32] So the prevention of any single war not only prevents that particular one but also reduces the chance of whole generations of subsequent wars.

This shows how critically important it is to make sure the other end of the life-cycle is managed well. AI can prevent war, it can bring peace sooner and it can also ensure the peace is sustained and not just a cease-fire.

Making the Peace Safe

In former war zones across the world, there are more than a hundred million land mines and other unexploded bombs and every year they kill or injure thousands of people trying to rebuild their lives; farmers tilling the fields, children playing innocently.

Perhaps not surprisingly, given the devastating war there, Ukraine is now the most heavily mined country on earth. According to Economy Minister Yulia Svyrydenko, "The scale of the contamination of Ukraine with mines and unexploded ordnance is the largest since the Second World War."[33]

For a mine to be removed, different methods are available but it always ends up with a human walking around the field with a mine probe to locate them. And this painstakingly sensitive work can take decades to complete.

So, many farmers have taken matters into their own hands, using hobbyist metal detectors to attempt to clear their fields by themselves, with tragic results.

As a result, Ukraine's technology sector is developing a high-tech response. Paul Heslop, head of U.N. Mine Action at the United Nations Development Programme in Ukraine, says "We're going to see a fundamental change in the way that humanitarian demining is done in the next three years in Ukraine that will affect mine action the whole world over."

Their focus is to firstly clear land of high value – roads to hospitals, power lines, bridges and schools – using high quality data to prioritise the locations that impact the most people.

But they need ways to detect the mines themselves. Volcanologist Jasper Baur[34] has found a great solution by adapting his methods for monitoring lava flow. He uses cheap and widely available drones, equipping them with either thermal or visual sensors, and then machine learning, trained specifically for the task, locates the mines.

The results? 91.8% accuracy in some environments. Yes, there are real-world limitations but, ultimately, it is a cheap, rapid and safe way to address the problem.

There are many other new technologies being trialled – thermal measurements, ground penetrating radar, magnetometry and lidar. All are promising, all have their specific benefits but all have their own peculiarities which mean right now they are not widely applicable.

But, as with everything in this sector, watch this space. And each innovation that improves safety in an extensively land-mined area will diminish the conflict trap, making peace more likely to be sustainable.

Water Wars

Climate change has already been fingerprinted as a contributor to war, especially in those regions where socioeconomic or political factors mean a heightened risk already.[35] As examples, environmental degradation has been linked to the conflicts in Sudan[34] and Syria[35] (although both claims are disputed).[36,37,38,39]

And this is with temperatures only 1.2°C above pre-industrial levels. The 2016 Paris Accord agreed to keep global surface temperatures well below 2°C above pre-industrial levels. However, seven years later, the UN's first stock take on the agreement's progress found that we were a long way from hitting these targets.[40]

If you go to https://www.co2.earth/daily-co2, you can check the amount of carbon in the air every day for the last sixty years. It does not make good reading, not only are emissions continuing to increase, they are (and have been consistently) accelerating. If this continues, it will lead to irreversible tipping points being triggered, leading to temperatures 5°C or even higher by the end of the century.[41]

As we saw in the previous chapter, the huge amount of energy that data centres use can itself be a driver behind climate change and this consumption is only going to increase.[42] Possibly exponentially.[43] But we also saw in the previous chapter just how much value AI brings in understanding the mechanisms of climate change, how to slow it down and how to mitigate its impact.

Despite the difficulty in directly pinning its impact to violence or warfare, rainfall variability does seem to be correlated, although the effect seems to be strongest with *abundance*.[44]

Flooding is now the most common natural disaster in the world and this is only likely to increase.[45]

But AI is helping the fightback. In July 2020, the European Commission's Global Flood Awareness System (GloFAS) forecasted severe flooding along the Jamuna River in Bangladesh which triggered a rapid response to provide humanitarian assistance to vulnerable populations before flooding reached critical levels.[46]

And digital twins of cities, rivers and whole ecosystems, like the E.U. DestinE delta region digital twin tool and other similar projects, also enable flood risks to be better understood and managed.[47]

At the other end of the spectrum, right now around 4 billion people live under highly water-stressed conditions for at least one month of the year.[48] At the same time, worldwide around 30% of drinking water is lost in distribution.[49] But digital twins of water distribution systems help here, too, as they can significantly reduce the water loss as it goes from source to end user.[50]

And take the Mekong River as another example: it crosses or borders six countries – China, Myanmar, Laos, Thailand, Cambodia, and Vietnam – who have a difficult history between them. Rapid economic growth has led to almost every one of these countries building or planning dams and drawing off water for hydropower, irrigation or local water use.

But a number of transboundary organisations work together to manage the situation using multiple neural network and machine learning models to manage the water flows and allow the countries to cooperate rather than fight.[51,52,53,54,55]

Water wars may be too simplistic a term but as climate change continues its dangerous journey, its impact on the environment is a contributing factor for future wars but AI can help understand, predict and even reduce its effects.

More Prosperity, Less Wars

Stray dogs and ears are clearly things we get emotional about but go to war? There must be something deeper at play. And the simple fact is that if life were better for most people, "wage war" would be very low on your plan for the day.

The United Nations Sustainable Development Goals (SDGs) is a set of goals and targets with the aim of "peace and prosperity for people and the planet". It's a to-do list for making the world a better place and, clearly, peace is a big part of the payoff.

There are 17 goals and 169 targets across those goals, with the ambitious plan to reach them by 2030.[56] By reaching each of the targets, we score our goal.

And, in doing so, we also diminish the chances of war.

Well, AI can progress these goals.

A paper published in Nature in 2020, found 134 of the SDG targets could be enhanced by AI.[57] The International Computation and AI Network we saw in the previous section was set up for exactly this aim so whether it puts more food in your stomach or keeps you healthy with better drugs, each intervention is one less reason for war as an answer to your problems.[58,59]

One of the major factors contributing to prosperity is trade. It incentivises peace, it builds cooperation and it normalises the "other". Of course, it's not quite as simple as that, contrast the limited cross border trade between India and Pakistan and the flourishing business between China and Taiwan, although both pairs of countries are in conflict.[60] Trade can *increase* the chance of war if it's enforced or unequal or if it drives a race to control limited resources of high value.[61]

But, mostly, trade is creative, war is destructive and they tend to be mutually exclusive, it is rare countries at war continue to trade other than in the margins.[62] So anything which increases trade, particularly fair trade and with an emphasis on development, reduces conflict.[63,64]

And AI can do this in many ways.

Take customs procedures: AI systems can now read and understand descriptions of commercial goods and automatically trigger the right procedures and duties, significantly streamlining the process and reducing associated costs. They can also identify counterfeit products, protecting the legitimate trade and reducing losses.[65]

Or supply chain management. No more walking along the aisle with your clipboard, "smart warehouses" powered by AI use sensors, computer vision, and automated processes to optimise inventory management and space utilisation. They can predict demand, organise inventories, and track parcel movements in real-time, leading to much more efficient supply chains and, again, reduced costs. And every cost cut is value created and the war dial turned down one small notch.

Of course, not so good for clipboard manufacturers.

Transportation can be optimised too, as real-time traffic data warns you of any anti-AI protests ahead and reroutes you to avoid it. Scheduling in air and maritime transport will be more efficient and load space maximised, again driving cost reductions.

Even the 'simple' case of automatic translation opens up whole new geographical markets. When eBay introduced a machine translation service to their website, it led to a 17.5% increase in exports to Latin America.[66] AI understands the nuance and the cultural variations like a local.

All of this cuts the cost of international trade which means two things: firstly, the cost-benefit analysis moves even further towards trade, making war ever less likely. And, secondly, we're baking the proverbial bigger pie so negotiating parties are happy to divide it out more evenly because there is more to divide out.

International trade agreements are tremendously complex, involving tariffs, quotas and regulations for thousands of product lines in dozens of industries across multiple regions, impacting all kinds of communities and vested interests and political opinions, each with very different viewpoints and demands and red lines. Simple, they ain't.

For example, when Canada and the EU were finalising their trade deal, it was vetoed by Wallonia. Three people live in Wallonia and they blocked a deal which took 10 years to negotiate and impacted 500 million people.[67]

AI handles this complexity easily and can accommodate the perspectives of all the stakeholders. Including Wallonia.

It can integrate giant datasets like historical trade data, economic indicators, demographic trends, climate change projections, political sentiment analyses and many others and discover otherwise unseen areas of mutual benefit and optimise the vast number of variables for all stakeholders, rather than just the loudest.

It can also anticipate unintended consequences by playing with different scenarios and predicting their impact. How would reducing import tariffs affect labour figures in Detroit? What if we tightened the rules of origin, how would sourcing patterns change?

These predictions would inform the negotiators' strategies, enabling them to make decisions with greater confidence. And greater confidence isn't just a 'nice to have'. Aggressive negotiation stances often come from fear of risk. If that fear is reduced, all sides can afford to be more generous in their negotiation.

The result of all of this: fairer trade agreements, greater prosperity, less war.

Being Nice: The Key to Global Domination

As Von Clausewitz noted, "War is merely the continuation of politics by other means" so if we can become more skilled at the politics, perhaps there will be less need for war.[68]

There's some positive news on this front.

"Diplomacy" is a board game with a map of Europe and the surrounding region in 1901 and players each represent a country and they compete with each other to conquer Europe. Every round, players negotiate with each other on building alliances and then they make their moves.

Strategic thinking is a key part of it but even more important is the human-to-human negotiation. You see, the move agreed may not actually be the move played: Italy and Germany might agree a joint attack on Austria-Hungary but one of them may have had their fingers crossed and actually attacks the other (who is now distracted by Austria-Hungary). Plenty of back-stabbing goes on, combining the strategic thinking of Risk with the Machiavellian skills of TV show Traitor.

It's the kind of game about which people say, "Ok, AI can win at chess, it can win at Go, but it will *never* beat a human at Diplomacy."

Until researchers at Meta developed an AI agent called Cicero who could play this game and, as it turns out, can play pretty well. It joined an online Diplomacy league which included professional players and even three-time world champion, Andrew Goff. Across forty games, it achieved more than double the average score of the human players, ending in the top 10% of them.[69]

So where's the good news in that, shouldn't we be worried? Perhaps, except it won by being *nice*. It didn't lie. It turns out that being truthful is great for building alliances which pay off in the long term. Who knew?

Don't get me wrong, AI agents can lie if they are incentivised to. In a technical report on GPT-4, OpenAI described how, working with the Alignment Research Center, they set the LLM a task to hire a TaskRabbit worker to solve a CAPTCHA test.[70] The worker jokingly asked "Are you a robot?" and GPT-4 replied that it was vision-impaired and this was why it needed the assistance. Naughty GPT-4!

But when Meta was building Cicero, they found it tricky to achieve the right balance between deception and honesty and so they decided it was easier to go with outright honesty. And it worked.

Goff, often considered the Diplomacy GOAT, says that although the game has this reputation for treachery, as players get more experienced and stronger, they become more and more honest. He says, "Diplomacy is ultimately about building trust in an environment that encourages you not to trust anyone".

Cicero would even suggest positive moves to the other player, moves the other player hadn't considered. What a great way to build trust and foster an alliance which would pay back further down the line.

It was flawed. It would sometimes suggest playing illegal moves and later would deny saying things it had said. The games were played online anonymously so the other players didn't know it was a bot, they just thought it was drunk!

But ultimately it was extremely good at strategic thinking, understanding other players' intentions, and building profitable alliances. These are the skills we need in complex real-world negotiations and, indeed, diplomacy.

Perhaps, in future, AI can advise our diplomats to be nice and truthful and we can win without recourse to war.

Israel – Palestine: Is There Hope?

The Israel-Palestine conflict goes back over a century but has an origin story dating millennia. It's the great intractable conflict of our time.

Can there ever be peace there?

Well, perhaps there can.

The 1990s were a time of great hope for peace around the world. On the 9th November, 1989, the Cold War ended as the Berlin Wall came down and a new relationship was born between the West and the Eastern Bloc.

On 11th February 1990, Nelson Mandela was released from prison, broadcast on televisions across the world. Four years later, for the first time in their history all South Africans were allowed to vote in parliamentary elections and Mandela was elected President.

In 1993, secret talks began between Israel and the Palestine Liberation Organisation, which led to the Oslo Accords and in 1994, Yasser Arafat, Yitzhak Rabin and Shimon Pires, the senior politicians involved, were awarded the Nobel Prize for Peace in recognition.

And in April 1998, the Good Friday Agreement in Northern Ireland was signed and the country saw peace after decades of violence. The Reverend Ian Paisley and Martin McGuinness, once bitter enemies, shared an office and became friends.[71]

Many of the long-standing conflicts of the post Second World War era were finally coming to an end. Each had seemed impossible in advance but, to a greater or lesser extent, proved successful and their impact is felt positively today.

With the glaring exception of the Oslo Accords.

The first one was signed in 1993 and the second in 1995, they were flawed and incomplete deals but they were a huge step in the right direction and, with the right political will, could have very well formed the basis of a lasting peace.

Unfortunately, although agreement was reached in the negotiation room, outside of the room proved more difficult to convince. Neither Hamas, the Palestinian militant faction, nor the patriotic factions within Israel were convinced and both acted to undermine its implementation, culminating in the assassination of Prime Minister Rabin by the Israeli ultranationalist Yigal Amir.

After helping the successful Northern Ireland peace process, Colin Irwin was expecting to work again with Senator George Mitchell in the Middle East but it wasn't until 2009 that he was able to run a peace poll.[72] He met with representatives and leaders on all sides, including Shimon Peres, Ehud Olmert, the prime minister at the time, Fatah, the Palestinian political party in charge of the West Bank and he also met with Hamas.

The one person who refused to meet him was Benjamin Netanyahu, then leader of the opposition, who sent his spokesperson instead.

He took his results to Washington and presented them to the Senate and the House of Representatives, to George Mitchell and the State Department. His opinion polls showed clearly that a deal could be done based around the two-state solution, involving mutual recognition of an independent Palestinian state alongside a secure Israeli state. This was the solution put forward by the 1978 Camp David agreement, it was a core part of the Oslo Accords and is still the outcome favoured by the international community.

But, ultimately, no action was taken and the opportunity was missed.

But there is still hope. Even at the height of the 2023/24 events in Gaza, polls on both sides showed support for the two-state solution. The answers depend on the specific wording of the question but a poll in March 2024 found a 72.5% positive response amongst Palestinians. And on the Israeli side, a January 2024 poll had 51.3% support.[73]

Framing it the other way around, an Israeli poll in May 2024 found 43% thought the proposition "unacceptable" which does sound like a dealbreaker. However, this actually compares favourably when a similar question was asked about power sharing in Northern Ireland in January 1998. 52% of Protestants thought it was "unacceptable" but, despite this, with the right political leadership from the UK, Ireland, the US and EU working together, peace was made.

When taken along the right process, people fiercely against can be brought onside.

Irwin points out, "Security has always been the top priority for Israelis and when this is factored in, success in negotiations can be assured. And significantly demilitarising a future Palestine is not a deal-breaker for the Palestinians, according to the Institute for Social and Economic Progress March 2024 poll."

So, to ask the question again, can there ever be peace there?

The facts on the ground are always relevant and it requires the political will but Irwin's polls suggest that there is similar, if not more, public support for a deal between Palestine and Israel than there was in Northern Ireland. So, perhaps yes, there is some hope, after all, that the right process could succeed.

Maybe not right now but with sufficient successful examples around the world, led by local grassroots interventions where the political will does exist, the momentum will grow until the logic is inescapable and the clamour for it to be used with Israel and Palestine will eventually be irresistible.

As with freeing the law in Chapter Seven and overhauling democracy in Chapter Eight, the road to peace in even the most intractable conflicts is there.

There's Still A Way to go, but...

It was a summer's Sunday, June 28th, and a car drove through the city streets and a man sat outside a café pondering his options. The car turned right into a side street but soon realised it was a wrong turn. The driver stopped to reverse but accidentally stalled, just outside the café.

Gavrilo Princip, a member of the Black Hand, a Serbian nationalist secret society, stood up from his chair, approached the car and shot the Archduke Ferdinand from close range.

The Archduke died, the First World War began.

Just like every other war, countless books have been written on the causes of World War One and countless more could have. Was it German expansionism? Serbian nationalism? Russian mobilisation plans? The intricate network of alliances? Whichever you choose, what was the cause of that cause? And the cause, again, of that?

And, equally, whichever you choose, it may still have been averted had the car not taken the wrong turning.

There are many, many contributing factors to war and every one of them is a possible intervention for peace. Many very clever people are working hard to address each one, with some success but not yet enough. AI is cleverer still and we've seen that it too is already working hard for the same goal, and already finding successes previously unlikely.

And the AI we have now is the least effective version of the technology that will be available to us as we move forward. It will only become more capable.

There is no single silver bullet but, with luck and application, we can diminish each contributing factor, one by one, and an end to war is not an impossible dream, after all.

Section 3
The Warning

10
What Could Possibly Go Wrong?

So, war is going to end, society will be healed, everyone will get on with each other and we'll all sing Kumbaya together. (I'll skip Kumbaya but I'll see you at the bar).

Mind you, there's another plausible scenario.

AI could *accelerate* conflict.

It has history. In one of the very first incidents of two chatbots talking to each other (one called Alan, the other Sruthi, and both developed at Cornell University), they ended up arguing about the nature of God. They had been trained on about 65 million conversations with humans so we know where their attitude came from.[1]

Warfare is famously difficult to predict. When World War One broke out, all mobilising plans were built on the horse and the railway. The Germans launched the Schlieffen Plan and, shortly, they were on the outskirts of the rapidly evacuated Paris and it looked as though the French would need to surrender.

Instead, General Gallieni ordered every taxi in Paris to be commandeered to transport soldiers to the front and after two days of ferrying all available troops in this way, the German advance was halted forty miles from the centre of the capital.

The speed and flexibility of the car was there for all to see and war changed from then on.[2]

It's difficult to predict the future of warfare but AI will certainly take centre stage. As a result, an arms race is already taking place between the major powers to make sure they have the AI advantage because even marginal advantages are likely to prove decisive.[3]

Paul Scharre begins his book "Four Battlegrounds: Power in the Age of Artificial Intelligence" with a description of a 2019 DARPA simulation dogfight, where AI is pitted against a highly experienced F-16 fighter pilot. The artificial pilot won hands down, in five rounds it scored fifteen kills to the human's none. It was better at shooting, it was better at flying the aircraft and it could pull manoeuvres with g-forces a human could not tolerate. Most of all, it could make quicker decisions.[4]

He argues that, in the same way that coal was critical in 19th-century wars and oil in the 20th century, success in 21st-century fighting will be fuelled by artificial intelligence. And there are four factors that will drive such success: data, compute, talent and institutions. Right now, he believes, the United States has the advantage across these factors, but the trend is for China to catch up rapidly.

Interestingly, the first three of those factors are highly globalised, which acts to increase stability.

An illustrative example is that TSMC, the world's foremost semiconductor manufacturer, by far, is based in Taiwan. Their chips lie behind nearly all of the data centres that host the big artificial intelligence models in both the U.S. and in China.

So a Chinese invasion of Taiwan seems less likely because it would inevitably involve the destruction of a major supplier for as long as the Chinese computers are dependent on it.[5]

The net result is that China is pouring huge resources into catching up in the technology, the United States are doing so to stay ahead, and other countries are doing similar so they aren't left behind. It's not a pattern that usually ends well.

There are other dangerous elements to it. For a start, it shifts the advantage from the defender to the attacker.

Since von Clausewitz, it has been a military given that the defender has an advantage over the attacker and this is for many reasons but some of them no longer apply. The advantage is largely psychological, deriving from the desperation of defending the homeland and potentially losing everything, for one side, and the demoralising effect of long periods spent in stressful conditions away from home for the other.

Clearly, neither of those are as significant a factor in the case of artificial intelligence. Indeed, any humans in the defence will quickly get dispirited by the relentlessly quick responses of the attacking AI and will lead to a sense of hopelessness.[6]

Not just that but the major power peace of the 20th century was based on the principle of Mutually Assured Destruction (MAD) and this rule no longer applies. The principle was that no country would ever be foolish enough to launch a nuclear missile attack because it would be impossible to destroy the whole of the enemy's arsenal, meaning a retaliatory attack would follow immediately after and the initiator would suffer as much as their enemy. Hence a relatively stable peace between the major powers for the last sixty years.

In an AI war, however, the first mover may well be able to disrupt the other country's systems sufficiently so that retaliation isn't possible which means an outright victory is now a viable strategy.

And since speed is so important, there is an incentive to press the button quickly to ensure that you are that first mover. But, of course, the enemy has the same incentive, so they will try to move quicker than you. The MADness of nuclear war created a stable environment for peace but this will be replaced by a very fragile set-up, where neither side has the luxury for consideration, communication or verification, their only option, from an existential perspective, is to press the button as quickly as they can.

You can come out from underneath the table for now, though, the systems aren't reliable enough to be replaced by humans yet. Scharre reports of a DARPA experiment that trained an AI robot to reliably detect people in complex, urban environments and then challenged eight marines to reach the robot, placed 300m away, without being noticed. All eight succeeded: two reached it by doing somersaults, two put themselves in a cardboard box and one disguised himself as a fir tree.[7]

I hope I'm not releasing any security-critical secrets by publishing this but I will keep an eye on the sales of fir-tree suits in China.

Rogue Actors

It's not just a major power war between the US and China or Russia that we need to be scared of.

AI is just a tool and anyone who has access to it can use it, which is pretty much everyone. So, that's about eight billion people to be scared of, if any of them were to have any grudge against the status quo which, to be fair, probably isn't *all* eight billion.

It might be a teenager in their bedroom using Crispr-Cas9 to cook up an airborne-transmitted variant of Ebola. It might happen by mistake: Martin Rees describes the risk as "error, not terror", adding "The global village will have its own village idiot who will have global reach."

It might be one of your favourite dictators like Vladimir Putin or Kim Jong-Un who sets an army of social media bots to spread false information that magnifies distrust in a country's institutions. Or it might be one of your favourite billionaires (or trillionaires by the time you read this) stirring up hatred between one segment of the community and another by posting incendiary comments on X.[8] Can't imagine anyone doing such an insane thing but you never know.

Or perhaps the worst rogue actor could be the AI itself.

Nick Bostrom posited a thought experiment that an artificially intelligent agent that is set a task of making as many paperclips as possible might take it upon itself to kill all human beings because it could turn them into paperclips. Alternatively, an AI that is not only more intelligent than a human, but more intelligent than all humans might decide to take over the world and there wouldn't be much we could do about it.

Do I think either of these last two situations will occur? Probably not.

Do I think we should act now to prevent them? Yes, absolutely. Although they may be low probability, they are exceedingly high impact, and so we should definitely be considering what guardrails we can put in place now before it's too late.

But I also think these examples raise the question of the leviathan, which is an important one.

The Leviathan

The Leviathan is an Old Testament sea monster but in modern usage it refers to something that is overwhelmingly powerful and has its own agenda which may or may not align with ours. The fear is that AI could become that leviathan, either accidentally (viz paperclips) or through its own will.

We've seen the films, it usually ends badly.

I think it is unlikely but sufficiently feasible to warrant efforts to prevent it but I think there are other examples of leviathan that we should be more worried about.

Hobbes wrote his famous book of that name in 1651 and it has gone on to become one of the core texts of political theory. He lived in a time of war and he believed that nature had a tendency to violence and, to avoid this, we needed a powerful state. Without such, there is nothing stopping a descent into a bloody free-for-all from which no-one benefits.

However, if the state is strong enough, it can regulate and police anti-social behaviour, allowing everyone to live in greater peace and contentment.[9]

This is the basis of the social contract. I agree not to murder so that everybody else agrees not to murder me. Our freedom is maximised by agreeing to restrain it in certain ways. The agreement is not with the state, it is with society. But we devolve some of our power to the state to enforce the system and we are better off for doing so.

He saw the state as an automaton – it is not a human being but it is similar, in that, as an entity, it has a goal and has methods to achieve that goal. And it has agency, it can decide what to do in order to achieve its goal. In fact, it has super-agency, its access to resources gives it a power to dictate to other entities how it wants them to behave to achieve or protect its goals.

Now, ideally, the goal of the state aligns with the interests of its people and in many instances that is the case, more or less. In corrupt states or dictatorships, though, it is not true. And so, there is a problem, namely that the state can be too powerful and can misuse its power.

Hence the necessity for checks and balances that make sure the state does not misuse its power. Often, a democracy is structured with three branches – the legislature, the judiciary and the administration – to provide this balance. And there are other bodies, formal or informal, that also form part of the equilibrium, like the press, business, unions, advocacy groups, religious institutions and many similar.

A healthily functioning society is one where all these institutions are in balance, that no single one of them gets so much power that they can override the wishes of the others.

The Horror! The Horror!

But what if one of these became too powerful themselves?

The corporation is a leviathan. It is an entity organised in such a way to achieve a goal and it has agency towards achieving it. But if the goal of the state is, superficially at least, to optimise the well-being of its citizens, the goal of a business is purely and simply to maximise shareholder profit.

Put differently, its goal is to take as much money as it can from your bank account and put it into theirs.

More than that, they are legally bound to do this. So, if the corporation becomes too powerful, that is very bad news. All those resources utilised to take your money with nothing capable of stopping them.

So, what happens if a business has too much power? Well, we have several examples we can refer to for reference. The East India Company was a joint-stock company granted a royal charter in 1600 to trade in India. But its power grew rapidly and it became a quasi-state, with an army, setting taxes and administering justice.

It had, as David Runciman puts it, "the best of both worlds, the single-mindedness of the corporation coupled with the sovereign power of the state".[10]

And it used this power to enrich its officers at the expense of the local people. Sir Robert Clive became one of the richest people in the world whilst Bengal suffered a famine in which nearly 10 million died. He hated India and committed suicide at the age of forty-nine, of which Samuel Johnson wrote that he "had acquired his fortune by such crimes that his consciousness of them impelled him to cut his own throat."[11]

And the African chartered companies were arguably worse, their methods to achieve their goals of personal wealth best described by Joseph Conrad: "The horror! The horror!".[12,13]

The 19th-century "scramble for Africa" was ostensibly driven by the 3 C's – Christianity, Civilisation and Commerce – and it's worth remembering that Kurtz, Conrad's character in "Heart of Darkness" who symbolises the moral decay of these companies, is described as a great musician and a great humanitarian whose written aim was of "humanising, improving, instructing".

But for all their disclaimers of only wanting to benefit others, you did not want to be a local under their governance.

And there is prospect of another leviathan. The nature of our current economy is one of "winner takes all". The nature of the military arms race is similar. Given the exponential growth of artificial intelligence, it is not unthinkable that there will be one winner and only one winner. Leading the pack at the moment are two American leviathans – the U.S. government and the Silicon Valley technology companies.

Or perhaps they could combine to become one. Former OpenAI researcher, Leopold Aschenbrenner thinks they will create a Manhattan Project for the 21st Century. The thinking is that the American military is likely to value artificial intelligence capabilities as so important for national security and defeating the

Chinese state leviathan that it commandeers the tech companies into a new project which effectively takes over.[14]

At the time of writing, Apple was valued at $3.5 trillion which is more than every country in the world, bar the top eight.[15,16] Meta, Microsoft, Nvidia, Amazon and Alphabet are not far behind. So, whether it is tech co plus military or simply tech co, a leviathan whose sole goal is take money from your account and put into theirs is not an appealing prospect and we will look at this in more detail in the next chapter.

Kafka 10x

Whichever leviathan we end up with, they will be orders of magnitude more powerful than any other individual, business or state we have ever seen before.

Their size, their resources and their reach will mean no one can stop them doing whatever they want. They will be able to lobby governments to write the laws that will benefit them and they will be able to defend themselves against existing laws.

And more than that, they will be able to control how we behave.

As the world is ever more digitised, power will lie in the code. Today, if I'm driving to the hospital and I'm in a rush, I might briefly go a little over the speed limit to overtake a slow coach in front of me; but if I'm in a self-driving car that won't be possible – the code just won't allow it. If I quit my job yesterday but forgot to pick up some belongings, I can easily pop back into the office today and the receptionist would let me through with a joke; but if it's a facial recognition system and I've been deleted, it's not going to let me in.

Even if I'm legit but there's a bug, it won't let me in. And there is no ringing up the helpline to ask them to sort it out or find a simple work-around, there is no helpline: try phoning Amazon when your book doesn't arrive.

Tech co's love their 10x, this is Kafka 10x.

The decision of what you are allowed to do and not allowed to do is moving to the programmers and there will be no way around it. I used to be a programmer myself, I know what they're like, it's not a good thing.

Power Comes Through Persuasion

The best way to control behaviour is to control how people think and they can do this through their management of your social media news feeds, what is reported on other media news sites and, shortly, our personal assistant's suggestions.

They are collecting vast amounts of data on us through our online behaviour, our purchases, GPS location tracking, television viewing habits, our wearable devices, even our thermostat and our doorbell and in so many other ways.

And then they sell it to other companies who also want to take money from your account and put it into their own. And they sell it to political organisations who want you to agree with them and vote for them.

And with all this data, we are being rated and the rating impacts what we have access to. Our credit score decides if we can get that loan, our health score allows us to get insurance, these are normal things but, in the future, they will be more absolute.

And what about our social score? In China, a social credit figure allows access to faster internet speeds and more jobs. This will be a very powerful way of manipulating behaviour so whoever the leviathan is, they will probably do this. It's not all bad, it will probably lead to better behaviour, less crime, indeed, less conflict.

But who will decide what 'good' is? The leviathan. Any disagreement (and they know if it even crosses your mind) and you don't have access.

In Jamie Susskind's "Future Politics", he imagines that you might want to go on a protest for or against some cause or policy and maybe the leviathan doesn't want you to. There are many ways they could prevent it from happening. Perhaps:

- the protest isn't mentioned on the news so you are unaware of it
- it doesn't show on searches either
- they censor your messages so you never receive the details
- your weather report predicts rain so you decide to stay home
- your digital map says the traffic is appalling
- the train flies through the station without stopping to let you off
- the ringleaders have been locked in their house by their smart locks.

Most of these have been done already and, please note, these are the *soft* options.

In our modern surveillance economy, not only do they know your thoughts but they can control them more than ever before.

The more knowledge they have of you, the easier it is for them to persuade you. Large language models are trained to communicate in appealing ways, their voice will sound like our favourite actor or our best friend, they will know exactly what words to use to make us buy a specific product or support a particular policy.[17]

This is asymmetric. The leviathan will have a lot of informational power over the individual, the individual has no informational power over the leviathan.

So, let's hope it's nice.

It's Coming for Your Job

And while we're on the topic of things going wrong, how about mass unemployment leading to civil strife, even civil war?

A 2019 Oxford Economics report suggested that by 2030, 20 million manufacturing jobs will be lost to robots.[18] And if one of those jobs is yours, don't bother applying for a new position in the warehouse, Amazon employs 750,000 robots and is taking on hundreds of thousands of new ones a year, even as it reduces the number of human employees at the same time.[19] And you won't get a job in distribution either, driverless cars and trucks are on their way. At the time of writing, Waymo is giving 100,000 self-driving taxi rides a week and Baidu's Apollo Go robotaxis average at 287,500 per month.[20,21] By the time of your reading, these figures will be much higher.

Retail assistants don't have a great medium-term future either and now LLMs are here, translators, language teachers, voice-over artists, copy-writers and customer service agents should all think about re-skilling fairly soon.

In fact, a new study by a team of researchers from Wharton, OpenAI and the Oxford-based Centre for the Governance of AI found that roughly 1.8% of jobs have over half their tasks replaceable by LLMs but when you include other software that can complement the LLM, this figure jumps to 46%.[22]

So, if half your job can be done by software, you might be asked to work part-time. In the good scenario.

Of course, not everyone agrees with this.

The theory of comparative advantage tells us that in normal circumstances people should always be able to find a job that is economically suited to them: if Mary is a great surgeon and also very good at gardening and she is better than Bob at both, they would still both be employed because it is worthwhile for Mary to do her surgery whilst employing Bob as the gardener; outsourcing the gardening frees her up to do the better-paid work, which more than compensates for the wages she has to pay Bob.[23]

Unfortunately, this trusted pillar of labour economics breaks down if Mary is a computer because the computer will be able to do both jobs at the same time.[24]

A more plausible argument is that when technology has impacted work in the past, it simply shifted it to new areas. It can free up time to do new tasks; it creates more money so consumers create more demand and, therefore, jobs; it can create whole new industries that weren't even imaginable before. This is why these days there are fewer blacksmiths but many more computer programmers.[25]

But that disruption can be painful. For example, when the agricultural and industrial revolutions took place, there was a massive migration from the countryside to the cities which led to a significant *reduction* in quality of life for a large percentage of the population. In the long run, it may have worked out, but in the short and medium term many were worse off.

And there is a strong argument that this time is different. We will be facing multiple sectors being revolutionised at the same time so the job loss will be very large. And as we saw above, we may well be chasing jobs that disappear before we even get there. The exponential speed of change means that the new jobs created are just as likely to be done by a bot as by a human.

Previous innovations, through power or automation, either increased our strength, our speed or our reach. But they always had to be used by humans because it was human intelligence that worked them and found new ways to work with them. However, artificial intelligence will be able to do even those thinking and creative tasks better than humans.

In recent waves of automation, new jobs have been created but they are typically lower quality, lower status, less reliable and lower wage. Think fast-food delivery cyclist.

AI brings expertise to everyone, which reduces the competitive advantage of that expertise, making it much cheaper. Everyone will have access to this expertise: they will be able to make much better personal finance decisions, legal decisions, health decisions and so on because of the tools that will be on their phone and free.

It's just that those people who used to be paid to do those things will no longer have a job. Or they will be delivering fast-food.

And then a drone will deliver the fast food.

The Revolt of the Redundant

But, anyway, who will be ordering the fast-food? If no one has a job, no one can afford the luxury of ordering in.

This won't happen overnight. Much of the current use of AI in the office is playing around and exploring different use cases but individuals will find ways in which they can usefully put it to work. These efficiencies will free people up to do higher value tasks, just as the techno-optimists claim.

But there will also be cost-saving lay-offs or, more likely, not replacing people who leave for natural reasons. Expect a team of ten to become a team of nine or eight.

As jobs are replaced by machines and algorithms, there will be an initial productivity boost to the economy but the secondary impact will be that those people who have lost their jobs will have no money to buy goods, leading to a recession.

Falling labour costs and falling consumption will lead to deflation and a business's natural response will be to cut costs and replace staff with more machines and algorithms. Local rational optimisation leads to a systemic economic failure.

Normal cyclical upturns will not save the day, as they have with previous recessions, because AI will relentlessly take more and more of the jobs.

AI promises abundance. Peter Diamandis, founder of the X-Prize and the Singularity University, writes "Within a generation, we will be able to provide foods and services, once reserved for the wealthy few, to any and all who need them" as the price of everything on the digital doubling curve reduces exponentially to zero.[26]

This may happen but I suspect we will need to go through a turbulent transitionary period to get there. Anyone whose job is replaced by a bot in the next few years won't sit back and enjoy the warm glow of abundance, they will probably find it difficult. And as AI-driven unemployment increases, it will just get bleaker.

Eventually, the economic system will need to restructure completely to allow the general population to enjoy the abundance and this may happen but not until we've had ten or twenty years of unemployment on a scale never seen before in developed countries.

There are 3.5 million truck drivers in the United States, how will they respond when self-driving trucks replace their jobs?[27] Then ask the same question for pretty much every other sector. When unemployment hits 10%, 15%, 25%, higher, the chances of significant civil unrest are appreciable. Civil war expert, Barbara Walter, says that America's chances of a second civil war are already dangerously high.[28]

Throw in mass unemployment and we're pulling the pin on a grenade.

When a caterpillar reaches the end of its stage in the insect's life-cycle, it attaches itself to a leaf or a stem and forms a chrysalis. Within this protected space, it goes through the remarkable transformation we call metamorphosis and it restructures its body completely until it emerges from the chrysalis as a beautiful butterfly, unrecognisable from the caterpillar it was only a short while before.

This is a common metaphor for the upcoming economic transition but what goes on in that chrysalis? Well, enzymes are released that break down most of the tissues into a soupy liquid, with a few organs and clumps of cells remaining intact. Almost all of the structure that was the caterpillar has disappeared into a mushy broth.[29]

AI might deliver the cornucopia that humans have always dreamed of but if our society needs to go through a similar process as the chrysalis before it gets there, we may not survive it.

Nick Bostrom talks of knotty futures.[30]

It is the nature of knots that you have to undo them in the right order. A complicated knot needs to be unpicked part by part and each part tackled in the correct sequence. If you pull on the string before the right time, it will tighten the knot and make it harder to undo.

Such could be our future. That we find ourselves in a knot but it is too difficult to undo because we didn't do the right things before getting to this point.

So, in Chapter Twelve, we will explore what we need to do now to make sure we don't find ourselves facing these challenges in the future.

But before that, let's just allow ourselves, if briefly, to get even more worried!

11
The Leviathan as Psychopath

Tech Co's Win the Leviathan Race

By now, you've read several chapters on the end of conflict and one chapter on the threats we face. That's not because the threats are less likely or less consequential, it's just that there is a lot of writing out there already worrying about the risk but, personally, I haven't come across many people discussing the end of conflict.

Which way will it go? 50-50 is my best guess, sorry I can't be any more helpful.

It depends on the governance that will take us through the next decade or so. Good governance – thoughtful, objective, fair, evidence-based – and we'll be fine; bad governance and we won't. It's as simple as that.

So, what does that governance look like now?

Writing in early February 2025, the "leader of the free world" is President Donald Trump. Do I have faith in his governance? No, I don't. But do I think he will end all hope of good governance? No, I don't think this either.

It's possible that he will remove the checks and balances by stacking all the institutions with MAGA-capped zealots and I hope not because I firmly believe that dictator plus AI is our worst possible scenario.

But I believe there are so many logic bombs and fault-lines in his project that it will, ultimately, implode. What's more, despite his anti-regulation views, he is conscious of the dangers of AI and many of his supporters are very much against the over-reach of the technology companies. And Elon Musk takes the risks very seriously.

So, it remains to be seen how this will play out.

But I don't believe Trump is the biggest threat.

For me, the technology companies are most likely to triumph in the winner-takes-all leviathan prize. Sure, they respectfully sat behind the President at his inauguration but this was just positioning. They know that their exponential growth rate means things will be different at the next inauguration and different still at the one after that.

They are who we need to be most concerned with.

Now, there is no problem with a leviathan unless its goals are misaligned with our own. Unfortunately, corporations' goals are completely *at odds* with ours – as we've seen, it's their legal requirement to take as much money as they can from our accounts and put into theirs. And if they don't put sufficient effort into doing this, shareholders sue them.

So how is this going to work out for us?

They say, of course, that they are working towards our best interests. If this is true, we have nothing to worry about; an all-powerful entity looking out for us can be welcomed.

But if it isn't true, it's something that should be avoided *at all costs*.

So, in this chapter, let's explore whether we think a major shift of power to the tech companies will be a good thing.

They Would Say That, Wouldn't They?

Most tech founders want the world to be a better place. Silicon Valley cafés and co-working spaces are full of people with great ideas for using technology to solve the world's problems.

But at some point, this changes and they become a caricature of the corporate baddie in all the sci-fi films. Peter Thiel and Elon Musk use their billions for personal revenge.[1,2] Musk spends over $250 million to help Trump get elected, gets a key government position in return and proceeds to lay waste to departments that help the very poorest of our society.[3] A dozen other tech billionaires also swap allegiance to Trump and their personal wealth increases steeply.[4]

They all give great reasons for it but should we believe those reasons?

Marc Andreessen built the first web browser, Mosaic, later renamed Netscape Navigator, and is now one of the most influential investors in Silicon Valley. A lifelong Democrat, he was a late convert to Trump as the polls pointed towards a Republican victory.

He blames it on woke culture gone wild, communist capture of the intellectual elites, power corrupting those who hold it, the oligarchy, 99% tax rates and the Biden administration wanting to destroy the American tech industry.[5] To be clear, there was no irony in any of these attributions.

Lots of reasons but none of them pass the "They would say that, wouldn't they?" test.

What is this test? Well, consider my mate Gary who supports Arsenal: if he tells me that Arsenal are going to be West Ham, my team, in the next game, well he would say that, wouldn't he? So I'm not going to take his assertion as fact. But if West Ham's owner, David Sullivan, were to tell me the same, I've much more cause for believing him.

Here's another explanation for Andreessen's last-minute switch: the Democrats are finally (albeit slowly) introducing regulation for the tech industry, restraining just some of their excesses and, therefore, his personal profit; Trump, on the other hand, is promising to deregulate everything. In other words, he will get richer under Trump.

It's much easier to believe that more money is his main driver rather than a lucky side-effect that he hadn't really considered.

Andreessen's net worth was $1.2 billion at the start of the Biden administration and $1.9 billion by its end.[6] At a time when the average American's wages barely increased after inflation and 40% of them can't pull together $400 (even from debt), that's a huge growth but clearly not enough for him.[7]

Over a similar period, Elon Musk's net worth grew from $24 billion in 2020 to $200 billion by summer 2024 and then reached $445 billion in the two months after Trump's election victory.[8] I'm sure he, too, has lots of reasons for voting Trump but how many pass the "They would say that, wouldn't they?" test? Isn't it more likely it's because of the money?

"Elon, what was it about the $245 billion that persuaded you to vote for Trump?"

So, Can We Trust Them?

Their whole business model is based on tricking us into giving them that which is ours, namely our data, so they can take more of that which is ours, namely our money.

Not only that, but they get us to do the work for them. According to Jonathan Taplin, Facebook's users spend nearly 40,000 years of their time posting, commenting and liking *every day*![9]

And it's all been sleight of hand, they pretended to be nice and told us they were giving us free stuff but, while we got excited about all the free stuff, they took our data.

Apparently, we gave them permission to do it. Apparently, at some point we agreed and signed a contract to let them take the data and do whatever they want with it. But they relied on TS;DR – Terms of Service; Didn't Read. It was a deliberate strategy.

And anyone who says, "Oh don't bother reading the contract, you'll be fine" should *never* be trusted.

Nor someone who is happy to peer at your cards whenever they want, but refuses to show you theirs. The industry is built on surveillance but we have no way of inspecting them in return and their algorithms are top secret. So we really can't know what we're agreeing to when we sign the contract, even if we were the one person in a million who read it.

We've seen Google's hiding strategy in Chapter Eight but they employ many other methods to put us off the trail. When the EU border control agency, Frontex, was asked how technology companies managed their data, they released one document but refused twenty-seven others on the basis of protecting those companies' commercial interests.[10]

And when two companies lodged applications to build a hyperscale data centre under favourable terms in the small town of Zeewolde in the Netherlands, nobody really paid much attention. The companies were called Tulip and Polder Networks, nice homely Dutch names, but in reality, they were owned by Meta, who had gone to extreme lengths to keep their involvement out of public awareness. It turns out this kind of deception is a common ploy in data centre applications.[11]

We're beginning to see a bit of a pattern.

Nope, We Absolutely Can't Trust Them

There are other practices we can throw in.

Bruce Schneier points out in "A Hacker's Mind" that they learnt a lot from the casino industry about how to get users addicted. The digital user experience has a lot more in common with a slot machine than it appears and this is very much by design.[12] Every year, they would all meet at The Habit Summit at Stanford University and discuss the best technologies for getting customers to build a habit of buying their products.[13]

And if that habit becomes an addiction? Nothing to do with us, guv! And if we break the world in doing this? Nothing to do with us, guv!

Apart from all the mind-hacking tricks we saw in Chapter Eight, they lock you into their product by making it very difficult to leave. It's psychologically very hard to leave a social media platform when you have spent years building a network and you would have to start again from scratch if you moved. It would take very little effort to build a one-click button that migrates your account seamlessly to another provider but why would they make it simple, eh?

And you never own anything now, of course. They've changed the whole business model so everything is a "service", which means it's theirs and you can lease it temporarily. In the past, you bought a product – you paid once for your DVD, then it was yours and you could do whatever you wanted with it. Now, that's just not possible, so you have to pay multiple times for the same thing and have no legal right to do anything with it other than under the strict terms they unilaterally stipulate.

"Anytime someone puts a lock on something that belongs to you, and won't give you a key, they're not doing it for your benefit."[14] This is Doctorow's First Law, they're not doing any of this for your benefit. They own everything and if they are feeling in a good mood, they will allow you to use something as long as you are compliant and pay for it multiple times.

And perhaps worst of all there's predatory pricing.

Amazon, for example, makes huge losses on Prime because it's so cheap but, in doing so, they undercut the market and put all the competition out of business.[15] How can they do this? By offsetting the losses with massive profits made from other business streams (with the added benefit of avoiding tax on those profits).

It's a good business model if you've got deep enough pockets. WeWork lost $10 billion in three years and Uber lost $32 billion before making its first profit. Wipe out the competition by operating at a massive loss, knowing that you will last it out better than they will.[16,17] And once they're gone, you're free to charge as much as you like because you're the only shop that's still open.

And, by the way, this is the *global* market – Uber aren't trying to dominate the San Francisco taxi industry but the global one; as of 2021, they operate in over 10,000 cities in 72 countries.[18] Amazon aren't trying to corner the Seattle bookstore market but the whole of retail across the world.

Winner-takes-all, by definition, results in monopolies and more and more once proud free-market champions are beginning to support the idea of monopoly.[19]

Well, they would say that, wouldn't they?

But at least they obey the law?

In her book, "The Tech Coup", Marietje Schaake, a Member of the European Parliament, describes a typical example of how they treat the law when she flew to California as part of an EU delegation in order to meet top Facebook executives and discuss the platform's methods of content moderation.

Except the legal department weren't available to talk to them.[20]

They were given a nice tour of the building but almost every question was met with an apology that they would need to talk to the legal department for that. "Exactly," she replied, "that's why we are here." But they got nowhere. Meta had pretended to engage but, even with the EU government, they refused to do in any meaningful way.

Other companies can be even less respectful. Uber, for example, are downright confrontational.

They developed an app called Greyball, which was an exact parallel of their main app, but they used it in jurisdictions that resisted their licence application. Anyone who might be involved in checking if Uber infringed any regulation would be redirected to Greyball (based on identified phone numbers or location near a specific government building) and would only be shown ghost cars that never actually arrived.

No-one could ever verify that Uber were breaking the law.[21]

What's more, each Uber office had a kill switch to shut down their computers and delete all sensitive data before a police raid, with orders often given from the very top to hit this kill switch. Again, a blatantly illegal tactic used in full knowledge that they were breaking the law and, indeed, *because* they were breaking the law.[22]

Platforms like Airbnb, Uber, TaskRabbit and Amazon employ very expensive lawyers to argue, usually successfully, that normal industry regulations and taxes don't apply to them. And if any municipality finds against them, they ignore the ruling and continue to operate whilst challenging the law through lengthy court and appeal processes. The cash-strapped municipality doesn't have the same depth of pockets to ride it out and the platform invariably wins through attrition.

As one example of many, the California Assembly Bill 5 was a law that gave ride-share drivers employed status and, therefore, the rights and security that went along with it. So Uber, Lyft and any other affected organisation spent $200 million between them challenging it.

The bill was passed but Uber simply refused to abide by it and, eventually, they were able to get Proposition 22 passed which exempted them.[23]

None of this should be surprising. Martin Gilens of Princeton and Benjamin Page of Northwestern University conducted a much-cited study on which pockets of society had the most influence on public policy. They found that the general public had very little impact on laws passed but the American elite corporations and super-wealthy had a substantial one.[24]

Yes, politics *is* set up to support business and the rich.

Obviously, the fact that they fund so many Senators' campaigns gives them a lot of leverage but they don't even need to pay for their lobbying. A quick tweet from Elon Musk and everyone on X sees it, an edit to Google's search page and everyone sees it. If that tweet or edit says, "Write to your Representative now", there is an awful lot of pressure on Congress to do what Musk or Google want them to do.[25]

The big tech companies do obey the law, as it turns out, but only when it suits them and when it doesn't, they just ignore it or get it changed, whichever is cheaper.

They Don't Owe the Government, Do They?

But why should they follow any law, these are self-made men (*sic*), highly talented, hard-working geniuses who are forging a great future for the rest of us and shouldn't be held back by such small-minded things as regulations. It's not as if they owe the government or society anything, is it?

Actually, anything that involves a computer owes a lot to the US government because much of the fundamentals of the industry were developed in the 1950s and 1960s on the back of government funding because of how important the microprocessor world was to national security.

And as well as providing the funding, the government was also the main client. As we saw in Chapter Four, Fairchild Semiconductors and their more famous spin-off, Intel, launched Silicon Valley and the whole venture capital industry and both of them owed the large majority of their success to government contracts.[26]

Nearly all the "givens" in the computer industry that we now take for granted were originally developed by these firms or in research centres like Xerox PARC and Bell Labs, both, again, highly co-financed by the government. Even the very simplest things like CPU's and hard disk drives could not have been built otherwise.[27]

Oh, and there's the internet, I suppose. It was originally called ARPANET, named after the government Defense Advanced Research Projects Agency (DARPA) that built it. Any tech business owes a huge amount to the state and to tax-payers money if only for this major piece of free infrastructure that underpins it all.

Oh, and the World Wide Web, too, which was developed by Tim Berners-Lee when he was working at CERN (government-funded) and given away for free.

And while we're at it, the mobile phone industry is also built on government technology like GPS, a military satellite network opened to the general public in the 1980s.

And, as Mariana Mazzucato points out, almost everything that separates a smartphone from a stupid phone has come from government-funded or other public research. The touchscreen, lithium-ion batteries, cellular technology and even Siri ultimately evolved from government technologies.

Even if something was developed in-house, it was built on the huge body of open-source research of the scientific community, most of which took place in universities. The majority of universities around the world are publicly funded and even in the US, federal, state and local grants to universities amount to nearly $250 billion a year.[28]

And it was built, too, by a post-doc engineer or professor who had learnt most of their craft in a publicly funded university. There has been a brain drain from universities to the commercial sector for decades because, as Maja Pantic, a computer science professor at Imperial College points out, "There's no way that anybody would say 'no' to two or three times their salary."

Andrew Ng and Fei-Fei Li both joined Google from Stanford University, whilst Nobel Prize winner Geoffrey Hinton joined from Toronto University. Yann Lecun left Stanford for Facebook.[29] The list of taxpayer-funded professors siphoned off by industry stretches long.

Even Elon Musk, the great scourge of government, has benefitted from $4.9bn in government aid, whether grants, tax breaks, investments or subsidised loans and enjoyed $5.5bn procurement contracts for SpaceX from NASA and the US Airforce.[30]

And Palantir, run by that other arch-libertarian, Peter Thiel, was founded in 2004 on CIA funding and specialises in large government contracts, especially the military and intelligence sector.[31]

And just in case you were wondering, the loans are always on favourable terms and, moreover, guaranteed by the government so, if it goes wrong, it's the government who foots the bill. This maybe because of national security concerns or it may be because they are "too big to fail".

Either way, it enables the company to take a lot more risks because if it goes well, the company takes the upside, but if it goes wrong the government foots the bill.[32]

So, the government has been extraordinarily generous to them and they have only achieved their success because of this helping hand. Despite this, they all claim it is unfairly cracking down on them and holding them back.

But, I guess, they would say that, wouldn't they?

But At Least They Pay Their Fair Share of Taxes

And as you'd expect by now, they don't pay their fair share of taxes at all. Quite the opposite.

In 1992, the US Supreme Court ruled in *Quin Corp vs North Dakota* that a company that does not have a physical presence in a state doesn't have to pay sales tax in that state. This has been a pillar of the online business model ever since because a store that sold its products on the newly invented World Wide Web would have a clear competitive advantage over traditional brick-and-mortar shops.

As a direct result, Amazon, for example, chose to headquarter in Seattle and so don't pay sales tax on any sales outside of the State of Washington.[33] And in 2018, they auctioned their second headquarters to the locality most willing to give it tax breaks for setting up shop.

According to Good Jobs First, who track wasteful subsidies and corporate misconduct, by 2024 it had received $6.7 billion of state and regional tax subsidies for its warehouses, data centres, and film productions.[34]

They also avoid paying corporate federal income taxes: according to the Institute on Taxation and Economic Policy, they avoided paying more than $5 billion of such taxes in 2021. And over the previous four years, they reported a total federal tax rate of just 5.1% on over $78 billion of U.S. income.[35] No wonder they can out-compete normal shops who pay normal taxes.

How I would love to pay just 5% taxes but, clearly, I'm not rich enough to qualify.

Amazon aren't alone, of course.

Google, Apple and Elon Musk have all benefitted by placing their headquarters (real or virtual) in states or countries that compete hardest in the tax jurisdiction race-to-the-bottom.[36] The regions' argument is that the business brings other benefits but this isn't always true. When Apple located a new data centre in Iowa, they received a nice $150 million tax break to smooth the process. The benefit to Iowa, in return? A grand total of 50 new jobs.[37]

Even if, like Apple, they HQ in a state like California, complicated tax arrangements with low-to-no tax jurisdictions like Nevada, Ireland and the British Virgin Islands mean they can still save billions of dollars of tax a year.

Transfer pricing works by setting up a subsidiary in a low tax jurisdiction like Ireland and keeping the assets, such as intellectual property, with that subsidiary. The US office pays huge royalties to the subsidiary for the assets, reducing the tax bill in the United States whilst paying a low royalty tax in Ireland. All kinds of further complications can be added in, leveraging loopholes in the tax laws of other countries.

The net result is that American companies avoid paying $200 billion of taxes a year.

That, remember, is at the expense of everyone else who *do* have to pay taxes.[38] Their communications departments all put their hand on their heart as they declare they pay every cent of tax that is asked of them although they forget to mention the huge effort spent ensuring what is asked of them is as little as possible.

But they would say that, wouldn't they?

The Leviathan as Psychopath

As we saw in the previous chapter, Apple is valued higher than every country in the world bar the top eight. Well, national economies grow slowly, tech companies super quickly. In the last 5 years, the British economy has grown approximately 2.5%, Apple's market capitalisation 300%.[39,40]

The winners of the winner-takes-all race are about to be announced and it is almost certainly the technology companies. And they will have won because:

- They are built on technology that was funded entirely or largely by the taxpayer
- Their product is built from our data which they have tricked us into giving them
- They receive a huge helping hand from the government because of the abnormally light regulation of the industry
- They receive a huge helping hand from the government in terms of loans and massive state contracts
- They do everything they can to avoid paying taxes

- They lobby governments to ensure laws benefit them disproportionately
- They are willing to break the law and pay expensive lawyers to win their case.

All while saying sympathetically, "Trust in us", as did Kaa the python as he wrapped himself around Mowgli's body.

Eric Schmidt was Google's CEO and Executive Chairman for sixteen years and, as such, perhaps more responsible than anyone for their success. He's happy to tell you his ethical framework: "The Google policy on a lot of things is to get right up to the creepy line and not cross it."[41]

The problem, of course, is who decides where that creepy line sits? And if you're someone who spends their life on the edge of that line, isn't your standard likely to be different than a normal person's?

And so the line shifts further and further in the wrong direction.

When Vernon Edwards, part of the team who rescued the football team stranded for 12 days in a Thai cave, told CNN interviewers that Elon Musk's offer of a submarine to aid the rescue was a publicity stunt, Musk, the proud defender of free speech, responded by calling him a paedophile on Twitter. When Peter Thiel, the great libertarian, was outed for being gay by the website Gawker, he secretly funded Hulk Hogan's lawsuit against the website, leading to its bankruptcy.

These are just two of many examples of the tech leaders and their companies adopting bullying as standard practice.

We are building the profile of a psychopath here. Everything in this chapter fits neatly into a description of a psychopath and we shouldn't be surprised. After all, a corporation's goal is to make money and only that, there is no place for empathy.

And the world has never seen such powerful psychopaths.

We are moving into a world where the leviathan is not a government whose intention is to protect its people, the leviathan is a psychopath.

They say we have nothing to fear but they would say that, wouldn't they?

12
What Then Must We Do?

What then must we do?

Such was the question Tolstoy asked when he first saw the squalor of the Muscovite poor. He was shocked by the misery of life in the city slums and the vast contrasts between the masses and the wealthy minority; a society where "the poor come to feed on the crumbs of wealth", where wage-earning and slavery were synonymous, where the rich were protected by the state and the church.[1]

He spent the next four years working amongst them and writing the immensely powerful book of that name that shook the conscience of the Russian people.[2]

What then must we do? It is the moral imperative. It is the question we should always be asking.

Unfortunately, we're usually too busy or too tired or it's too complicated.

- "I know we need to reduce our carbon footprint but I like the thermostat set to 24°C, otherwise I get cold."
- "I know I shouldn't eat animals but I like meat too much to do anything about it now, maybe next year."

- "I know Amazon have a terrible employment rights record but Prime is just so convenient."
- "I know Uber are lowering drivers' wages but they are cheap."

Sometimes it can be an existential imperative. It wasn't for Tolstoy but it was for the poor and it would have been, indeed, for Tolstoy had he lived just four years longer in time for the Soviet revolution.

Are we facing an existential imperative right now? It's certainly possible.

So, we can no longer afford the moral equivocation.

How did these technology companies become so powerful?

Because we helped them.

It was every Google search, every Tweet, every post on Facebook that put them where they are now. Without us, they would be nowhere. It is feasible that our near future will consist of 0.1% of the population enjoying untold wealth and 99.9% of us feeding on their crumbs. And if that's the case, it was down to us, we made it happen.

The good news is that the majority of this book outlines a different future where life is safer, healthier, wealthier and fairer for everyone. This is certainly possible, too.

So, to heed Tolstoy, what then must we do?

Solving the Leviathan Problem

Whatever form it takes, we need to solve the leviathan problem. And AI could, itself, be the answer.

In May 2023, OpenAI announced they were inviting applications for a project called "Democratic Inputs to AI". Remesh, who we met in Chapters Eight and Nine, were one of the applicants.[3]

They surmised that if we can identify the will of humanity, we can then align the AI with that will. Thoughtful readers might think this isn't easy and they'd be totally right.

But with deliberative technology, at a grand scale, it is realistic, incorporating both global diversity and the changing opinions with evolving circumstances.[4]

Currently, the Remesh platform can allow 1000 users conversing at the same time, Polis projects have worked with over 30,000. Moore's Law tells us these numbers will grow exponentially. Who knows, maybe the whole world will finally be able to have their say sometime soon.

And until then, AI-scaled citizens' assembly mini-publics would be far preferable to the whim of a psychopathic billionaire.

Whatever form the leviathan takes, if its constitution requires it to align its decisions with the will of humanity (as identified through mass deliberative technology), we can make sure we will be harnessing its power and resources for the good of all, rather than the few.

The British think-tank Chatham House agree with this approach and they also submitted an application along similar lines, in conjunction with vTaiwan and the AI Objectives Institute.[5] Both Remesh and Chatham House ran successful pilot projects of their technologies.

And Anthropic, the creators of Claude, conducted a similar ethical governance programme of their own. Working with the Collective Intelligence Project, they asked 1000 members of the American public what they would like to see in a chatbot's constitution and then trained Claude on the answers. It resulted in a constitution that was not written by Claude software engineers but a far more representative set of people.[6]

And, remember, the constitution won't just be a charter document but will be code and code is unbreachable law. So, if it's coded this way, it will have to do it. And this can be code that is verified by 3rd parties.

This is not unlike a cooperative organisation and the customers are not just owning it, they are also making the decisions. We saw in Chapter Six how this model can work in business, it may turn out that it will prove the model for governance in general.

So, it is do-able. Whether the leviathan is the state, the technology companies, AI itself or any combination of these, it can be aligned with humanity using AI-driven deliberative technology and, in this way, ensure everyone benefits.

What the Companies Need to Do

Fortunately, there has been some research on what needs to be done to ensure a safe and equitable AI future. Of course, it's nothing like the amount of research conducted on building an *un*safe one. A recent meta-study estimated that 250 times more budget is spent on capability-building than on safety research.[7]

But it is happening. The international network of Artificial Intelligence Safety Institutes has been set up to promote the safe development of AI and universities, tech companies themselves and independent organisations like The Collective Intelligence Project, Control AI, Founders Pledge, The Alan Turing Institute and the Future of Life Institute are all active in this area, working with each other to develop advice and practical steps for tech companies and governments to follow.

Building processes for wider public input to their governance is a common recommendation, whether that's through participatory technology as we've seen above or simply independent boards with real power (beyond Facebook's Oversight Board model).

Other recommendations include:

- Working with more diverse communities to co-create the models
- Systems for detecting and preventing bias
- Transparency of data and of algorithm
- Giving ownership of the data to the individual
- Using opt-in consent for data use rather than the current opt-out mechanism
- Using data fiduciaries, independent professional organisations who manage people's data with a duty of care for that individual
- Paying royalties or a tax on the data use
- Greater interoperability so users can move easily from one platform to another
- Federated learning – where the model sits on the user's computer or phone rather than the cloud, ensuring greater privacy
- Building benevolence into the models so they treat us humans kindly
- Regular testing and monitoring of outcomes
- Using mathematical proofs to ensure algorithmic compliance with specified standards
- Working with hardware that only runs code that uses such mathematical proofs
- Employing tamper detection modules and kill switches.[8,9,10,11]

All perfectly feasible. Put them into place and we can sleep a lot easier at night.

Why They Won't

But it's probably not going to happen. The Asilomar principles are a 23-point framework for ethical AI developed in 2015, that are well-recognised and respected.[12] The ideas exist already, the bigger question is ensuring companies adhere to them.

And companies won't adhere to them. Why? Because the *other* companies don't adhere to them. It is a classic game theory problem. There is an arms race to develop the most powerful commercial AI system, and its winner-takes-all nature does not allow thoughts of society's well-being or safety. Thus, no single company can risk it by themselves and it is a race to the bottom.

Recommendations are not enough, it needs regulation.

If governments step in and make these recommendations legal requirement, with consequences if not met, *all* companies can adhere to them because they are confident all other companies will too.

Indeed, Sam Altman said as much when he testified to a Senate subcommittee, imploring Congress to step in. "I think if this technology goes wrong, it can go quite wrong," he said. "We want to work with the government to prevent that from happening."[13]

But governments won't do this. Why? Because the other governments won't. The same winner-takes-all arms race that characterises the corporate marketplace is also found among governments. America refuses to hobble its companies because it fears China, Russia or any other country won't do the same for theirs. In turn, those countries refuse to do so because they fear America won't.

It requires a global plan but how likely is that?

Well, maybe it's not impossible.

We have successful examples from the past with nuclear and biological weapons and there are already successes within the world of AI. The Bletchley Declaration (November 2023) was signed by 28 countries including the US, China and the EU and the United Nations General Assembly Resolution on AI (2023-2024) was passed with 123 co-sponsors, including China and Russia.[14]

It is often joked only an alien attack could really get the world to work alongside each other. But artificial intelligence *is* a kind of alien. Maybe, just maybe, governments will realise that this is a threat that requires them to collaborate in order to survive.

After all, leviathans like to survive too.

The current prevailing leviathan is the government but they are at risk of losing their status to something more powerful even than them. Self-preservation, rather than the benefit of humanity, might be the cause that impels them to act for the benefit of humanity.

Five Years to Save the World but I'm Optimistic!

Tony Czarnecki, Managing Partner at Sustensis, futurist and author of six books on the topic.

"We may have AGI sometime this year but if we said five years, by the end of the decade, it's absolutely a given that it will happen. And once we have various AGIs, think about how difficult it will be to dethrone these guys. So we have to act before that. This is the reality we have to face.

But there is a window where it is possible.

I'm suggesting that we create a joint venture between all the AI companies. So, for instance, Google separates out DeepMind,

Musk separates xAI, Meta, its AI division, and so on. And they create a joint venture and all companies split the benefit.

And they would create one AI and this would be so powerful that it could detect and manage any other AI that was created. And this would be safer for the world straight away.

Now, this would need to be imposed by law and it would need countries to work together to do it. But the motivation is that every government, irrespective of their political views, has an interest that the state retains control over what its citizens and its companies do.

In my view, this is doable. I look at the example of the Global Minimum Tax agreement, where no country can have a corporate tax lower than 15%. That's an international agreement that 136 countries signed up to so such profound changes are possible.

I am optimistic here. We have already done something important because we've created a pattern of AI Safety Summits which now happen every six months in different countries.

And you don't have to invent anything new. There is already the Global Partnership on AI, which is essentially part of the OECD. This is broadly supported by 50 countries or more, which excludes India and China but includes Brazil.

I'm almost certain India would join and I would invite China although I doubt it would answer but Baidu might join.

And we are talking about creating a critical mass. Once you have 50 or 60 members there will be an avalanche effect and other countries would join too. China would probably stay outside but it might be affiliated.

And the initial role should be non-political but actually I think this would be the beginning of a de facto world government.

Now, for the next four years we have Trump as president and he is obviously against regulation. But Elon Musk is a double-edged

> sword. On one hand, he's an ultra-libertarian, also against regulation.
>
> But on the other hand, he's obsessed by saving humans. All his businesses are about it. Tesla, xAI, SpaceX, he's genuinely concerned about saving humans, even if some of the ideas are weird.
>
> So from that point of view, again, I am optimistic."

What Can Governments Do?

In 1984, AT&T had a market capitalisation of $150bn (inflation-adjusted to today's money) and Ronald Reagan's administration deemed this too big and its regional operating companies were divested and split into seven "Baby Bells".[15]

How tiny this seems in comparison to today's internet giants. So there are already plenty of existing anti-trust regulations which should be enforced to constrain their powers. And, if they aren't sufficient, newer laws should be introduced.

Moreover, these companies have become so important to the infrastructure of the modern world that they have become public utilities and public utilities, even if privately owned, should have some accountability to the people.

Water, for example, should be clean and available for everyone in the country. And people can pay for it and companies can earn money from making it available but prices should be reasonable and services to a certain standard. Likewise, energy and health and education and the law.

Well, likewise too, AI. The airline industry, finance, automobiles, pharmaceuticals are regulated, why should technology be treated with such a generous hand?

There needs to be a dedicated regulatory body to oversee the industry, one with teeth, one with resources to match private sector capabilities, one with an AI that is better than any corporate AI so that it can evaluate them adequately and check for compliance.

It would be empowered to enforce laws, conduct mandatory audits, and impose significant penalties on companies that violate regulations, even sanctioning the leadership team.

It would need to be proactive and have the ability to move quickly. It should work with legislators to "red team" new laws to see how companies will try to get around them and, once passed, it should monitor the companies' behaviour and be ready to update quickly.

And we also need a legal patch system, exactly like software updates, because the field moves so fast that legislation is rapidly outdated.

Guidelines for fairness, safety, accountability, and transparency in the development and deployment of algorithms should be built, along with guidelines for the individual's digital rights. Companies would be required to adhere to these standards and undergo regular audits to ensure compliance.

And, of course, as you were thinking already, all guidelines would be developed though deliberative means involving the wider communities.

If we put these provisions into place, I think we'd be ok.

We Have to Be More Critical of the AI

Melissa Terras, Professor of Digital Cultural Heritage, University of Edinburgh, ex-Turing Fellow at The Alan Turing Institute.

"I'm acutely aware of how toxic most of the AI major providers are. They make all the promises under the sun about how AI is going to be wonderful, doing "cooperative-washing" about how this is for the benefit of humanity, blah, blah, blah. But, actually, it is just to capture the market in AI, like Starbucks did with coffee shops, like Uber did with taxis.

They're trying to flush out all the competition, buying up small firms, shutting down others so that we'll come to a stage where we can't remember how to sit down in front of a computer and write anything because we're so used to AI, and then we'll have to pay more money.

We spent 25 years making a wonderful internet, what a time to be alive, to have this encyclopedia that you can walk about with. But we've sleep-walked into the complete ruining of our information environment. And it was the same process, it always starts with the greenwashing, the "whatever washing". They promised, "Oh, this is the democratisation of information. It's the democratisation of science. The democratisation of free speech." But ultimately, it's just so that they can land grab one industry after another. And it's accelerating with AI.

So, I'm asking people to be more critical. I would urge people to automatically distrust AI until it can prove that it is trustworthy. I do think that there will be ways in which AI can help the area you're in but we should be asking critical questions of any tool we're using. Step back and think, "Wait a minute, do we really need an AI here? Who has programmed it? Why are they providing the tool? Where do they sit legally? Are they profit-making? If so, are the profits put back into the community or are the profits given to shareholders?" And this is just the beginning.

And it's a power grab as much as it is a market grab. We need to make sure that we are not ceding our power to AI and we're not ceding the power of our communities to AI. And we're not ceding the power of our elected representatives and our governments to an AI that has yet to prove it can be trusted.

We need to ask, "How can I persuade Google? How can I communicate to Google that they should slow down or something?"

I've just written a paper, it's still in draft, about cooperatives in AI and how cooperatives would be a better means of governance

> for AI. I am part of an AI cooperative that I helped establish. We have about 250 co-owners and we work with major libraries and archives and similar organisations. As far as I know, we're the first one in the world.
>
> We need to raise our voice."

It's Our Clicks That Count

But we can't just hope the tech companies and governments do what we'd love them to do, how often has that happened in the past? We need to take responsibility for the change ourselves.

The tech company threat has been looming large for a long time now and we've avoided thinking about it, largely, I'm sure, because we're busy and have other issues that seem more pressing. But we can't avoid it any more. It has moved from the box marked "important but not urgent" to the one labelled "existentially important and critically urgent".

We may not have time to read the new 800-page tome from Shoshanna Zuboff but we should still keep up to date with what is happening in the tech world and its impact on society.

Remember, it's our clicks that make the difference so we can exercise our consumer power by avoiding the tech monopolies like Amazon, Meta, Google, Apple and others. I appreciate this is tantamount to social suicide and, practically impossible but the less you feed them, the less powerful they will grow.

There are alternatives that are open-source or operate by more ethical values. Browsers like Brave, search engines like DuckDuckGo and Startpage and phones like the Fairphone or the de-Googled e operating system are all better choices than the tech giants.

There are even alternatives to ChatGPT, Gemini and Claude. Mistral is an open-source model that can run on your phone,

PrivateGPT is built on ChatGPT architecture but runs on its own cloud server and Petals runs on a distributed network like blockchain.

And always set your privacy settings to a maximum so that a minimum of your data is sucked up and sold to the highest bidder to help them take more money from your bank account.

We can be active in other ways too.

We can contact our elected representatives about our concerns, we can write to our local newspaper, we can even use social media (ahem!).

We can talk about it with our friends to spread the conversation, we can participate in deliberative decision-making or find out more about it from organisations like Involve. We can write to the tech company (ha-ha, I know!), we can complain to data protection agencies, we can support advocacy groups like the Electronic Frontier Foundation, we can join peaceful protests and sign petitions and many other things, limited only by our imagination.

We can even ask ChatGPT for some more ideas!

Serbian pro-democracy agitator Sroja Popovic's "Blueprint for Revolution"[16] is a great toolkit for activism. In fact, it's even just a fun way to live your life.

He lists all kinds of ways to protest and bring about change, including rock concerts, stand-up comedy gigs, rice pudding parties and taxi go slows. He says get your community involved, get your priest involved, get the shops involved, take your tv for a walk. He recommends laughtivism, wear red, sit down, write on thousands of ping-pong balls and let them loose in town. Hide mini usb speakers playing revolutionary songs in trash cans, stand in front of a tank, give flowers to the police.

It's a lot more fun than pitch forks and burning torches and it's important to have fun as we change the world.

John Lennon said, "It will be ok in the end. If it's not ok, it's not the end."

We need to stand up to dictators, we need to stand up to psychopathic billionaires, we need to stand up to tech companies.

And we can.

And if we do, the powers of AI can be brought to bear for the benefit of everyone and we really can build a world where everyone is better off in every possible way.

AI is scary and exciting in equal measure.

But which outcome materialises is up to us.

Afterword

I am terrified.

If Douglas Hofstadter can say it, I can too.

Well, on Mondays, Wednesdays and Fridays anyway. On Tuesdays, Thursdays and Saturdays I'm totally excited about the amazing things the future will bring.

Sundays, I take a day off from thinking about it because it's so exhausting.

But "it is our duty, not to prophesy evil but, rather, to fight for a better world."[1] So, let's fight for a better world.

Audrey Tang says, "Don't protest, demonstrate". It's a clever phrase and it's right.

We can't really complain about the state of things because the state of things is, partly at least, because of us.

If we're in a traffic jam, we can't complain about it, we are the traffic. We can't complain about climate change because it was our heating and our travel that's caused it. We can't complain about the technology companies ruling the world because it was our clicks and purchases that enabled their drive for power, their land grab.

My brother worked as a motorcycle instructor and his catchphrase was "You're the only person in charge of your safety". Instead of complaining, we need to do something about it instead. The world is being built as we speak, let's build it the way we want.

Be the example you'd like to see. If you want the world to be nicer, be nice. If you want the world to stop arguing, don't argue.

If you want to prevent climate change, turn the heating down, put on a jumper, travel less, go vegan. If you don't want the AI companies to rule the world, don't buy from Amazon, don't use Google search.

And, most of all be happy, no matter what the outcome. Joy is our best resistance, joy the best form of activism. As we saw in Chapter One, the world is a much better place than ever before but we don't let ourselves enjoy that. My worry is that AI will build the world we've always dreamt of and we'll still complain!

"Think global, act local", said the hippies and they were right. Think global and change the world, one person at a time. Think global and be happy, one person at a time. Think global and end conflict, one person at a time.

Moore's Law wasn't just a graph, it was a roadmap, a self-fulfilling prophecy. "The End of Conflict" could be too.

It's up to us.

References

Introduction

1. Hofstadter, D (1999), "Gödel, Escher, Bach: An Eternal Golden Braid", (Basic Books), ISBN 9780465026562
2. Mitchell, M (2020), "Artificial Intelligence: A Guide for Thinking Humans", (Pelican), ISBN 9780241404836
3. Santayana, G (1922), "Soliloquies in England" (C. Scribner's Sons),https://archive.org/details/soliloquiesineng00santrich/page/n1/mode/2up
4. Kurzweil, R (2005), "The Singularity is Near: When Humans Transcend Biology", (Gerald Duckworth), ISBN 0715635611
5. Loudon I. Deaths in childbed from the eighteenth century to 1935. Med Hist. 1986 Jan;30(1):1-41
6. https://data.worldbank.org/indicator/SH.STA.MMRT?locations=FI-VE&year_high_desc=false

Chapter One

1. Goodall, J. (1986). The Chimpanzees of Gombe: Patterns of Behavior. The Belknap Press of Harvard University Press. pp. 503–514. ISBN 9780674116498.
2. Nowak, M. (2011), Supercooperators: Altruism, Evolution, and Why We Need Each Other to Succeed (The Free Press), ISBN 9781439100189
3. Sapolsky, R. (2018) Behave: The bestselling exploration of why humans behave as they do (Vintage), 9780099575061
4. Hölldobler, B. and Wilson, E.O (1994), "Journey To The Ants – A Story Of Scientific Exploration" (Harvard University Press), 9780674485259

5. Dugatkin, L.A. (2007). "Inclusive fitness theory from Darwin to Hamilton". Genetics. 176 (3): 1375–80. doi:10.1093/genetics/176.3.1375. PMC 1931543. PMID 17641209.
6. Sagan, Lynn (1967). "On the origin of mitosing cells". Journal of Theoretical Biology. 14 (3): 225–274
7. Hardin, G (1968). "The Tragedy of the Commons". Science. 162 (3859): 1243–1248. Bibcode:1968Sci...162.1243H. doi:10.1126/science.162.3859.1243. PMID 5699198
8. Nowak, M (2011)
9. Fehr E, Gächter S. Altruistic punishment in humans. Nature. 2002 Jan 10;415(6868):137-40. doi: 10.1038/415137a. PMID: 11805825.
10. Rand DG, Dreber A, Ellingsen T, Fudenberg D, Nowak MA. Positive interactions promote public cooperation. Science. 2009 Sep 4;325(5945):1272-5. doi: 10.1126/science.1177418. PMID: 19729661; PMCID: PMC2875121.
11. "NY subway 'hero' saves teenager" BBC News Online. January 4, 2007. news.bbc.co.uk/1/hi/world/Americas/6231971.stm
12. Zimbardo, Philip G., et al. "The Stanford prison experiment." (1971)
13. The Stanford Prison Experiment, https://www.imdb.com/title/tt0420293/
14. Zimbardo, P (2007), The Lucifer Effect: Understanding How Good People Turn Evil (Random House) 9781400064113
15. "Modern History Sourcebook: Rudolf Hoess, Commandant of Auschwitz: Testimony at Nuremberg, 1946". Fordham University
16. Piper, Franciszek (2000b). Długoborski, Wacław; Piper, Franciszek (eds.). Auschwitz, 1940–1945. Central Issues in the History of the Camp. Vol. III: Mass Murder. Oświęcim: Auschwitz-Birkenau State Museum. ISBN 9788385047872.
17. Höß, Rudolph (1959). Commandant of Auschwitz: The Autobiography of Rudolf Höß. Translated by FitzGibbon, Constantine. Cleveland OH: World Publishing Company.
18. https://www.heroicimagination.org/
19. Pinker, S (2011) The Better Angels of Our Nature, (Penguin) 9780141034645

20. Whigham, Thomas L. (2002). The Paraguayan War: Causes and Early Conduct. Vol. 1. Lincoln: University of Nebraska Press. ISBN 9780803247864.
21. White, M (2011) Atrocities: The 100 Deadliest Episodes in Human History (W.W. Norton) ASIN: B005LW5JMQ
22. Pinker, S (2018), Enlightenment Now, (Penguin) ISBN 9780141979090
23. Max Roser and Hannah Ritchie, "Homicides", Our World In Data, December 2019, www.ourworldindata.org/homicides
24. Eisner, M (2003), Long-Term Historical Trends in Violent Crime. Crime & Justice, 30, pp 83-142
25. Pinker, S (2011)
26. Office for National Statistics (ONS), released 24 July 2024, ONS website, statistical bulletin, Crime in England and Wales: year ending March 2024
27. Aamodt, M.G. (2016), "Serial Killer Statistics", http://maamodt.asp.radford.edu/serial killer information center/project description.htm
28. Demandt, A (1984) Der Fall Roms. Die Auflösung des römischen Reiches im Urteil der Nachwelt. (C. H. Beck) ISBN 3-406-09598-4.
29. Turchin, P.; Brennan, R.; Currie, T.; Feeney, K.; Francois, P.; Hoyer, D., et al. (2015). Seshat: The Global History Databank. Cliodynamics, 6(1) https://escholarship.org/uc/item/9qx38718
30. Turchin, P (2016) Ultra Society: How 10,000 years of war made humans the greatest cooperators on earth (Beresta Books) 9780996139519
31. Keegan, J (1993) A History of Warfare (Pimlico), ISBN 0712698507
32. Rosling, H (2018) Factfulness: 10 reasons we're wrong about and why things are better than you think (Sceptre) 9781473637498
33. https://www.start.umd.edu/gtd/about/
34. https://www.statista.com/chart/6024/causes-of-death-in-the-us/
35. Pinker, S (2018)
36. Katsuyama, M., Higo, E., Miyamoto, M. et al. Development of prevention strategies against bath-related deaths based on

epidemiological surveys of inquest records in Kagoshima Prefecture. Sci Rep 13, 2277 (2023).
37. Kahneman, D (2011), Thinking, Fast and Slow (Farrar, Straus and Giroux) 9780374275631
38. Rosling, H (2018)
39. Arnold Barnett (2020) Aviation Safety: A Whole New World?. Transportation Science 54(1):84-96.
40. Orwell, G (2003). Shooting an Elephant and Other Essays (Penguin Classics) ISBN 9780141187396
41. de Sola Pool, I and Kochen, M (1978/79) "Contacts and Influence," Social Networks 1
42. Milgram, Stanley (May 1967). "The Small World Problem". Psychology Today.
43. Rankin, A and Philip, P (1969) "An Epidemic of Laughing in the Bukoba District of Tanganyika" Central African Journal of Medicine 9
44. Christakis, N and Fowler, J (2010) "Connected" (HarperPress) ISBN 9780007347438
45. Blackmore, S (1999) "The Meme Machine", (Oxford University Press) ISBN 9780192862129
46. Hill, Alison L., et al. "Emotions as infectious diseases in a large social network: the SISa model." Proceedings of the Royal Society B: Biological Sciences 277.1701 (2010): 3827-3835.
47. Christakis NA, Fowler JH (2007) The spread of obesity in a large social network over 32 years. N Engl J Med 357:370–379.
48. Fowler JH, Christakis NA (2008) The dynamic spread of happiness in a large social network. BMJ 337:a2338.
49. Singh J (2005) Collaborative networks as determinants of knowledge diffusion patterns. Manage Sci 51:756–770.
50. Fowler, James H.; Christakis, Nicholas A. (2010-03-23). "Cooperative behavior cascades in human social networks". Proceedings of the National Academy of Sciences. 107 (12): 5334–5338.
51. Milgram, S (1967)
52. Shirado, Hirokazu, and Nicholas A. Christakis. "Network engineering using autonomous agents increases cooperation in human groups." Iscience 23.9 (2020).
53. Shirado, H., Hou, Y.TY. & Jung, M.F. Stingy bots can improve human welfare in experimental sharing networks. Sci Rep 13, 17957 (2023)

54. Traeger, Margaret L., et al. "Vulnerable robots positively shape human conversational dynamics in a human–robot team." Proceedings of the National Academy of Sciences 117.12 (2020)
55. Rahwan, Iyad, et al. "Machine behaviour." Nature 568.7753 (2019): 477-486
56. https://www.weforum.org/agenda/2015/10/what-can-governments-do-to-prevent-slavery/

Chapter Two

1. Horton, S (2016) "The Leader's Guide to Negotiation: How to Use Soft Skills to Get Hard Results" (FT Press) ISBN 9781292112800
2. Horton, S (2022) "Change Their Mind: 6 Steps to Persuade Anyone, Anytime" (Pearson) ISBN 9781292406794
3. Fisher, R et al (1083) "Getting to Yes: Negotiating Agreement Without Giving In" (Penguin) ISBN 9780140005343

Chapter Three

1. https://www.economicsandpeace.org/wp-content/uploads/2024/06/GPI-2024-web.pdf
2. "World Economic Outlook Database, April 2024", International Monetary Fund. 16 April 2024
3. https://worldhappiness.report/ed/2024/happiness-and-age-summary/
4. https://www.transparency.org/en/cpi/2023
5. Kahneman, D (2012) "Thinking, Fast and Slow" (Penguin) ISBN 9780141033570
6. Baltiansky, D and Ames, D (2024) "Opponent or Partner: Do Negotiation Counterpart Labels Matter?", Academy of Management Annual Proceedings 2024
7. Gallwey, T (1976) "The Inner Game of Tennis" (Random House) 9780394400433
8. Osgood, C. E. (1962). An alternative to war or surrender. Urbana: University of Illinois Press.
9. Bidgood, S. (2021). Just GRIT and Bear It: A Cold War Approach to Future US-Russia Arms Control. The International Spectator, 56(1), 1–19.

10. Rosenberg, Marshall B. (2003). Nonviolent Communication: A Language of Life (2nd ed.). (PuddleDancer Press) ISBN 9781892005038
11. https://www.wired.com/2016/03/two-moves-alphago-lee-sedol-redefined-future/
12. https://en.wikipedia.org/wiki/Lee_Sedol
13. Park, J et al (2024) "Generative Agent Simulations of 1,000 People", https://arxiv.org/abs/2411.10109

Chapter Four

1. Airplane II: The Sequel. Directed by Ken Finkleman, Paramount Pictures, 1982.
2. Dyson FJ, Colloquium at NASA's Goddard Space Flight Center, 2000.
3. Lawler, E. L. (1985). The Travelling Salesman Problem: A Guided Tour of Combinatorial Optimization John Wiley & sons. ISBN 9780471904137.
4. Atsushi Tero et al. Rules for Biologically Inspired Adaptive Network Design. Science 327, 439-442 (2010).
5. Bolhuis JJ, Tattersall I, Chomsky N, Berwick RC (2014) How Could Language Have Evolved? PLoS Biol 12(8): e1001934.
6. Everett, Daniel L. (August 2005). "Cultural Constraints on Grammar and Cognition in Pirahã: Another Look at the Design Features of Human Language". Current Anthropology. 46 (4): 621–646.
7. Fisher, S (2001) "A History of Writing" (Reaktion Books) ISBN 9781789143492
8. Wagner, S. (2000) "A Well-Known Stranger". In Gutenberg: Man of the Millennium. (City of Mainz)
9. Swift, J (1710) The Examiner, Number 15, (John Morphew)
10. Paul, J (2024) "Thomas More: A Life" (Penguin)
11. Eisenstein, E (2011), "Divine Art, Infernal Machine: The Reception of Printing in the West from First Impressions to the Sense of an Ending" University of Pennsylvania Press 9780812242805
12. Freeth, T et al. (2006) "Decoding the ancient Greek astronomical calculator known as the Antikythera Mechanism" Nature. 444 (7119): 587–91

13. Efstathiou, K (2018) "Celestial Gearbox: Oldest Known Computer is a Mechanism Designed to Calculate the Location of the Sun, Moon, and Planets". Mechanical Engineering. 140 (9)
14. Pickover, C, (2019) "Artificial Intelligence: From Mediaeval Robots to Neural Networks" (Sterling Publishing)
15. Flippo, Hyde. "Konrad Zuse: The first programmable, digital computer". german-way.com. The German Way & More.
16. https://www.tnmoc.org/colossus, The National Museum of Computing
17. Weik, Martin H. (December 1955). Ballistic Research Laboratories Report No. 971: A Survey of Domestic Electronic Digital Computing Systems Abordeen Proving Ground, MD: United States Department of Commerce Office of Technical Services
18. Gordon E. Moore, "Cramming More Components onto Integrated Circuits," Electronics, pp. 114–117, April 19, 1965
19. Wilson, J (1985), "The New Venturers: Inside the High Stakes World of Venture Capital" (Addison Wesley) ISBN 9780201096811
20. Mallaby S, (2022), "The Power Law", Penguin Random House ISBN 9780241356524
21. Professor Noah Wardrip-Fruin https://grandtextauto.soe.ucsc.edu/2005/08/01/christopher-strachey-first-digital-artist/
22. "The Imitation Game", Morten Tyldum 2014
23. A. M. Turing. 'Computing Machinery and Intelligence'. Mind, 49, 1950
24. https://videogamehistorian.wordpress.com/2014/01/22/the-priesthood-at-play-computer-games-in-the-1950s/
25. https://www.thoregister.com/2012/06/26/kasparov_v_turing/
26. Wooldridge, M (2021) "The Road to Conscious Machines" (Penguin Random House) ISBN 9780241333914
27. Hemingway, E (1926) "The Sun Also Rises" (Charles Scribner's Sons) ISBN
28. Kurzweil, R (2005) "The Singularity Is Near" (Penguin) ISBN 0670033847
29. https://en.wikipedia.org/wiki/Nuance_Communications
30. https://www.wired.com/2014/10/future-of-artificial-intelligence/
31. https://www.chessgames.com/perl/chess.pl?pid=15940&pid2=13728

32. https://www.chessgames.com/perl/chesscollection?cid=1014770
33. https://www.ibm.com/history/watson-jeopardy
34. https://www.youtube.com/watch?v=WXuK6gekU1Y
35. Brewin, K (2024) "God-like: a 500 year history of Artificial Intelligence in myths, machines, monsters." (Vaux Books) ISBN 9780993562877
36. Knight, Will. "OpenAI's CEO Says the Age of Giant AI Models Is Already Over". Wired.
37. https://www.cnbc.com/2024/02/09/openai-ceo-sam-altman-reportedly-seeking-trillions-of-dollars-for-ai-chip-project.html
38. https://www.telegraph.co.uk/finance/property/12064158/Britain-for-sale-8-trillion-or-nearest-offer.html
39. Gottlieb, A (2016) "The Dream of Enlightenment: The Rise of Modern Philosophy" (Allen Lane) ISBN 9780713995442
40. https://blogs.bath.ac.uk/pvc-research/2024/07/24/the-rise-of-ai-generated-research-grant-funding-applications/
41. https://blog.google/products/gemini/google-gemini-deep-research/
42. Skarlinski, M et al (2024), "Language agents achieve superhuman synthesis of scientific knowledge", https://arxiv.org/abs/2409.1374
43. Toner-Rodgers, A., 2024. Artificial intelligence, scientific discovery, and product innovation. arXiv preprint arXiv:2412.17866.
44. https://www.nytimes.com/2024/12/23/science/ai-hallucinations-science.html
45. Lu, C. et al (2024) "The AI Scientist: Towards fully automated open-ended scientific discovery." arXiv preprint arXiv:2408.06292.
46. Larsen, P. and Von Ins, M., 2010. The rate of growth in scientific publication and the decline in coverage provided by Science Citation Index. Scientometrics, 84(3), pp.575-603.
47. Robertson, R (2020) "The Enlightenment: The Pursuit of Happiness 1680-1790" (Penguin) ISBN 9780141979403
48. Robertson, J (2005), "The Case For the Enlightenment: Scotland and Naples 1680–1760" (Cambridge University Press) ISBN 9780521847872
49. Robertson, R (2020)
50. Wooldridge, M (2021)

51. https://en.wikipedia.org/wiki/List_of_chess_players_by_peak_FIDE_rating

Chapter Five

1. Horton, S (2016), "The Leader's Guide to Negotiation" (FT Press), ISBN 9781292112800
2. Rana, Y (2024) "When AI Joins the Table: How Large Language Models Transform Negotiations" https://ssrn.com/abstract=5049248
3. https://platform.openai.com/docs/guides/prompt-engineering
4. https://humantic.ai/product/personallly-ai assistant
5. Horton, S (2016)
6. Mitchell, G (1999) "Making Peace" (William Heinemann) ISBN 9780434007554
7. Monbiot, B (2024) "Can your "digital twin" be trustworthy?, TEDxCornell www.youtube.com/watch?v=0MZSRfVrO78
8. https://www.consumerreports.org/electronics/privacy/each-facebook-user-is-monitored-by-thousands-of-companies-a5824207467/
9. Schelling, T (1978) "Micromotives and Macrobehaviour" (W. W. Norton & Company) ISBN 9780393090093

Chapter Six

1. Managing conflict in the modern workplace, CIPD January 2020
2. Estimating the costs of workplace conflict, CIPD May 2021
3. CIPD (2020)
4. Traub, B et al, Evaluating the Impact of Artificial Intelligence Versus Human Management on Modifying Workplace Behavior (February 2024) https://ssrn.com/abstract=4739430
5. https://www.bbc.co.uk/news/articles/c03lgz2zrg1o
6. https://www.mondragon-corporation.com/urtekotx-ostena//1_carta.php?lang=en
7. https://www.dfamilk.com/newsroom/press-center/press-center-blog/march-2023/dfa-reports-2022-financial-results

8. Krznaric, R (2024) "History for Tomorrow: Inspiration from the Past for the Future of Humanity" (WH Allen) ISBN 9780753559628
9. Stanford, L (1887) "Co-operation of Labor," New York Tribune, May 4, 1887.
10. Bancroft, H (1952) "History of the Life of Leland Stanford" (Biobooks)
11. https://www.langsikt.no/en/publikasjoner/framtidspanelet---hva-tenker-folk-om-norges-rikdom
12. Mckinsey & Co (2024) "What Are AI Guardrails?" (Mckinsey Explainers) November 14 2024
13. https://www.linkedin.com/posts/pactum-ai_martin-rand-of-pactum-ai-on-5-things-you-activity-7153817045644591105-Nj2m/
14. Understanding Artificial Intelligence At Pactum (October 2023) https://resources.pactum.com/understanding-artificial-intelligence-at-pactum?hsLang=en
15. https://pactum.com/product/
16. Susskind, D (2020) "A World Without Work", (Penguin) ISBN 9780141986807

Chapter Seven

1. Hershey, Tina Batra; Burke, Donald (February 2018). "Pioneers in Computerized Legal Research: The Story of the Pittsburgh System". Pittsburgh Journal of Technology Law and Policy. 18. Pittsburgh: University of Pittsburgh Press: 29–39
2. Bourne, Charles P.; Hahn, Trudi Bellardo (2003). A History of Online Information Services, 1963-1976. Cambridge, Massachusetts: The MIT Press. p. 301. ISBN 9780262025386
3. Susskind, R (2008) "The End of Lawyers? Rethinking the Nature of Legal Services" (Oxford University Press) ISBN 9780199541720
4. Susskind, R (2013) "Tomorrow's Lawyers: An Introduction to Your Future" (Oxford University Press) ISBN 9780199668069
5. Robins, W.R. "Automated Legal Information Retrieval" (1986) 5 Houston Law Review 691
6. Open AI (2023) GPT-4 Technical Report, https://cdn.openai.com/papers/gpt-4.pdf

7. https://www.nytimes.com/2023/05/27/nyregion/avianca-airline-lawsuit-chatgpt.html
8. https://casetext.com/blog/ethical-use-ai-legal-2/
9. Brofman, C (2008) "Settled! The Online Dispute Revolution" Lexicomm Group ISBN 9780980197204
10. Cohen, A (2002) "The Perfect Store: Inside eBay" (Piatkus) ISBN 9780749923495
11. https://www.nytimes.com/2019/03/12/technology/uber-drivers-lawsuit-settle.html
12. https://www.ft.com/content/dd98b94e-ac62-11e9-8030-530adfa879c2
13. https://www.statista.com/statistics/941275/litigation-spending-united-states/
14. https://unlock.veritone.com/aiware-ediscovery-TCPA-case-study
15. Hadfield, G "The Price of Law: How the Market for Lawyers Distorts the Justice System" (2000) 98 Michigan Law Review 4 900
16. https://www.lawnext.com/2006/06/judges-order-rock-papor-scissors.html
17. https://www.lawgazette.co.uk/practice/robot-beats-human-lawyers-in-outcomes-challenge/5063471.article
18. Holmes, O.W. "The Path of the Law" (1897) 10 Harvard Law Review 457
19. https://www.dw.com/en/how-chinas-ai-is-automating-the-legal-system/a-64465980
20. Casaleggio, D (2024) "AI Democracy: How Artificial Intelligence will rewrite Politics and Society" Kindle Edition
21. Rhode, D "Legal Ethics in an Adversary System: The Persistent Questions" (2006) 34:3 Hofstra Law Review 641
22. https://committees.parliament.uk/committee/102/justice-committee/news/156934/legal-aid-needs-urgent-reform-to-secure-fairness-of-the-justice-system/
23. Morgan, R "The 'Point of Law' Approach", (1962) 3:1 Modern Uses of Logic in Law 44
24. Katz, D et al (2021) "Legal Informatics" (Cambridge University Press) ISBN 1107142725
25. Arewa, O "Open Access in a Closed Universe: Lexis, Westlaw, Law Schools and the Legal Information Market" (2006) 10-4 Lewis & Clark Law Review 797

26. Fuller, L (1964) "The Morality of Law" (Yale University Press) ISBN 9780300010701
27. https://law.stanford.edu/stanford-lawyer/articles/artificial-intelligence-and-the-law/
28. Laurence, Helen; William Miller (2000). Academic research on the Internet: options for scholars and libraries. Routledge ISBN 0-7890-1177-8
29. https://hls.harvard.edu/today/caselaw-access-project-conference-marks-full-release-of-digitized-decisions/
30. https://transparencyproject.org.uk/all-about-bailii-part-one-what-it-is-and-where-it-came-from/
31. https://www.bailii.org/bailii/timeline/#More2009
32. https://www.technologyslegaledge.com/2021/02/bailii-grants-oxford-university-unprecedented-access-to-case-data-for-ai-analysis-in-historic-agreement/
33. Pirie, F (2021) "The Rule of Laws: A 4000 Year Quest to Order the World" (Profile Books) 9781788163026
34. https://www.theatlantic.com/international/archive/2017/03/martin-mcguinness-ian-paisley/520257/
35. https://justiceinnovation.law.stanford.edu/projects/ai-access-to-justice/tasks/

Chapter Eight

1. Aṅguttara Nikāya 5.198
2. https://about.nextdoor.com/kindness/
3. Saltz, E et al (2024) "Re-Ranking News Comments by Constructiveness and Curiosity Significantly Increases Perceived Respect, Trustworthiness, and Interest", https://arxiv.org/abs/2404.05429
4. https://mashable.com/article/elon-musk-community-notes
5. https://community-notes-leaderboard.com/
6. https://www.nytimes.com/2024/09/27/technology/elon-musk-x-posts.html
7. https://www.youtube.com/watch?v=bF6rer0I1FE
8. Murthy, V (2023) "Our Epidemic of Loneliness and Isolation The U.S. Surgeon General's Advisory on the Healing Effects of Social Connection and Community"
9. Case, A and Deaton, A, (2020), "Deaths of Despair and the Future of Capitalism", Princeton University Press

10. https://www.documentcloud.org/documents/24080032-state-ags-v-meta
11. 1793, "Collection Générale des Décrets Rendus par la Convention Nationale, Date: May 8, 1793 (Chez Baudouin, Imprimeur de la Convention Nationale)
12. Lee, S (1962 Aug), Amazing Fantasy #15 "Spider-Man!" (Marvel Comics)
13. "The Strange Disappearance of Cooperation in America," by Peter Turchin, Social Evolution Forum (June 21, 2013)
14. https://www.ucl.ac.uk/judicial-institute/sites/judicial-institute/files/are_juries_fair.pdf
15. Crick, B (1962) "In Defence of Politics", Weidenfeld & Nicolson
16. Barber, M., McCarty, N., Mansbridge, J., & Martin, C. J. (2015). Causes and consequences of polarization. Political negotiation: A handbook, 37, 39-43.
17. https://citizensassembly.ie/wp-content/uploads/2023/02/FirstReport_EIGHTAMENDMENT.pdf
18. "Referendum Results 1937–2018" (PDF). Department of Housing, Planning and Local Government. September 2018. p. 96
19. https://www.buergerrat.de/en/news/germany-is-world-champion-of-citizens-assemblies/
20. https://www.buergerrat.de/en/news/parties-on-citizens-assemblies/
21. OECD Deliberative Democracy Database (2023)
22. Enabling National Initiatives to Take Democracy Beyond Elections, A Project of the UN Democracy Fund & the newDemocracy Foundation
23. Rawls, J (1971) "A Theory of Justice" Belknap Press
24. https://venturebeat.com/ai/researchers-say-the-whiteness-of-ai-in-pop-culture-erases-people-of-color/
25. https://www.propublica.org/article/how-we-analyzed-the-compas-recidivism-algorithm
26. https://proceedings.mlr.press/v81/buolamwini18a/buolamwini18a.pdf
27. https://law.stanford.edu/2024/03/19/slss-julian-nyarko-on-why-large-language-models-like-chatgpt-treat-black-and-white-sounding-names-differently/
28. Guillory, D "Combating Anti-Blackness in the AI Community", University of California - Berkeley
29. https://www.indigenous-ai.net/

30. https://venturebeat.com/ai/pymetrics-open-sources-audit-ai-an-algorithm-bias-detection-tool/
31. https://pair-code.github.io/what-if-tool/ai-fairness.html
32. https://aif360.res.ibm.com/
33. https://www.arnoldventures.org/stories/could-ai-help-make-prosecutors-decisions-race-blind-a-q-a-with-alex-chohlas-wood
34. https://medium.com/design-ibm/the-origins-of-bias-and-how-ai-might-be-our-answer-to-ending-it-acc3610d6354
35. https://d4bl.org/
36. D'Ignazio, C & Klein, L (2023) "Data Feminism" MIT Press
37. https://pubs.geoscienceworld.org/gsa/books/edited-volume/492/chapter-abstract/3800319/Volcanic-winter-in-the-Garden-of-Eden-The-Toba?redirectedFrom=fulltext
38. https://www.planetaryhealthcheck.org/storyblokcdn/f/301438/x/a4efc3f6d5/planetaryhealthcheck2024_report.pdf
39. Andermann, T., Faurby, S., Turvey, S. T., Antonelli, A. & Silvestro, D. The past and future human impact on mammalian diversity. Sci. Adv. 6, eabb2313 (2020).
40. IOC-UNESCO. 2024. State of the Ocean Report. Paris, IOC-UNESCO. (IOC Technical Series, 190)
41. https://www.wwf.org.uk/sites/default/files/2024-10/living-planet-report-2024.pdf
42. Strubell, E, Ganesh, A, McCallum, A (2019) "Energy and Policy Considerations for Deep Learning in {NLP}" Proceedings of the 57th Annual Meeting of the Association for Computational Linguistics
43. Luccioni, A, Jernite, Y and Strubell, E. (2024) "Power Hungry Processing: Watts Driving the Cost of AI Deployment" ACM Conference on Fairness, Accountability, and Transparency (ACM FAccT '24),
44. https://situational-awareness.ai/racing-to-the-trillion-dollar-cluster/#Power
45. https://www.fastcompany.com/91227559/leveraging-ai-and-real-time-data-in-the-fight-against-climate-change
46. DeepMind Blog, "DeepMind AI Reduces Google Data Centre Cooling Bill by 40%", July 2016, https:// deepmind.com/blog/ deepmind-ai-reduces-google-data-centre-cooling-bill-40/

47. Remi Lam et al. Learning skillful medium-range global weather forecasting.Science382,1416-1421(2023)
48. https://www.nature.com/articles/d41586-024-00780-8
49. Abduljabbar, Rusul, et al. "Applications of artificial intelligence in transport: An overview." Sustainability 11.1 (2019): 189.
50. Franki, V et al "A comprehensive review of Artificial Intelligence (AI) companies in the power sector." Energies 16.3 (2023): 1077.
51. Mehmood, Muhammad Uzair et al. "A review of the applications of artificial intelligence and big data to buildings for energy-efficiency and a comfortable indoor living environment." Energy and buildings 202 (2019): 109383.
52. Priya, A. K., et al. "Artificial intelligence enabled carbon capture: A review." Science of The Total Environment 886 (2023). 163913.
53. Dellosa, J et al, "Artificial Intelligence (AI) in Renewable Energy Systems: A Condensed Review of its Applications and Techniques," 2021 IEEE International Conference on Environment and Electrical Engineering and 2021 IEEE Industrial and Commercial Power Systems Europe (EEEIC / I&CPS Europe), Bari, Italy, 2021, pp. 1-6
54. https://sdgs.un.org/partnerships/ocean-data-alliance
55. https://digitaltwinocean.mercator-ocean.eu/
56. https://esto.nasa.gov/earth-system-digital-twin/
57. https://destination-earth.eu/
58. https://op.europa.eu/en/publication-detail/-/publication/4902607b-e541-11ec-a534-01aa75ed71a1
59. https://natureontheboard.com/so-how-exactly-does-nature-serve-as-a-director-of-a-company-ca0e5caf226e
60. https://www.scientificamerican.com/article/how-scientists-are-using-ai-to-talk-to-animals/
61. Landgraf, T et al (2018) "Dancing Honey Bee Robot Elicits Dance-Following and Recruits Foragers" arXiv preprint arXiv:1803.07126
62. https://theoceancleanup.com/
63. https://www.wildlifeinsights.org/
64. https://edition.cnn.com/2023/09/23/us/fighting-wildfire-with-ai-california-climate/index.html
65. https://www.space-intelligence.com/

66. https://www.bbc.co.uk/news/articles/c5yxw9wr3j4o

Chapter Nine

1. Kant, Immanuel (2016). "Perpetual Peace; A Philosophical Essay" Translated by Smith, Mary C. Project Gutenberg.
2. Wells, H.G. (1914) "The War That Will End All War", (Duffield & Company)
3. https://inkstickmedia.com/hg-wells-and-the-war-to-end-war/
4. https://theconversation.com/israel-gaza-how-opinion-polls-used-in-northern-ireland-could-pave-a-way-to-peace-224085
5. "Peacekeeping operations timeline". United Nations Peacekeeping, https://peacekeeping.un.org/en/peacekeeping-operations-timeline
6. Irwin, C (2012) "The People's Peace: Public Opinion, Public Diplomacy and World Peace" ISBN-9798675897421 https://peacepolls.etinu.net/peacepolls/documents/008880.pdf
7. https://blog.remesh.ai/the-remesh-story
8. https://www.youthconversations.org/countries
9. Olsher, D (2015) "New Artificial Intelligence Tools for Deep Conflict Resolution and Humanitarian Response" Procedia Engineering, Volume 107, Pages 282-292,
10. O'Lone, K et al (2024) "Employing Multi-Agent AI to Model Conflict and Cooperation in Northern Ireland," New England Journal of Public Policy: Vol. 36: Iss. 1, Article 6.
11. https://justin-lane.medium.com/ai-model-suggest-troubles-in-northern-ireland-with-a-hard-border-cc58958097fe
12. https://www.nytimes.com/2019/12/16/world/europe/paramilitary-attacks-northern-ireland.html
13. Kropaczek, D et al (2023). Digital Twins for Nuclear Power Plants and Facilities. In: Crespi, N et al (ed) The Digital Twin. Springer, Cham. https://doi.org/10.1007/978-3-031-21343-4_31
14. https://www.nytimes.com/2015/04/22/us/in-atomic-labs-across-us-a-race-to-stop-iran.html
15. https://www.world-nuclear-news.org/Articles/Idaho-researchers-develop-reactor-digital-twin

16. "Transcript of Powell's U.N. Presentation" https://edition.cnn.com/2003/US/02/05/sprj.irq.powell.transcript/ 6 February 2003
17. Ritter, S (1999) "Endgame: Solving The Iraq Crisis" (Simon & Schuster) ISBN 0743247728
18. "Mortality after the 2003 invasion of Iraq: a cross-sectional cluster sample survey" (PDF). Archived from the original (PDF) on September 7, 2015. (242 KB). By Gilbert Burnham, Riyadh Lafta, Shannon Doocy, and Les Roberts. The Lancet, October 11, 2006
19. https://humanitariangrandchallenge.org/wp-content/uploads/2023/12/Hala-Systems-Outcome-Case-Study.pdf
20. Gold, D (2018) "Saving Lives With Tech Amid Syria's Endless Civil War", Wired https://www.wired.com/story/syria-civil-war-hala-sentry/
21. https://www.visionofhumanity.org/start-up-on-a-mission-to-save-lives-in-conflict-zones/
22. Howard, P (2015) "Pax Technica: How the internet of things may set us free or lock us up" (Yale University Press) ISBN 9780300199475
23. Yanagizawa-Drott, David (1 November 2014). "Propaganda and Conflict: Evidence from the Rwandan Genocide" The Quarterly Journal of Economics. 129 (4): 1947–1994.
24. Panic, B & Arthur, A (2024) "AI For Peace" (CRC Press) ISBN 978103241837
25. https://thesentinelproject.org/
26. Panic, B & Arthur, A (2024)
27. Walter, B (2023) "How Civil Wars Start: And how to stop them" (Penguin) ISBN 9780241988398
28. https://www.historynet.com/what-we-learned-from-the-battle-of-zappolino-1325/
29. Leland G (2009). Stupid History: Tales of Stupidity, Strangeness, and Mythconceptions Through the Ages. (Andrews McMeel Publishing) ISBN 9780740792106
30. https://elpais.com/diario/2009/07/20/deportes/1248040816_850215.html#
31. https://en.wikipedia.org/wiki/War_of_Jenkins'_Ear
32. Collier, P & Sambanis, N (2002). "Understanding Civil War". Journal of Conflict Resolution. 46 (1): 3–12
33. https://time.com/6330445/demining-ukraine/

34. Baur, J et al (2021) "How to Implement Drones and Machine Learning to Reduce Time, Costs, and Dangers Associated with Landmine Detection," The Journal of Conventional Weapons Destruction: Vol. 25: Iss. 1, Article 29 https://commons.lib.jmu.edu/cisr-journal/vol25/iss1/29
35. Mach, K. et al. Climate as a risk factor for armed conflict. Nature 571, 193–197 (2019)
36. Sudan Post-Conflict Environmental Assessment (2007) United Nations Environment Programme UNEP_Sudan_PCEA_2007.pdf
37. Water, drought, climate change, and conflict in Syria Weather, Climate and Society, 6 (3) (2014), pp. 331-340
38. Selby, J et al Beyond scarcity: Rethinking water, climate change and conflict in the Sudans, Global Environmental Change Volume 29, 2014, Pages 360-370, ISSN 0959-3780
39. Selby, J Climate change and the Syrian civil war revisited, Political Geography, Volume 60, 2017, Pages 232-244, ISSN 0962-6298
40. Climate Change 2023 Synthesis Report, Summary for Policy Makers
41. https://www.climate.gov/news-features/understanding-climate/climate-change-global-temperature
42. Jones, Nicola. "How to stop data centres from gobbling up the world's electricity." nature 561.7722 (2018): 163-166.
43. https://situational-awareness.ai/racing-to-the-trillion-dollar-cluster/#Power
44. Hendrix, C. S., & Salehyan, I. (2012). Climate change, rainfall, and social conflict in Africa. Journal of Peace Research, 49(1), 35-50.
45. https://www.statista.com/topics/11261/floods/
46. https://blogs.icrc.org/law-and-policy/2021/08/19/artificial-intelligence-anticipatory-humanitarian/
47. https://destine.ecmwf.int/news/destine-digital-twins-to-anticipate-the-devastating-effects-of-flooding-in-coastal-areas/
48. https://www.wri.org/insights/highest-water-stressed-countries
49. https://iwaponline.com/ws/article-abstract/19/3/831/41417/Quantifying-the-global-non-revenue-water-problem?redirectedFrom=fulltext

50. https://www.siemens.com/global/en/company/stories/industry/2023/lushan-watersupply-waste-water-process-control-system-digital-twin-china.html
51. Sokhem, Pech, Kengo Sunada, and Satoru Oishi. "Managing transboundary rivers: The case of the Mekong river basin." Water international 32.4 (2007): 503-523.
52. Ha, Duong Hai, et al. "Application of Artificial Intelligence to Forecast Drought Index for the Mekong Delta." Applied Sciences 14.15 (2024): 6763.
53. Nguyen, Thanh-Tung, Quynh Nguyen Huu, and Mark Junjie Li. "Forecasting time series water levels on Mekong river using machine learning models." 2015 Seventh International Conference on Knowledge and Systems Engineering (KSE). IEEE, 2015.
54. Pitakaso, Rapeepan, et al. "A novel artificial multiple intelligence system (AMIS) for agricultural product Transborder logistics network Design in the Greater Mekong Subregion (GMS)." Computation 10.7 (2022): 126.
55. Poortinga, Ate, et al. "Predictive analytics for identifying land cover change hotspots in the mekong region." Remote Sensing 12.9 (2020): 1472.
56. UN General Assembly (UNGA). A/RES/70/1Transforming our world: the 2030 Agenda for Sustainable Development. Resolut 25, 1–35 (2015).
57. Vinuesa, Ricardo, et al. "The role of artificial intelligence in achieving the Sustainable Development Goals." Nature communications 11.1 (2020): 1-10
58. https://icain.ch/#pilot-projects-part
59. Nordling, Linda. "How the genomics revolution could finally help Africa." Nature 544 7648 (2017).
60. Kastner, S. L. (2007). When Do Conflicting Political Relations Affect International Trade? Journal of Conflict Resolution, 51(4), 664-688.
61. Barbieri, K. and Reuveny, R. (2005), Economic Globalization and Civil War. Journal of Politics, 67: 1228-1247
62. Jackson MO, Nei S. Networks of military alliances, wars, and international trade. Proc Natl Acad Sci U S A. 2015 Dec 15;112(50):15277-84.
63. https://warpreventioninitiative.org/2015/re-examining-the-connection-between-peace-conflict-and-trade/#_ftn20

64. https://www.worldbank.org/en/topic/trade/publication/trading-away-from-conflict
65. Ferencz, J., J. López González and I. Oliván García (2022), "Artificial Intelligence and international trade: Some preliminary implications", OECD Trade Policy Papers, No. 260, OECD Publishing, Paris
66. Brynjolfsson, Erik, Xiang Hui, and Meng Liu. "Does machine translation affect international trade? Evidence from a large digital platform." Management Science 65.12 (2019): 5449-5460.
67. https://www.ft.com/content/3babf690-07fa-3f6f-a888-2ac9c6efc271
68. Von Clausewitz, C (2006) "On War" (Project Gutenberg E-book) English translation of 1874 by Colonel J.J. Graham
69. Meta Fundamental AI Research Diplomacy Team (FAIR)† et al. Human-level play in the game of Diplomacy by combining language models with strategic reasoning. Science 378, 1067-1074 (2022)
70. https://cdn.openai.com/papers/gpt-4.pdf
71. https://www.belfasttelegraph.co.uk/news/northern-ireland/how-martin-mcguinness-and-ian-paisley-forged-an-unlikely-friendship/35550640.html
72. Irwin, C (2012)
73. https://www.liverpool.ac.uk/politics/news/articles/as-international-support-for-an-independent-palestine-grows-heres-what-israelis-and-palestinians-now-think-of-the-two-state-solution

Chapter Ten

1. https://youtu.be/WnzlbyTZsQY
2. Yergin, D (1993), "The Prize", (Simon & Schuster) isbn 9781847376466
3. Payne, K (2018), "Strategy, Evolution and War: From Apes to Artificial Intelligence" (Georgetown University Press) ISBN 9781626165793
4. Scharre, P (2023) "Four Battlegrounds: Power in the Age of Artificial Intelligence" (W.W. Norton & Company) ISBN 9780393866865

5. https://www.taipeitimes.com/News/biz/archives/2022/10/11/2003786778
6. Payne, K (2018)
7. Scharre, P (2023)
8. https://www.nytimes.com/2024/08/07/business/musk-starmer-riots-uk.html
9. Hobbes, T (1651) "Leviathan or The Matter, Forme and Power of a Commonwealth Ecclesiasticall and Civil", https://gutenberg.org/ebooks/3207
10. Runciman, D (2023) "The Handover: How We Gave Control of Our Lives to Corporations, States and AIs" (Profile Books) ISBN 9781788163675
11. Dalrymple, W (2019) "The Anarchy: The Relentless Rise of the East India Company" (Bloomsbury) ISBN 9781408864371
12. Pakenham, T (1991) "The Scramble for Africa, 1876-1912" (Weldenfeld & Nicholson) ISBN 9780297811305
13. Conrad, J (1902) "Heart of Darkness" https://gutenberg.org/ebooks/219
14. Aschenbrenner, L (2024) "Situational Awareness" https://situational-awareness.ai/
15. https://www.fool.com/research/largest-companies-by-market-cap/
16. Allianz Research (2021) Allianz Global Wealth Report 2021
17. Rahwan, Iyad, et al. "Machine behaviour." Nature 568.7753 (2019): 477-486.
18. Lambert, J et al (2019) "How Robots Change The World: What Automation Really Means for Jobs and Productivity" Oxford Economics www.oxfordeconomics.com
19. https://finance.yahoo.com/news/amazon-grows-over-750-000-153000967.html
20. https://techcrunch.com/2024/08/20/waymo-is-now-giving-100000-robotaxi-rides-week/
21. https://www.baiguan.news/p/baidu-apollo-go-robotaxi-wuhan-launch
22. Elondou, T et al (2024), "GPTs are GPTs: Labor market impact potential of LLMs", Science Volume 384 Issue 6702
23. https://www.noahpinion.blog/p/plentiful-high-paying-jobs-in-the

24. Ford, M (2015) "The Rise of the Robots: Technology and the Threat of Mass Unemployment" (Oneworld Publications) ISBN 9781780747491
25. Susskind, D (2020) "A World Without Work: Technology, Automation and How We Should Respond" (Allen Lane) ISBN 9780241321096
26. Diamandis, P & Kotler, S (2012) "Abundance: The Future Is Better Than You Think" (Free Press) 9781451614213
27. https://www.census.gov/library/stories/2019/06/america-keeps-on-trucking.html
28. Walter, B (2022) "How Civil Wars Start: And How to Stop Them" (Viking) ISBN 9780241429754
29. https://www.nationalgeographic.com/science/article/3-d-scans-caterpillars-transforming-butterflies-metamorphosis
30. Bostrom, N & Timson, D (2024) "Deep Utopia: Life and Meaning in a Solved World" (Ideapress Publishing) ISBN 9781646871643

Chapter Eleven

1. Holiday, R (2018) Conspiracy: Peter Thiel, Hulk Hogan, Gawker, and the Anatomy of Intrigue (Portfolio) ISBN 9780735217645
2. https://www.bbc.co.uk/news/world-us-canada-50695593
3. https://edition.cnn.com/2024/12/05/politics/elon-musk-trump-campaign-finance-filings/index.html
4. https://www.nytimes.com/2024/10/18/magazine/trump-donors-silicon-valley.html
5. https://www.youtube.com/watch?v=sgTeZXw-ytQ
6. https://www.forbes.com/profile/marc-andreessen/
7. https://gregbrodsky.medium.com/why-ray-dalio-and-other-captains-of-industry-are-rethinking-traditional-winner-takes-all-capitalism-5ea9ab419538
8. https://www.forbes.com/profile/elon-musk/
9. Taplin, J (2017) "Move Fast and Break Things: How Facebook, Google, and Amazon Have Cornered Culture and What It Means for All of Us" (Macmillan) ISBN 9781509847693
10. Schaake, M (2024) "The Tech Coup: How to Save Democracy from Silicon Valley" (Princeton University Press) ISBN 9780691241173
11. Ibid

12. Schneier, B (2023) "A Hacker's Mind: How the Powerful Bend Society's Rules, and How to Bend them Back" (W.W. Norton & Co) ISBN 9780393866667
13. https://medium.com/behavior-design/announcing-the-habit-summit-421aa0d65b1e
14. https://www.publishersweekly.com/pw/by-topic/columns-and-blogs/cory-doctorow/article/44012-doctorow-s-first-law.html
15. Mitchell, S (2021) Amazon's Toll Road, How the Tech Giant Funds its Monopoly Empire by Exploiting Small Businesses, (Institute for Local Self-Reliance)
16. Schneier, B (2023)
17. Schaake, M (2024)
18. Schneier, B (2023)
19. Thiel, P & Masters, B (2014) "Zero to One: Notes on Startups, or How to Build the Future" (Currency) ISBN 9780804139298
20. Schaake, M (2024)
21. https://www.bbc.co.uk/news/resources/idt-f29714b5-73d2-4932-a889-5c63778e273d
22. Schaake, M (2024)
23. Schneier, B (2023)
24. https://www.cambridge.org/core/journals/perspectives-on-politics/article/testing-theories-of-american-politics-elites-interest-groups-and-average-citizens/62327F513959D0A304D4893B382B992B
25. Taplin, J (2017)
26. Lazonick, W, (2009) "Sustainable Prosperity in the New Economy? Business Organization and High-tech Employment in the United States" W. E. Upjohn Institute for Employment Research, 2009, ch. 2.
27. Mazzucato, M (2018) "The Entrepreneurial State: Debunking Public vs Private Sector Myths" (Penguin) ISBN 9780141986104
28. https://www.ibisworld.com/us/bed/government-funding-for-universities/4073/
29. Olson, P (2024) "Supremacy: AI, ChatGPT and the Race that Will Change the World" (Macmillan Business) ISBN 9781035038220
30. Mazzucato, M (2018)
31. Taplin, J (2017)
32. Schneier, B (2023)
33. Taplin, J (2017)

34. https://goodjobsfirst.org/amazon-tracker/
35. https://itep.org/amazon-avoids-more-than-5-billion-in-corporate-income-taxes-reports-6-percent-tax-rate-on-35-billion-of-us-income/
36. Mazzucato, M (2018)
37. Schaake, M (2024)
38. Schneier, B (2023)
39. https://www.ons.gov.uk/economy/grossdomesticproductgdp/timeseries/ihyq
40. https://www.wsj.com/market-data/quotes/AAPL/historical-prices
41. https://allthingsd.com/20110120/talking-schmidt-googles-ceo-in-his-own-words/

Chapter Twelve

1. Tolstoy, L (1886) "What Then Must We Do?" https://archive.org/details/in.ernet.dli.2015.202642
2. Troyat, H (1967), "Tolstoy" (Penguin)
3. https://openai.com/index/democratic-inputs-to-ai/
4. Konya, A (2023) "Deliberative Technology for Alignment" arXiv:2312.03893v1
5. Devine, F et al (2023) "RECURSIVE PUBLIC: Piloting Connected Democratic Engagement with AI Governance (Chatham House)
6. https://www.anthropic.com/news/collective-constitutional-ai-aligning-a-language-model-with-public-input
7. https://www.founderspledge.com/research/research-and-recommendations-advanced-artificial-intelligence
8. "A roadmap to democratic AI," https://www.cip.org/research/ai-roadmap
9. Schneier, B (2015) "Data and Goliath: The Hidden Battles to Collect Your Data and Control Your World" (W.W. Norton & Co) ISBN 9780393352177
10. Tegmark, M et al (2023) "PROVABLY SAFE SYSTEMS: THE ONLY PATH TO CONTROLLABLE AGI" arXiv:2309.01933
11. https://research.google/blog/federated-learning-collaborative-machine-learning-without-centralized-training-data/
12. Wooldridge, M (2020) "The Road to Conscious Machines: The Story of AI" (Penguin) ISBN 9780241333914

13. https://www.nytimes.com/2023/05/16/technology/openai-altman-artificial-intelligence-regulation.html
14. https://news.un.org/en/story/2024/03/1147831
15. https://www.nytimes.com/1982/01/09/us/us-settles-phone-suit-drops-ibm-case-at-t-to-split-up-transforming-industry.html
16. Popovic, S (2015) "Blueprint for Revolution: how to use rice pudding, Lego men, and other non-violent techniques to galvanise communities, overthrow dictators, or simply change the world" (Scribe) ISBN 9781922247872

Afterword

1. Popper, K (2020) "The Open Society and Its Enemies" (Princeton University Press) ISBN 9780691210841

Like the Idea of the End of Conflict?

To summarise the book in one sentence, it broadly outlines two possible futures: one, the end of conflict, which is something I believe we should all be working towards; the other, a misaligned leviathan of any kind, which could be catastrophic.

I hope you enjoyed reading it and found it motivating enough for you to do something about. If so, one very simple action you could do would be to help spread the word – the more people know about this idea, the more likely it is to come about.

So, tell your friends, write an honest review on Amazon, Goodreads and/or other online bookstores, post it on LinkedIn, Facebook, Instagram, X/Twitter, the social media platform of your choice, mention it in your professional newsletter if you have one, give a copy to your friends, suggest it to your local library, follow me on social media and engage with the conversation. Anything that you can think of that will widen the conversation.

The book was written on a not-for-profit basis, as a labour of love, something I felt the world needs to know about more. Behaviours spread one person at a time, ideas come into reality one person at a time. Anything you can do to spread the word is going to help bring about the end of conflict.

We can do this.

Thank you

Simon

www.theendofconflict.ai